Urbanization in Developing Countries

Urbanization and Social Change in West Africa

Urbanization in Developing Countries

edited by Kenneth Little

The first books in the series are:

V. F. Costello: *Urbanization in the Middle East*
J. Gugler and W. G. Flanagan: *Urbanization and Social Change in West Africa*

Other titles are in active preparation.

Urbanization and Social Change in West Africa

JOSEF GUGLER
University of Connecticut

WILLIAM G. FLANAGAN
University College, Cork

CAMBRIDGE UNIVERSITY PRESS

Cambridge
London   New York   Melbourne

Published by the Syndics of the Cambridge University Press
The Pitt Building, Trumpington Street, Cambridge CB2 1RP
Bentley House, 200 Euston Road, London NW1 2DB
32 East 57th Street, New York, NY 10022, USA
296 Beaconsfield Parade, Middle Park, Melbourne 3206, Australia

First published 1978

Printed in the United States of America
Typeset by the Fuller Organization, Inc., Philadelphia, Pa.
Printed and bound by the Murray Printing Company, Westford, Mass.

Library of Congress Cataloging in Publication Data
Gugler, Josef.
Urbanization and social change in West Africa.
(Urbanization in developing countries)
Bibliography: p.
Includes indexes.
1. Urbanization – Africa, West.   2. Africa,
West – Social conditions.   I.   Flanagan, William G.,
joint author.   II.   Title.
HT148.W4G83   1976   301.36'0966   76–9175
ISBN 0 521 21348 7   hard covers
ISBN 0 521 29118 6   paperback

To the men and women who successfully fought
to end colonialism in West Africa,
to the future of Guinea-Bissau

Contents

Maps

Figures

Tables

Preface

By now, the literature on urbanization in Subsaharan Africa in general, and West Africa in particular, is substantial, both in volume and in the richness of observation and analysis it contains. We have chosen to review this literature and to interpret its disparate findings, focussing on a number of key issues in the urbanization process and on change in several particularly important social contexts. The issues involved lie within the domain of no single discipline. Of necessity, we have not limited ourselves to the writings of fellow sociologists and social anthropologists but have drawn heavily on work conventionally labeled political science, economics, demography, geography, history, and social psychology. Not surprisingly, we found some of the most penetrating observations in the writings of West African novelists and playwrights who have given vigorous expression to the experiences of people living in a period of rapid change.

So that this reality may come to life for our readers, we have let a number of its observers speak for themselves. Most of them are foreigners with considerable research experience in West Africa, a couple are distinguished Nigerian social scientists, and one is a prominent Nigerian novelist. We are grateful for their permission to reprint from their works.

We are sensitive to the argument as to whether it is proper for outsiders like us to comment on the policy issues facing West Africans today. However, we hold that it is incumbent upon social scientists to address these issues and reject the facile pose of foreigners who prefer to take a "neutral" stance and thus endorse the status quo, whatever the implications for the lives of those they write about. Concern with the outcomes of the pattern of urbanization we studied led us to take positions on what are indeed controversial matters.

This study is one outcome of the authors' association over a number of years. Its general framework originated in a graduate seminar that Josef Gugler first taught at what was then Makerere University College, Uganda. It is informed by research he carried out in Nigeria, under the auspices of the German Research Foundation, and in East Africa, when on the staff of the Makerere Institute of Social Research. The authors met, and their interests fused in the analysis of a survey of urbanization and social change in Dar es Salaam, Kampala, and Nairobi, which was sponsored by the Makerere Institute of Social Research and The University of Connecticut Research Foundation. Their joint endeavor drew heavily on William G. Flanagan's Ph.D. thesis on the role of the extended family in urbanization.

Our work is indebted to numerous people. The help we received along the way is immense and we are unable to acknowledge individually the warm hospitality extended by Nigerians in their village homes, the criticisms of our students, and the lively exchange among faculty and visitors that made work on Makerere Hill a stimulating experience. Our profound intellectual debt to a great many students of social life in West Africa and beyond will be readily apparent to the reader. Here we wish to thank Raymond Apthorpe, who gave this study vital encouragement in its early stages, and Floyd Dotson, who commented in great detail on portions of the manuscript. Both shall be absolved from our errors of commission and omission. Alick Newman drew the maps, and Dorothy McDonald applied her remarkable skills to the index. We also thank Betty G. Seaver and Patricia Murray, editors whose changes and observations went beyond recasting our prose to making us rethink some of our arguments, and Selma Wollman, who carried the main burden of impeccably typing more drafts than we care to remember.

London, June 1977

Josef Gugler
William G. Flanagan

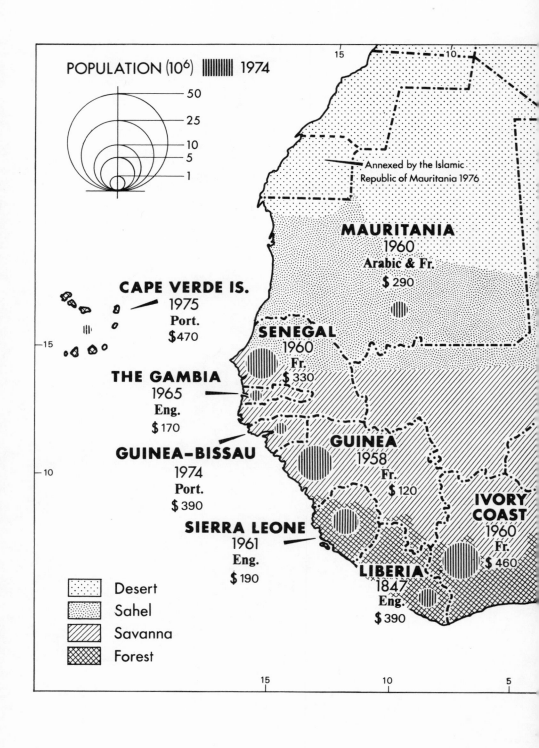

POPULATION (10^6) ||||||| 1974

50
25
10
5
1

CAPE VERDE IS.
1975
Port.
$470

THE GAMBIA
1965
Eng.
$170

GUINEA–BISSAU
1974
Port.
$390

SIERRA LEONE
1961
Eng.
$190

Annexed by the Islamic
Republic of Mauritania 1976

MAURITANIA
1960
Arabic & Fr.
$290

SENEGAL
1960
Fr.
$330

GUINEA
1958
Fr.
$120

IVORY
COAST
1960
Fr.
$460

LIBERIA
1847
Eng.
$390

Desert
Sahel
Savanna
Forest

15

10

15   10   5

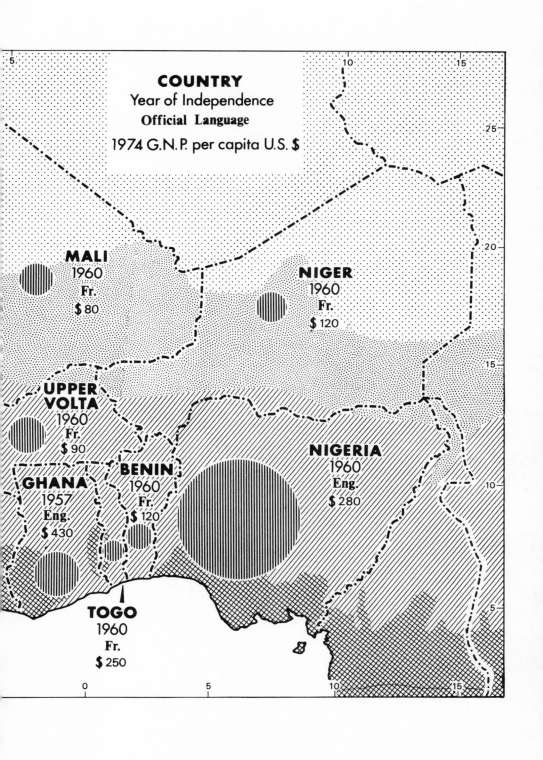

COUNTRY
Year of Independence
Official Language

1974 G.N.P. per capita U.S. $

MALI
1960
Fr.
$ 80

NIGER
1960
Fr.
$ 120

**UPPER
VOLTA**
1960
Fr.
$ 90

NIGERIA
1960
Eng.
$ 280

GHANA
1957
Eng.
$ 430

BENIN
1960
Fr.
$ 120

TOGO
1960
Fr.
$ 250

Introduction: Exploding cities in poverty-stricken countries

The Europeans came and assumed command of African history; and the solutions they found were solutions for themselves, not for Africans.

Basil Davidson (1974, p. 17)

The two foremost characteristics of the countries of West Africa[1] are the attributes that they share with many other countries on the continent and beyond: They were under colonial rule until recently, and they are extremely poor. Except for Liberia, each was part of the British, the French, or the Portuguese colonial empire. Ghana gained Independence in 1957, and the other countries followed in quick succession. By 1965, all West Africa was independent except for Guinea-Bissau, where it took more than a decade of armed struggle to achieve Independence from Portugal. Today, these young nations experience various degrees of economic, political, and cultural dependency on outside powers, and they have only very limited resources at their command to meet the aspirations of their peoples. By one conventional measure, gross national product (GNP) per capita, some West African countries are among the world's poorest, and most rank among the poorer of what are euphemistically called "developing countries."[2] The highest GNP per capita recorded for any country in the region amounts to about one-eighth of the comparable figure for Great Britain and about one-fourteenth of that for the United States.

The political and economic contexts of urbanization

West Africa is not only one of the poorest regions of the world but also one of the least urbanized.[3] Four out of five West Africans continue to live in rural areas, deriving their livelihood from various forms of agriculture that range all the way from subsistence farming to concentration on the production of a single crop for the world market. Despite this, urban patterns are long established in several parts of West Africa, a feature that distinguishes the region from much of the remainder of Subsaharan Africa.

Some of the old West African urban centers expanded, others withered away with the growth of maritime trade and the imposition of colonial rule. But this new epoch found its most dramatic expression in the many cities that were created. Rapid urban development occurred in many parts of the region, especially along the coast. At the same time, there has been a measure of continuity with earlier patterns of urbanization in one fundamental aspect. That

1

is, the primary functions of West African cities continue to be administration, commerce, and transshipment; no industrial city has yet emerged, and only a few of the less populous centers are focused on mining. But the fortunes of West African cities were now shaped by foreigners who came to impose the will of European powers and by world markets controlled by overseas economic interests. Today, administration and commerce in most West African countries are concentrated in seaports that double as capital cities, and the urban systems of many West African countries are characterized by the absence of towns of intermediate size.

In spite of a lack of commensurate industrial growth, West Africa experienced the most rapid rate of urban population growth of any region in the world between 1950 and 1970. Widespread unemployment and underemployment indicate that its cities have outstripped their economic foundations. Although urban employment has become difficult to secure for all but the best-trained, urban growth continues unabated, fed by both a high rate of population growth and substantial rural–urban migration that has its source in rural poverty.

To the extent that anyone designed and controlled the new cities and the extensions of the old, that was done by Europeans. The impact of Western culture in general was strong, especially through the missions and their schools. Residence and access to certain public facilities tended to be racially segregated de facto, if not de jure. But the climate of West Africa, for all its diversity, appeared sufficiently inhospitable to the intruders to preclude the establishment of substantial settler communities. This is in contrast with other parts of Subsaharan Africa, where white settlers established themselves and influenced colonial policy (if they did not gain control over the polity, as in South Africa).[4] West Africans acquired rights to urban land and built their own houses; they traded freely in the markets and in the streets; they moved without restrictions between rural and urban areas. Opportunities for the growing of cash crops for foreign markets developed and were taken up, giving a new impetus to commerce. Today, the reputation of West Africa's traders carries across the entire continent.

The social concomitants of urbanization

Rapid growth in the twentieth century was based on rural–urban migration. It brought together people of diverse origins, preponderantly young men. The new cities and the new extensions to the old stood in marked contrast with the old cities, which were characterized by balanced age structures and a preponderance of women.[5] The population of the old cities had stabilized; the elderly ascended to their secure place in extended families, and women were drawn from the countryside into the polygamous households of the more affluent. But the political and economic order of the new centers attracted primarily young men, who were more likely than either their elders or their sisters to be hired because of their physical strength or their education. All were confronted by an economic regime that cared little about supporting them, once their productive capability had been exhausted.[6] Not only short-term labor migrants but also many of those who spent a working life in town had, of necessity, to maintain links with their extended families and their village communities which offered them a measure of security and eventually welcomed them back. Except in the old cities, relatively few families have been permanently established in the urban environment for several generations.[7]

The new political and economic order was and is characterized by stark socioeconomic differentiation. In colonial days, attention focused on the contrast in standard of living between the small group of Europeans and the mass of Africans. With the approach of Independence, Africans moved into the positions formerly monopolized by the foreigners and assumed the privileges they had enjoyed. Today, competition is sharp, whether the goal is to reach an elite position or to make the jump from unemployment or underemployment into a secure job. In economic competition and political conflict in the urban arena, ethnic identities frequently become salient. These are new identities shaped out of an interaction of the factors of recognized common origin, the pursuit of efforts to advance the region of origin to which most urban dwellers anticipate returning eventually, and the perception of economic and political interests within the urban context. Tensions can reach the flash point where political power and/or economic privilege are perceived to be monopolized by one ethnic group.

West Africa shares a heavy burden with the remainder of Black Africa. The prejudice against Africans that was nourished in the days of the slave trade and cultivated under colonial rule sometimes appears impossible to overcome. General statements about "Africa" or "Africans" need to be predicated with the recognition that the real picture is so heterogeneous that there is often no typical or average case. On the other hand, many current generalizations about Africans apply, in fact, to all human beings. The particular fallacy of comparing actual norms of behavior in Africa with ideal norms of behavior in the West is still perpetrated all too frequently. Where genuine differences do exist between Black Africa and the West, there is typically a double failure: the neglect to explore which is the peculiar case and which is the near-universal pattern—and the tendency to fantasize about the so-called African mind instead of inquiring into structural constraints. We hope to contribute to a better understanding of present-day West Africa as we proceed to explore in depth the multifaceted process of urbanization there.

1 Empires and trade

It is particularly important to call attention to the danger of confusing urbanism with industrialism and modern capitalism . . . Different as the cities of earlier epochs may have been by virtue of their development in a preindustrial and pre-capitalistic order from the great cities of today, they were, nevertheless, cities.

Louis Wirth (1938, pp. 7f.)

The view that European history constitutes the mainstream of human history has often obscured or caused us to ignore important episodes of history played out in other areas of the world. During Europe's Dark Ages and Renaissance, the Western Sudan below the Sahara was the scene of rivalries among empires that at times surpassed in wealth and strength the European counterparts to which they were linked indirectly by a web of trade in gold.

Actually, there were a number of West African civilizations that flourished long before European contact. The origin of the earliest known of these, the empire of Ghana, remains shrouded; but by the eighth century its fame had reached as far as Bagdad, where it was mentioned by the Arab geographer al-Fazārī (Levtzion 1973, p. 3). Ancient Ghana's emergence was the result of several factors, but chief among them was the gold trade, with routes across the Sahara radiating from territories under its control. And with the beginning of Ghana's decline during the Muslim crusades of the eleventh century, the gold trade attracted a succession of new black states with ever expanding frontiers, foremost among them Mali, then Songhay.

In considering the question of why an urban civilization emerged at this time and in this place – the far reaches of West Africa, farthest across the Sudan from Egypt, and far to the south across the Sahara from North Africa – one is struck first by the sheer presence of the great desert. It apparently existed in the middle of the first millennium A.D. much as it does now, but its desiccation is a relatively recent (as these things go) and continuing event. Until about the fourth millennium B.C., the Sahara was humid and well watered; rock engravings dating from that period depict elephants, rhinoceroses, giraffes, hippopotamuses, crocodiles, and fish. Then, first the aquatic, and later the big wild animals disappear from more recent rock paintings, their places taken by the tended herds of the pastoralists. By the fifth century B.C., Herodotus was describing the Sahara that is familiar to us today (Levtzion 1973, p. 5). Thus, we know that although the Sahara was recently fertile, even lush, by the time ancient Ghana emerged, it did so on the borders of the desert.

5

The part played by the desert in determining the location of early West African population centers is very similar to that of the ocean in the location in modern times of the largest West African cities, most of which are found along the coast. It has been argued that Africa has, in fact, two natural northern borders, the Sahara and the Mediterranean. The early towns were actually desert ports at the termini of trade routes that crossed the desert from north to south. Located in the Sahel (*sāḥil* is the Arabic word for "shore") on the habitable edge of the desert, these towns grew up as commercial centers at the points where different means of transport (the camel of the Sahara and the donkeys and porters of the Sudan) met, and goods from the North and the South changed hands.

The journey across the desert was apparently at least as treacherous as any ocean crossing. A widely traveled Arab scholar, Ibn Baṭṭūṭa, described the desert passage in these terms:

The *takshīf* is the name given to every man of the Massūfa who is hired by the people of the caravan to go ahead to Walata with the letters of the people to their friends there, so as to rent houses for them and to come out to meet them with water a distance of four days. He who has no friend in Walata writes to a person who is known among the merchants of Walata for his generosity and he enters into a partnership with him. If perhaps the *takshīf* perishes in this desert, then the people of Walata do not know about the caravan, so its people, or most of them, perish. That desert has many devils, and if the *takshīf* be alone, they play with him and lure him on until he loses his way and perishes since there is no way which is clear there and no tracks. There is only sand blown by the wind. You see mountains of sand in a place, then you see they have moved to another. [(1355) 1975, p. 25]

Despite the rigors of the journey, the desert was traversed before 1000 B.C. Saharan rock paintings of that era record the passage of war or hunting chariots, and other archaeological evidence shows that two main routes crossed the desert by this date. Roman and Carthaginian trade with the Subsaharan region is also documented. Bullocks and horses apparently were the early beasts of burden, but it was the camel, introduced to the Saharan trade sometime in the early centuries A.D., that provided a vast improvement in desert transport and sustained commercial contact. Among the camel's remarkable attributes are its capacity to withstand great heat, its renowned ability to store energy, and its capacity to consume over fifty gallons of water at a time. Insofar as ancient West African urbanization was spawned by trade and trade is dependent upon transportation, history is bound to acknowledge the camel's unique contribution in early urban development in the region.

If these facts are properly taken into account, the "why" of the early West African towns has a classic answer. To the north and south were producers and markets separated by a magnificently hostile terrain. Along the edge of the desert, trading centers grew up, far-flung termini attracting diverse products and fulfilling the critical function of the middleman in extensive and large-scale networks of trade. The camel provided an efficient means of transport, the promise of wealth supplied the basis for ambition and entrepreneurship, and the spread of Islam, with its firm codes of behavior afforded the necessary unity and trust for long-distance transactions.[1] The early West African population centers emerged from the rich trans-Saharan trade; they were transformed into flourishing cities by the might of empire.

Three empires: Ghana, Mali, and Songhay

The properly cautious conscience of the group of scholars concerned with the early history of West Africa, Raymond A. Mauny, has made the point that "all that can be said of the history of Ghana before the coming of the Arabs in the eighth century must, in the present state of our knowledge of West Africa, be merely speculation" (1954, p. 207).[2] The origins of Ghana may forever remain mysterious. We can only surmise that the ruler of a trading center came to establish control over a network of such towns and to enforce security on the trading routes. Some written records do exist from the more prosperous later years, but there are enough contradictions, vague references, and exaggerations in these documents to warrant extreme caution in interpretation.[3] When Ghana was first mentioned toward the end of the eighth century by al-Fazārī, he referred to it as the "Gold Country." In the first half of the tenth century, Ibn al-Faqīh al-Hamadhānī, a southern Arabian scholar, reviewed the gold sources that replenished the Muslim treasuries and mints and concluded that the most productive gold mine in the world was that of Ghana. At that time, gold from the Sudan was minted in Sijilmāsa at the northern end of the Sahara. The geographer Ibn Ḥawqal, who visited Sijilmāsa in 951, was impressed by the volume of trade with the Sudan. He was shown a bill certifying that an Awdaghust trader, a native of Sijilmāsa, owed 42,000 dinars, a level of credit unheard of anywhere in the Muslim world at that time (Levtzion 1968).

A network of trade routes across the Sahara linked Ghana not only with the Maghrib but also with Egypt. Lured by the promise of gold, merchants braved the hazards of the desert. The main commodity they brought in exchange was salt extracted from deposits in the Sahara.[4] On its way south, salt became an increasingly valuable commodity. It is said to have sometimes been exchanged in equal amounts for gold. The prosperous trade diversified. Slaves, skins, gum, and spices were sent to the North; horses, copper, silver, tin, lead, and beads arrived in the South. European and Arab textiles were imported to the Sudan; at the same time, locally woven cloth was sent to the Sahara and the Maghrib.

The *Kaya Magha* ("Gold King") controlled an aggregate of tributary kingdoms, each with its own ruler. Allegiance to the king was ensured in part by the practice of keeping the sons of rulers of vassal states in the king's court as hostages to continued fidelity. At its peak, in the eleventh century, the king's authority reached as far north as Awdaghust. At that time, the empire of Ghana seems to have covered a roughly circular territory resting in the cradle of the Senegal and Niger rivers along its southern borders, with an average radius of about 250 miles.

The king and the state appear to have acquired revenue in two main ways. Ghana controlled the varied trade generated by the existence of the gold fields lying to the south, rather than directly managing the extraction of the gold.[5] A tax was levied on all products entering and leaving the country, with the apparent exception of gold. The king's share of the gold trade consisted of his right to all nuggets weighing more than one ounce in their natural state; the remainder was for the market.

By the year 1000, Ghana was attaining the peak of its power and influence. al-Bakrī [(1068) 1975, p. 102], one of the great geographers of Western Islam, claimed that the king could field a force of 200,000 warriors on short notice. Although that figure may be something of an overestimate, there is little doubt that the military might of Ghana was exceptional for that time, certainly by European standards.[6] But Ghana fell victim to the waves of a religious war that washed around its economic foundations, eroding them and finally causing the collapse of the empire.

Ghana did not actually fall, in the sense of a dramatic defeat. Rather, it withered and dwindled in a process that took approximately two centuries. In the middle of the eleventh century the Almoravids, a zealous sect of Islam that was gaining wide success in its religious war to the north, descended on Ghana's borders. The Almoravid jihad (Islamic holy war) was undertaken to teach the "true" faith of Islam to wavering Muslims and to gain converts among the heathen. Islam had ordered and strengthened commerce by providing a common bond of identity and a code of ethics for traders. But now Ghana – and its ruler, who remained traditional in his beliefs and continued to proclaim his own divinity as leader of his people – became an ideal target of the Islamic crusade, its wealth providing added incentive for conquest and control. With its trade disrupted and its territories in revolt, the people of Ghana's capital received the stern lesson from the Almoravids in 1076 or 1077, when the city fell and was sacked.

Ghana rose again within a few years and drove out its quarreling conquerors. Yet it never quite regained its former prosperity. The trade had been disrupted, and with it, the centralizing strength of the state. Eventually, the state broke up into its component parts. What was left of Ghana was finally overthrown early in the thirteenth century by the Soso kingdom, a former vassal state. Within a few years the Soso kingdom was incorporated by the expanding empire of Mali.

Ghana proved to be the prototype for successively larger empires in the Western Sudan. During the period of its greatest expansion, in the fourteenth century, Mali extended from the Atlantic eastward past the great bend of the Niger River. It engulfed the former territory of Ghana in its northern limits, incorporating the gold-producing area of Bambuk, to which Ghana had merely controlled access, and bulged well below the arching Niger and Gambia rivers on the southern border.

Mali had evolved over generations from a small Malinke kingdom to a condition of moderate strength that allowed it to fill the trading vacuum left by Ghana's decline. The forceful leadership of Sundjata is remembered in an epic that is told far and wide among Malinke to this day. The political center of the Sudan thus shifted south, most likely to Niani, below the Niger River, far beyond the former southernmost reaches of Ghana.[7] This location gave close control over Bure, on the upper Niger, which had become the principal source of gold in the eleventh and twelfth centuries. And the more hospitable savannah belt here provided richer agricultural support for trading activity. As Mali expanded north, it integrated the savannah with the Sahel. During the reigns of Mansā Mūsā (1312–37) and Mansā Sulaymān (circa 1340–60), embassies and gifts were exchanged with the Morrocan sultan.

The rulers of Mali are said to have been Muslim from before the days of Sundjata. A number of them made the pilgrimage to Mecca and visited the Mamluk sultan of Egypt on their way. The pilgrimage of Mansā Mūsā in 1324–5 brought universal fame to the empire. His visit to Cairo was recorded in Egyptian chronicles as one of the principal events of the year. Different accounts mention between 8,000 and 60,000 followers accompanying him. When he approached Cairo he sent a present of 50,000 dinars to the sultan of Egypt. Again, estimates of the amount of gold Mansā Mūsā brought along vary, but several sources agree that so much gold was distributed as presents and spent in the markets that the value of gold decreased considerably in Cairo.

What Mansā Mūsā brought back to Mali had a more lasting effect than that which he had left in the East. On his pilgrimage, he resolved to strengthen Islam and to complement the prosperity of his country with suitable cultural achievements. To this end, he persuaded the Spanish poet and architect Abū Isḥāq al-Saḥilī, the Ismaili missionary al-Mu'ammar Abū'Abdallāh ibn Khadīja al-Kūmī, and four shurafā' (i.e., descendants of the Prophet) to return with him to Mali. After his return, he ordered mosques built and sent Sudanese ulama (Muslim scholars) to study in Fès, Morocco.

Ibn Baṭṭūṭa, who visited Mali in 1352–3, several years after Mansā Mūsā's death and during the reign of Mansā Sulaymān, remarked upon the justice and security that prevailed there. His report said of the people of Mali:

Amongst their good qualities is the small amount of injustice amongst them, for of all people they are the furthest from it. Their sultan does not forgive anyone in any matter to do with injustice. Among these qualities there is also the prevalence of peace in their country, the traveller is not afraid in it nor is he who lives there in fear of the thief or of the robber by violence. They do not interfere with the property of the white man who dies in their country, even though it may consist of great wealth, but rather they entrust it to the hand of someone dependable among the white men until it is taken by the rightful claimant. [(1355) 1975, p. 47]

Yet, for all its outward signs of order and soundness, the empire was already in trouble during Ibn Baṭṭūta's visit; he remarked, in fact, that Mansā Sulaymān was unpopular among his people, who remembered the generosity of Mansā Mūsā. However, it was not lack of popular support that mortally weakened Mali but the turbulence and intrigue that characterized much of the history of the rule of Mali. Over the course of the next few centuries, Mali's territories were slowly whittled away on all sides by invasion and secession.[8] Like Ghana, it withered and faded; but in Mali's case, internal weaknesses and division seem to have played a greater part.

Mali was succeeded by Songhay, an old kingdom based in Gao that had been active in the trans-Saharan trade since the eighth century. Songhay had come to be controlled by Mali; with the decline of Mali, it expanded into the last and greatest of the Sudanic empires. From beginning to end, the brief record of Songhay's hegemony is the most violent of the ancient period. Songhay grew to prominence under Sonni 'Alī the Great (1464–92), who began his reign with a campaign of expansion. One year after Sonni 'Alī's death, the throne was seized from his successor by Askiyā Muḥammad (1493–1528). Numerous expeditions took him as far west as the northwestern provinces of Mali beyond the upper Senegal and as far east as Agadès and Katsina. The power of the empire was based on the institution of a large standing army, a system of market inspection to ensure honest dealings, and the creation of a decentralized administration in which chief officeholders were either from or married into the royal family.

As was the case with Mali, Songhay suffered from internal intrigues; but when it was defeated in 1591, at the Battle of Tindibi, it was apparently at the peak of its power. Its end came when the sultan of Morocco commissioned an expedition in the eternal quest, the search for the city of gold. Moors, Italians, Greeks, French, English, and Spanish made up the force, equipped with harquebuses and cannons, that set out to conquer Songhay. Those who survived the arduous journey across the desert succeeded only in the destruction of the last Sudanic empire. They found no "city of gold" in their easy victories (mainly the result of their introduction of the man-made plague, the firearm, to the Western Sudan), but they did disrupt the order that had provided the necessary security for trade. As al-Sa'dī recorded:

The Moroccan army found the Sudan one of God's most favoured countries in prosperity and fertility. Peace and security reigned in all provinces . . . . Then all that changed: security gave place to danger; prosperity made way for misery; tranquility was succeeded by trouble, calamities and violence. Over the length and breadth of the land people devoured one another; raids and war destroyed the people's wealth, subjugated them into slavery, took their lives. Disorder spread and intensified until it became universal. [(1655) 1900, pp. 222f.]

Centers of trade and seats of empire

The ancient West African cities grew out of the interaction between the lucrative trans-Saharan trade and the fortunes of empires. If they had their origin in trade, they gained prominence when, and for as long as, they could draw on the resources of far-flung empires. The cities, in turn, were necessary organizational units for the intersection and coordination of state activity. The cities were thus both the product and the producers of sociocultural change; they reflected it and were the points from which it emanated. Then as now, the city received most of the wealth generated by trade and was the arena for the exchange of ideas and new materials carried there from distant places by traders, travelers, scholars, and specialists. From the chronicles of visitors and inhabitants and from archaeological evidence, more is being learned of what these places were like.

Writing in distant Córdoba, al-Bakrī gives this account of the capital of Ghana:

The city of Ghana consists of two towns in a plain. One of these towns is inhabited by Muslims. It has a dozen mosques in one of which they assemble for the Friday prayer. The mosques have all their imams, their muezzins, and their readers of the Koran. Lawyers and learned men live in the town. Close by are wells of sweet water from which they drink and near which they cultivate vegetables. The royal town, called al-Ghāba ["the grove"], is six miles away from the Muslim town, and the area between the two towns is covered with dwellings. Their houses are made of stone and acacia wood. The king has a palace and huts with conical roofs, surrounded by a wall-like enclosure. In the king's town, not far from the hall for royal audiences, is a mosque where pray the Muslims who come there on business. [(1068) 1975, p. 99]

Koumbi-Saleh has been identified as the likely site of the Muslim section of the capital of Ghana, but the royal city, presumably of more poorly constructed or less durable buildings, has proved impossible to locate. Excavations at Koumbi-Saleh have revealed a large town consisting of two parts. One, about 800 by 800 yards, was constructed in stone; the second, about 550 by 800 yards, was entirely inhabited but shows only isolated ruins of stone houses. The city, with narrow lanes except for a single great avenue that was about 40 feet wide as it passed the mosque, appears to have been densely populated. Mauny (1961, pp. 481f.) estimates, from the archaeological evidence at Koumbi-Saleh, that what is thought to have been the Muslim section of the capital of Ghana had a population of 15,000 to 20,000. That this was an important city over a long period of time is attested to by two cemeteries that are even larger than the residential areas. Stone was used extensively in construction, for floors as well as for walls. Mauny describes the finds:

The houses had upper storeys, and when these subsided they filled in the ground-floor rooms which when uncovered were found to be magnificently preserved under a mass of rubble averaging 12 feet in thickness. . . . P. Thomassey . . . lived on the site for several months and cleared two groups of buildings of very fine architectural style. The flagged floors, the wall-tablets painted with passages from the Koran, the graceful lines of the niches carved in walls and pillars, the stone staircases, and the wealth of skillfully-fashioned objects (iron tools and weapons, pottery, beads, grindstones, and some extremely rare glass weights used for weighing gold) give us a good idea of the type of civilisation that flourished here. (1959, pp. 24f.)

If Koumbi-Saleh is the biggest city that existed in the Sahara in the Middle Ages, the other major cities were located on or close to the Niger and functioned as river ports. There is an architectural similarity among the cities of the three empires, in that well-made buildings of stone are found along with buildings of the familiar mud or clay construction of the Sudan. Mud houses easily conjure the notion of an overgrown village, but 7,626 houses, not counting straw huts, were enumerated in Gao in about 1585 [Ibn al-Mukhtār (1665) 1913, p. 262]. On this evidence, Mauny (1961, p. 499) estimates that the capital of Songhay had 75,000 inhabitants.

Timbuktu was a smaller city. Mauny (1961, pp. 497f.) estimates a population of 25,000 in the fifteenth and sixteenth centuries, to which may be added the population of the river port proper. But it was Timbuktu that became the famous center of religion and learning. Abū Ishāq al-Sahīlī, who accompanied Mansā Mūsā on his return from pilgrimage, built a magnificent palace in the capital, then settled in Timbuktu, where he died in 1346. He is presumed to be the architect of the Great Mosque, and his style of building has had a lasting influence upon the architecture of the Western Sudan. The descendants of al-Sahīlī, however, settled in Walata, then the principal terminus of the trans-Saharan trade. In the second half of the fourteenth century, the trade shifted farther east, and the cosmopolitan commercial and religious elite began to move from Walata to Timbuktu, strategically located at the northernmost reaches of the Niger. Toward the end of the rule of Mali, the town emerged as a center of trade and Islamic learning. Its golden age came under the askiyās of Songhay, who made it their second capital (Levtzion 1973, pp. 201 and 157f.). Some 150 to 180 Koran schools were dispersed about the town; one of them had 123 students [Ibn al-Mukhtār (1665) 1913, pp. 315f.]. The mosque university of Sankore offered a range of studies from religion to the Maliki code of laws, and its fame spread throughout the Muslim world.[9] After the decline wrought by the Moroccan invasion, sons of Timbuktu, al-Saʿdī (1655) and Ibn al-Mukhtār (1665), wrote the two great chronicles, the Taʾrīkh al-Sūdān and the Taʾrīkh al-Fattāsh, which continue to be principal sources of information about the Western Sudan.[10]

When Songhay fell to the Moors, many of the traders and scholars from the Western Sudan migrated east to Bornu and the Hausa states, where the remnants of Sudanic political and economic power had shifted. The Hausa states, which actually comprised a number of peoples and cultures, have their own history of rivalry and city-state building, but not on the scale of the earlier empires. Still, according to one estimate, Kano had 75,000 inhabitants or more in the sixteenth century, after the city had recovered from a Songhay invasion (Mauny 1961, p. 501). Bornu, a larger state that encircled Lake Chad, was coheir to the traditional trade that had been developed to the west. But it appears that the smaller Hausa states, not the larger kingdom, gained the greater advantage from the eastward shift in trade routes (Fage 1969, p. 33). In 1826, Richard Lander (1830, pp. 200f. and 260) put the population of Kano at over 40,000, that of Sokoto, at that time the capital of the victorious Fulani army, at 120,000.

The seventeenth and eighteenth centuries, after the fall of Songhay, have sometimes been characterized as the Dark Ages of the Western Sudan. Indeed, Morocco proved unable to administer such a distant region effectively, but the invasion quite possibly increased commercial and religious contacts with the Maghrib. The steady influx of shurafā' from the North affirms the maintenance of strong religious links with North Africa, and the pace of Islamic diffusion accelerated (Willis 1971). Not only did the Muslim community grow in numbers, but from about the second half of the eighteenth century, social criticism received unprecedented impetus. Muslim leaders and their followers came to demand reform in consonance with their conception of a just society. Eventually, they provided the ideological basis for the jihad led by a learned theologian and pious Sufi, 'Uthmān dan Fodiye, who was heir to a centuries-old tradition of learning and social respectability in his family (Adeleye 1971).

Similarly, there is no substantial evidence to suggest that the wealth of the middle Niger region diminished. The redirection of trade was certainly not immediately and dramatically felt in the interior. There were brief periods during which the value of trans-Saharan trade increased, and in fact, its overall value may not have peaked until 1875 (Anthony G. Hopkins 1973, pp. 80f.). Still, with the fall of Songhay, the monumental era of Sudanic civilization had come to a close.

Trade and urban centers in the coastal and forest belts

The Portuguese were the earliest Europeans to come to the coasts of West Africa, arriving in mid-fifteenth century and establishing the first of a number of forts at Elmina (modern Ghana) in the early 1480s. Like the English and French who followed them in the next century, they were traders and missionaries rather than colonists. Later came the Dutch, Swedes, Danes, and Prussians, all of whom remained for only brief periods.

Again, it was West African gold that attracted traders and generated enterprise that led to prosperity and the growth of states and kingdoms, but ivory, wax, and pepper also contributed to commerce. As elsewhere on the African continent, it would take the Europeans a long time to penetrate much beyond the coast. In West Africa, political control remained in the hands of the Africans, at least for several centuries. The Europeans traded and established posts only by leave of the local rulers, whose position was strengthened over time through the acquisition of firearms, a commodity that the Saharan route did not supply efficiently. But the Europeans played one kingdom against another, supporting weaker peoples along the coast in order to prevent the emergence of a single powerful state, either there or in the interior.

Even before the European maritime activity, states had begun to emerge and expand between the Niger and the Volta rivers. These developments had started as early as the fourteenth century as a result of the traffic between the Akan gold fields and Mali and Songhay. By 1600, the Mossi states had many years of growth and consolidation behind them. But except for the northern Mossi, they were to be conquered and incorporated by the mid-eighteenth century into the powerful and well-organized trading state of Ashanti (Wilks 1971).

At the heart of Ashanti, on the crossroads of overland trade routes, was the seat of government, Kumasi. In 1839, Thomas B. Freeman (1844, pp. 54ff. and 169ff.) was the first European to visit and describe the city. He found wide streets, which he estimated to be 30 yards across, planted at intervals with banyan trees. There was a large open marketplace without permanent stalls, in which he saw goods of local and long-distance trade. Houses constructed of traditional materials were raised off the ground and roofed with reed and thatch. On another visit to the town, he witnessed a fire that leaped from house to house, ultimately consuming an area a half-mile long and 750 yards wide. He urged the king, who resided in the only stone dwelling Freeman saw, to "secure property by building more substantial houses." The king answered, "By God's help, I will try and do so, by and by." Such fires were common occurrences, and Europeans who followed Freeman, increasingly concerned about their growing property investment in the highly combustible towns, were eventually successful in replacing thatch with corrugated iron as roofing material.

Between 1821 and 1874, Ashanti's power was sapped as the result of a number of clashes with the British, who pragmatically sought to protect the autonomy of smaller coastal states over which Ashanti was attempting to assert or reassert control. Ashanti defeated the British in 1824, but in subsequent years the reach of its effective dominion was drastically reduced. In 1873–4, the last Ashanti campaign to the South was beaten back, and the British seized and burned Kumasi, blowing up the stone-built Palace of Culture (Wilks 1975, pp. 166ff.).

Dahomey was another powerful, although compact, state that arose in the period of coastal trade. Described as a small black Sparta, it had a well-drilled standing army consisting of both men and women, and it maintained an active ministry of intelligence and propaganda. Conquered territories were Dahomeanized, rather than allowed to maintain their own institutions and customs (as had been the practice of other conquering states in West Africa). A kind of income tax was imposed, and agriculture, livestock, hunters, saltmakers, craftsmen, and gravediggers were taxed; this, in addition to customs, tolls, and proceeds of the royal estates, made up the state's revenue. Dahomey took a regular census of its population, and provincial governors were kept honest by the assignment of a spy to each one's office (Boahen 1966, pp. 86ff.).

A visitor to Abomey, the capital, in 1772 described it as a large town with a population of about 24,000 people (Norris 1789, p. 92). When Freeman visited the capital in 1843, he did not record a numerical estimate but remarked that it was about as populous as Kumasi, which he had seen earlier. All buildings described were constructed of red clay with thatch roofing; some struck Freeman as being rather like English cottages. He also reported that what he saw of the interior of a royal residence was in the European style and presented "a very respectable appearance." Freeman's overall impression of the town was that, given its winding streets and close walls, it was not a particularly striking place (Freeman 1844, pp. 266ff.). Nonetheless, it was the headquarters of a very durable state that did not yield to European conquest until the French took it in 1894.

A large part of the wealth upon which coastal and forest states grew was generated by the slave trade. The exploitation of mineral and agricultural resources in the Americas had been increasing in scale, spurred on by an ever-growing demand in Europe, and the indigenous population of the Caribbean islands and the surrounding areas had been virtually exterminated by the diseases carried there by Europeans and by the harshest kind of slavery. It took no time at all for Europe to recognize the African alternative, and in 1518, the first slaves were shipped direct to the Americas. An estimated 10 million Africans were to follow; the majority were from West Africa (Curtin 1969, p. 268 and passim).[11] Although some Africans as well as Europeans and Americans prospered from the trade – the human merchandise of which was obtained through kidnapping, warfare, and criminal sentence – West Africa as a whole suffered from the loss of its most productive individuals and the general disorder entailed in their procurement. Once the trade was established, more and more leaders were drawn into it, either through successfully defending their domains, which resulted in the taking of prisoners, or simply in order to satisfy the appetite they had acquired for European items of trade.[12] Europeans or Americans rarely participated in the actual capture of slaves. Instead, they provided the market that led Africans to prey upon each other, thus bringing about an amtosphere of aggression and causing immeasurable damage to what had been for centuries an arena for the development of advanced black cultures.[13]

The Yoruba

In the southwest of what is now Nigeria and in adjoining parts of present-day Benin (formerly Dahomey), a system of large indigenous towns developed that most likely did not originate in trade either with the North or with the South.[14] The Hausa states (mentioned earlier in this chapter) arose out of trading centers as they inherited the trans-Saharan traffic from Songhay. However, the origin of Yoruba towns is much less clear. They are mentioned in records dating from the beginning of the sixteenth century. Traders and explorers in the early nineteenth century provide more detail about these large population centers. But just how the Yoruba became a city-building and city-dwelling people remains an open question.

Their early emergence makes it clear that these towns did not develop as protective communities in response to slave raids, although they certainly served this function during the intra-Yoruba wars. And although these walled towns offered protection (inadequate though it proved to be) against the Fulani jihad that swept down from the Hausa states, the oldest Yoruba cities predated the attacks. However, many of the new centers, notably Ibadan and Abeokuta, were established as an indirect result of the crusade.

Tradition has it that the Yoruba migrated from the northeast, probably between the seventh and tenth centuries, under their leader Oduduwa, who established Ile-Ife, "to which town even today most other Yoruba towns trace their origins" (Akin L. Mabogunje 1968, p. 76). From here, Oduduwa's sons were sent to found their own cities and kingdoms. Ile-Ife became and has remained the spiritual capital, but Old Oyo evolved under the rule of the Alafin as the political capital of Yorubaland, giving the whole territory its highest level of organization, probably prior to the eighteenth century (Mitchel 1961, p. 282). It was this growth in power that led formerly coequal chiefs to support the revolt of the commander-in-chief of the imperial army, who courted Fulani help as well, in the overthrow of the Alafin at Old Oyo (Awe 1967, p. 12). The Fulani, pursuing their own religious ends and vowing to dip the Koran into the sea, had, in fact, achieved a Fulani rather than Yoruba-allied victory (Old Oyo fell about 1835) and sent waves of refugees fleeing south to swell the population of old towns and villages and to found new ones. Ibadan would, after much internal struggle, emerge as the Yoruba metropolis; but the political cohesiveness of Yorubaland, which was tenuous at any time, had been "dismembered," as Bolanle Awe (1967, p. 13) aptly phrases it, into a number of fragments.

Akin L. Mabogunje (1968, pp. 76ff.) speculates that Yoruba towns, which apparently have always contained a large proportion of farmers who commute to their fields, evolved as the product of imperial expansion that gathered in formerly dispersed populations in order to minimize problems of control and that these towns came into being as "colonial settlements." According to this interpretation, Yoruba towns were first administrative centers and only afterward became the centers of the trade upon which their continued existence depended. "Unequal distribution of natural resources was soon capitalized upon and specialized centers of production emerged. Considerable movements of peoples and goods became a major factor linking the towns and determining the nature of their interaction one with the other" (Mabogunje 1968, p. 79). Trade also extended beyond Yorubaland, north to the Hausa states and south to the coast, and it involved Dahomey, Ashanti, and Accra as well. In Ife, Abeokuta, and Ijebu-Ode, wholesale guilds held monopolies over trade and over items imported from Europe. These monopolies were eventually broken by the British, who sought, as they had elsewhere, to establish the widest possible market for their imports (Bascom 1955, p. 449).

Within towns, an organic interdependence developed as the Yoruba city dwellers specialized, although this occurred to a lesser extent than it does in industrial cities. Nonetheless, specialization was sufficiently advanced to make each individual economically dependent upon the society as a whole (Bascom 1955, p. 450). Hugh Clapperton, who was the first European traveler in Yoruba country, described the industry that he encountered:

We have observed several looms going here: in one house we saw eight or ten – in fact a regular manufactory. Their cloth is good in texture, and some very fine. . . . We visited several manufactories of cloth and three dyehouses, with upwards of twenty vats or large earthen pots in each, and all in full work. The indigo here is of an excellent quality, and forms a most beautiful and durable dye; the women are the dyers, the boys the weavers; the loom and shuttles are on the same principle as the common English loom, but the warp only about four inches wide. (1829, pp. 14ff.)

Other Yoruba crafts that developed early include ironworking, smelting and blacksmithing, wood carving, bead manufacture, brass and coppersmithing, leatherworking, musical instrument manufacture, carpentry, building, and herbalist trades (Mabogunje 1968, pp. 82ff.). These varied enterprises, located within the walled compounds that constituted the basic units of the Yoruba town, were scattered throughout the urbanized areas.

Any catalog of Yoruba achievement is not complete without mention of the high level attained by Yoruba artwork in wood, terra cotta, and bronze. The most remarkable and justifiably famous works, metal castings created through the lost-wax method, were produced at Ife in the fifteenth century by masters who remain anonymous. The measure of art is certainly not taken in the level of technology it makes use of, but this advanced technique of modeling, as employed at Ife, rendered the human form with a realism that is quite astonishing, despite the somewhat idealized features. These figures, comparable to works created in classic Greece, bear lasting testimony to the sophistication of Yoruba urban culture.

The towns themselves, before their appearance had become affected by European contact, were much like those of Ashanti or Dahomey. Buildings were of mud with thatched roofs; they were clustered together in compounds, which in turn were enclosed in walls of the same construction.

The compounds and not the roads, were the most important element in the Yoruba town plan. Each compound was the visible expression of a lineage or extended family, and might have between 20 and 2,000 inhabitants but with an average of between 100 and 200. The town was composed of groups of these compounds formed into quarters, each with a quarter chief . . . The size of each often depended on the prestige of its chief, and, as a result, could vary considerably within each town and from town to town. (Mitchel 1961, p. 286)

It appears that the towns originally had overall street plans of radial or grid design. The formula included broad, straight streets crossing at the center, where a palace adjoined the most important market. The congested, haphazard pattern that exists today is the result of the settlement of refugees during the wars of the nineteenth century and the tendency for all kinds of migrants to seek to locate within rather than on the edge of the city (Mabogunje 1968, pp. 96ff.). The main roads, palace, and central market have remained, but the indigenous Yoruba areas are characterized by a connecting maze of narrow, crooked lanes that run among residences.

Farmers constitute a considerable part of the population of Yoruba towns to this day. R. A. Akinola (1963, pp. 105ff.) describes this situation for Ibadan. Even during the intra-Yoruba wars of the nineteenth century, many Ibadan warriors sent members of their households out to farm, and farm hamlets continued to spring up. With the establishment of the Pax Britannica these settlements grew rapidly, became more permanent, and extended the farming area to the limit of the territory available to the town. At the same time, the farmers continued to owe allegiance to the ruler of Ibadan. Akinola refers to daily commuting to the farm as a thing of the past and notes the exhaustion of the soil surrounding the town, particularly that within a four-to-five-mile radius. But the hamlets continue to be regarded as daughter settlements, most of the farmers having rooms or houses in Ibadan. They look to their residences in the city as their homes; born in the hamlets, spending their working lives there, they still expect to be buried in their ancestral compounds in Ibadan. Those in nearby hamlets spend an average of five nights every week there and the remaining two in Ibadan, the spiritual center for all. Certain traditional religious rites and festivals can be performed only in Ibadan, and the Christian and Muslim celebrations also draw many people from the hamlet into the town. Important family ceremonies are sometimes performed in the city.

Like most Yoruba towns, (new) Oyo differs from Ibadan in that land four to five miles from the town is available for farming. Such land, the *oko etile* ("farms of the outskirts"), is farmed by men who go out from their town homes, traveling either on foot or, to an increasing extent, by bicycle. Most are only part-time farmers whose principal economic concern (carpentry, sewing, bicycle repairing, or one of the many other trades) lies with the town itself. Beyond about five miles from the town, on land called the *oko egan* ("bush farm"), one finds hamlets where the full-time farmers and their families live, still owing social allegiance to Oyo (Stephen Goddard 1965). G. J. Afolabi Ojo (1970, p. 466) reports that the average distance of the *oko egan* varies depending on the size and extent of land available to the town, the population size of the town, and the degree to which the farmers grow cash crops and have adopted modern methods.[15]

Past censuses of Yoruba towns have included many members of urban compounds who lived in the *oko egan*. This accords with the position taken by Peter C. Lloyd (1962, pp. 55 and 58), who holds that the farmers in the *oko egan* belong to the sociological population of the town. Ojo (1970, p. 470) similarly emphasizes that Yoruba do not normally give up town life, no matter how long they stay on the farm. He goes on to suggest that those who stay for extended periods compensate for this by spending equally long periods at home in town. But even if the farm-dwelling population is excluded, there remain a number of Yoruba towns that have been urban in size for a long time.

Defining the city

These Yoruba cities presented an odd picture to those who were accustomed to the character of urban areas in Europe or America. The preindustrial city is part of Western experience, but the cities of Yorubaland contained such large numbers of farmers and the buildings were so villagelike that to the foreign eye they seemed no more than dense rural settlements. Even though estimates in the 1850s placed the population of Ibadan at between 70,000 and 100,000, Abeokuta at 60,000, and Oyo at 25,000, some have questioned the urban status of these places.

There have been many attempts to arrive at a theoretical definition of the city and city life. Marx and Engels, Durkheim, and Weber all dealt in more or less detail with the issue of what it was that characterized their modern, increasingly urban, society. Yet, in 1938, Louis Wirth stated quite correctly that a satisfactory definition was yet to be formulated. In his classic paper, "Urbanism as a Way of Life," he posited size, density, and heterogeneity in permanent settlement as the core of criteria to be used in the definition of urbanism.

Gideon Sjoberg (1960, pp. 32f.), following V. Gordon Childe (1957), accepts Wirth's criteria but goes on to say that "these are insufficient. We add the requirement of a significant number of full-time specialists, including a literate group, engaged in a relatively wide range of non-agricultural activities."

Accordingly, he finds that "the traditional Dahomey, Ashanti, or Yoruba in Africa . . . we must also class as 'quasi urban.' All of these were complex folk orders that were perhaps on the way to becoming feudal, or literate pre-industrial, societies."

An acceptable classification of the indigenous coastal and forest centers of West Africa as either city or noncity appears to be an issue of debate for three reasons. The first is a matter of operational imprecision; that is, what did Wirth intend by "heterogeneity" in his definition, and what proportion of specialists satisfies Sjoberg's criterion of "a significant number"? Second is the issue of literacy, which Childe and Sjoberg find critical to city status. Third, because a large segment of the population of Yoruba town dwellers is engaged in agriculture, does this mean these places are nonurban?

By "heterogeneity," Wirth meant that the individual's allegiance is segmented in the modern (American) city, in which an individual belongs to a number of groups. It does not refer to ethnic differences nor necessarily to the degree of stratification present (two ways in which the term has often been interpreted). Eva Krapf-Askari (1969, pp. 82ff.) has emphasized the vitality and variety of interest groups and associations among the Yoruba. Apart from their kin group, Yoruba owe allegiance to traditional crafts associations and the new guilds based on recently introduced crafts; to market guilds; to credit associations; to traditional politico-religious, Muslim, and Christian groupings; to ethnic associations; to political parties; to traditional age-sets; and to the social clubs that have come to replace them. Krapf-Askari observes that heterogeneity of allegiance and membership is valued by Yoruba and suggests that it is part of the high esteem in which Yoruba hold town life. It is the mark of an urbanite to belong to many associations; the ridiculed country boor has no such opportunities.

Although the historical experience of occidental cities indicates the presence of a number of full-time specialists, it may be asked what the criterion of full-time specialization adds to a theoretical definition of cityhood. Yoruba specialists and merchants, as we have noted, were dependent on other specialists for materials and services; yet, it is not clear whether, at an early date, all or most supported themselves through farming as well. Whatever the case, they were able to draw and administer long-distance trade from around West Africa and beyond in volume that caused early European travelers some surprise. Instead of assuming that commerce and manufacture must be carried on by agents who are specialized or full time, a more constructive approach to defining the city would be to ask: Under what alternative modes of organization is the economic work of cities carried out?

The most suspect qualification in this index of urban traits is the requirement that at least a minority of residents be able to write in order to keep records and thus fix traditions and strengthen cohesion among a ruling elite.

Again, the nature of the trade indicates the capacity to keep adequate records outside of the device of writing. Writing was not a cause in the rise of metropolitan centers and empire in the Sudan; rather, writing followed what trade had created (which is unfortunate, of course, because we would otherwise know so much more about the early period). The Europeans who arrived on the coast armed with this device have recorded with it the difficulty they encountered in dealing with illiterate Africans, who, they thought, made their calculations only too well. Writing as a criterion for urbanism would seem to be based, as Mabogunje (1968, p. 41) has charged, largely on the ethnocentrism of those who make that argument.

Finally, there is the serious question of whether population centers where agriculture is the predominant occupation can be considered cities. Again, the most fruitful way to answer the question is to look at the early West African cities and ask if they carried on the business of the city, despite the fact that large numbers of the inhabitants were farmers. Mabogunje goes to great lengths to describe the craft production of Yoruba centers, in order to make two points:

first to emphasize the large number of people for whom craft production for trade must have provided employment in the past; and secondly, to make patent the illogicity of assuming that, because many Yoruba towns today are occupied by a majority of farmers, this majority was always so numerically important in the past. (1968, p. 85)

Mabogunje cites two disorganizing factors as reasons for the decline of indigenous manufacture: the disruption caused by the nineteenth-century intra-Yoruba rivalry and warfare that drove townspeople to farm in order to at least be ensured of subsistence[16] and the introduction of the cheap manufactured articles of European factories, especially iron and cloth. It is possible, according to this view, that Yoruba centers fit the standard definitions of the city better in the earlier than in the later periods. This in itself would argue for the inclusion of traditional Yoruba towns in any catalog of such places. William R. Bascom (1955, p. 449) reminds us further that the Yoruba pattern of trade included large markets, true middlemen, and true money (cowrie shells). Finally, at some stage, a sense of otherness between city and rural folk also developed. Bascom observed that "the city dwellers ridicule the unsophisticated 'bush' people; their attitudes, as expressed in conversation and proverbs, closely parallel our concept of 'rube' or 'hick.' The attitudes of the rural Yoruba toward the city dweller also seem to resemble those in our society" (1955, p. 451).

Rather than constituting some sort of an exception, the cities of the Yoruba provide us with an opportunity to strengthen the sociological definition of the city. The lesson contains a caution against constructing an exclusive theoretical model derived from one historical experience. The definition of the city has to flow from what it is that the city does. In other words, the city is what the city does in social-organizational and economic terms, and the examples of the ancient Sudan and coastal West Africa serve to broaden our experience in the forms such organization may take.

Traditional cities in changing times

In general, the towns of West Africa did not survive as such but were transformed with increasing European contact and control. Some, such as Kumasi, which remained an important crossroads, became integral parts of an expanded city with modern as well as traditional features. Others, such as Abomey, were superseded as the focus of urban development shifted toward the coast. Lagos, which was at first an indigenous fishing village, was engulfed and obliterated as the process that created modern Lagos took place. Many of the once important centers of empire in the Sudan shrank to mere villages or were lost entirely, but the Hausa city of Kano remains an important commercial and administrative center to this day. The Yoruba cities of Nigeria have also persisted, some shrinking, some continuing to grow. Foremost among the latter is Ibadan, whose population reached an estimated three-quarters of a million in the early 1970s.

Mabogunje describes the transition that took place in the appearance and organization of the traditional cities of the northern and southern sections of Nigeria.

Changes in the physical structure of Nigerian towns*

Everywhere the roofs of the houses were constructed of thatch, but quite early in the development of Northern Nigerian towns, the thatched roof was replaced by the flat, mud roof . . . This has given most towns in the north a distinctive appearance reminiscent of cities in North Africa. While the flat roof has survived in northern towns, the thatched roof has virtually disappeared from the southern towns. Its disappearance was consequent on the fire hazards to which it made a town frequently liable. Payne (1893, p. 8), for instance, calculated that between 1859 and 1892 there were as many as forty major outbreaks of fire in Lagos. One of the most disastrous was that of 1877. An eye-witness described it as astonishing even to the people of Lagos themselves, much as they were accustomed to witnessing such annual ravages.[1] The casualties involved two churches, one chapel, three mosques, between 1,000 and 2,000 houses, much property, and seven lives.

Traditional houses in Nigeria are more correctly referred to as 'compounds'. A compound . . . housed an extended family, comprising a man's immediate, though polygamous, family, the families of his grown-up male children and sometimes the families of his brothers as well as the slaves

*Excerpt from Akin L. Mabogunje, *Urbanization in Nigeria*, 1968, pp. 116–20, by permission of the author. Footnotes have been renumbered.
1 Archdeacon H. Johnson, letter to Henry Venn, 8 February 1877, Church Missionary Society Archives, CA2/055.

belonging to each of these families. A compound could thus be a very elaborate building containing many rooms and sometimes occupying several acres.

The basic unit of traditional residential organization in Nigerian towns, however, was the 'quarter'. A quarter consisted of groups of compounds occupied by members of one or more extended families. Each quarter was centred around a chief who performed social and jurisdictional functions within the limits of the quarter. Usually the chief was a descendant of one of the oldest families in the town. Old Lagos, for instance, had as many as twenty-two quarters; Ibadan had over seventy quarters, while the 1952 Census listed as many as ninety-three quarters in Abeokuta. Barth also listed some seventy-four quarters in Kano in 1851.

In the last hundred years, Nigerian cities have undergone tremendous changes in every aspect of their construction and physical organization. Many of these changes had their origin in Lagos and have gradually diffused inland from the coast. One of these was the replacement of the mud wall by baked-brick wall. As early as 1859, a certain Mattieu de Cruz established a brick kiln in Lagos at Ebute Metta (Payne 1893, p. 10). Another kiln was established in 1863 by the American Baptist Mission. These examples were soon followed by other missionary bodies and finally by the government in 1896. The result was that not only public buildings, but also numerous private houses began to be built of bricks. Even by 1865 Eales reported that in Lagos 'the European merchants have very fine brick houses; there were some that would not disgrace the best part of London, houses that cost £2,000 in the building'.[2]

In the succeeding years, brick walls were gradually displaced by those built of cement blocks. Cement, however, can be used not only to produce blocks, but also to plaster mud and brick houses. In this way, the latter are given a better protection against the elements of climate and a longer lease of life. Houses in present-day Nigerian towns thus vary from purely mud houses, mud houses with cement plaster, and brick houses with cement plaster to houses built of cement blocks. Generally the rate of change has been quicker in the southern than in the northern towns. In the latter, one often notices that, while houses in the traditional city (the *birni*) are still largely of mud, in the southerners' quarters (*sabon gari*) of the city, they are of more diverse materials.

The roofing material for houses has also been affected by great changes. As with the building material, the direction of change has been from Lagos inland, the effect being hardly felt in the traditional city of the north. The background to this change, as already stated, was the incessant hazard of fire which was becoming a real threat to the commercial life of Lagos in the mid-nineteenth century. As early as 1862, the European merchants in Lagos sent a letter to the British Governor advocating, 'first, that native houses throughout the town be within a given time covered with some less combustible material than is now used, and we recommend the bamboo mat as made at Calabar . . .; secondly, that all houses between the water side and the next street running parallel should be covered with slates, tiles, shingles or felt.'[3] Nothing was done at the time, but in 1877 it was proposed that the

2 Report of Select Committee on Africa, London, 1865, No. 7065, p. 279.
3 Letter by merchants and residents of Lagos to Governor Freeman, December 1862, CO 147/4, Vol. 2.

houses of the poorer people should be covered with corrugated iron, and that they should be made to pay the cost of it to the government by easy instalments.[4] The suggestion was turned down by the Governor-General of the colony who was then resident in Freetown, Sierra Leone. Later, however, towards the end of the century, corrugated iron had become very popular roofing material and with time it came to give to most Nigerian towns the appearance of an extensive, rusty-brown junk-spread.

The introduction of both cement and corrugated iron sheets into the building technology of the country had far-reaching consequences. Both were imported articles and to purchase them meant accumulating capital for the purpose. Fortunately by the end of the nineteenth century legitimate commerce had made great strides. Increasingly varied exports of palm oil, palm kernel, cocoa, groundnuts and cotton had served to put substantial sums of money in the hands of many individuals. However, the economic progress of individuals did not mean uniform progress among all members of an extended family. Differences in income and wealth began to give rise to differences in tastes, standards of living and expectations. The effect of this development was felt on kinship ties and family authority. It was more visibly reflected in the strains and stresses which were imposed on the form and design of the compounds. As with the enclosure movement in British agriculture in the nineteenth century, the 'improving' members of the family were anxious to break up the compound and to enclose and improve their portion of it. The disintegration of the compound into a number of houses containing a unit family is thus a feature of Nigerian towns in the last sixty years.

The disappearance of the family compound was hastened by the emergence of an architectural design which was more aesthetically exciting. This design, known as the Brazilian-style . . ., was introduced into the country by ex-slaves returning from Brazil. It involved the use of numerous ornamental frills to doorways, windows, pillars, balconies and verandas, as well as the application of bright colours to the house. Its layout consisted simply of a central corridor on to which rooms opened on both sides. This design has been in vogue for nearly a century, and is particularly dominant in the Yoruba country. Its popularity, however, is being increasingly challenged by new developments in the country, especially since 1956.

With the disappearance of the compound went many other forms of town organization. The 'quarter system' is remembered only through the fact of the existence of a chief, but it has today little functional significance. The functions of the quarter chief himself have been taken over by numerous other bodies: his representational role by the elected local councillor, his ritual role by the various churches and mosques, and his jurisdictional role by the courts. The quarter itself has been submerged in the new electoral wards which form the basis of modern political organization in the towns.

Changes in the form and layout of the city itself are more complex . . . In general, however, increasing exposure to modern Western technology and economic institutions has resulted in a greater demand for wide, straight roads and for buildings of multi-storey dimensions serving other than residential functions . . . Furthermore, the vehicular traffic which these functions generate has brought with it new problems and given new mean-

---

4 Archdeacon H. Johnson, letter to Henry Venn, 8 February 1877, Church Missionary Society Archives, CA2/055.

ing and importance to different parts of the city. The result is that specialized areas are beginning to emerge in Nigerian cities. Their control and regulation pose challenging problems to city administrators throughout the country.

African urbanization, like urban growth everywhere, was never a totally independent and isolated development. Nonetheless, the precolonial cities were African; they were not only the products of contact with the outside world but also the monuments of indigenous enterprise and cultures. For almost 100 years, however, since the European scramble for Africa, the big story of West African urbanization has been largely dictated by foreigners.

French and British influence grew throughout the nineteenth century in the pursuit of trade, but full colonial expansion and consolidation of territory did not come until the last few decades. The precipitating event may have been Britain's occupation of Egypt to prevent its old rival, France, from gaining control of the important link with India, the then newly opened Suez Canal (Webster and Boahen 1970, p. 217). Or it may have been ambitions of Belgium in carving out an expansive territory in the Congo in the late nineteenth century that inspired the stampede that left Africa with new boundaries demarcating not African states but European colonies. The French moved quickly across the Sudan and Sahara; Germany declared sovereignty over Togoland, Cameroun, South West Africa, and Tanganyika; and Britain suddenly found its interests closely circumscribed by claims of the other imperial powers. In 1884–5 the Europeans met in Berlin to "proclaim what was quite obvious" (Webster and Boahen 1970, pp. 218) by then: to acknowledge a shared fait accompli and agree upon the boundaries. The principle of ownership was "effective occupation" of territories by Europeans. The transition from African to European sovereignty in West Africa and the rest of the continent, as we shall discuss in Chapter 2, has to date been the most important factor in urbanization, itself a by-product of the larger political-economic process of colonialism.

2 Urbanization and economic development

The colonial city developed . . . as a centre of commerce and administration, rather than industrial production. It originated as a means whereby the metropolitan rulers established a base for the administration of the countryside, and the exploitation of its resources, and consequently the transfer of the surplus extracted from the countryside to the metropolis. At the same time, the city itself engaged in the parasitical exactions of a surplus from the countryside.

Gavin Williams (1970, p. 236)

West African urbanization took a new direction in the seventeenth century with the development of maritime trade. The commercial function of the seaports was complemented in the nineteenth century by the implantation of the colonial structure, first on the coast and then gradually inland. Public administration was further boosted by the advent of Independence. Commerce and government continue to overshadow industry in the cities of West Africa.

The proportion of the population living in urban centers (i.e., the level of urbanization) is rather low in West Africa when compared with that of other continents. However, urban growth (i.e., the rate of urbanization) has been extremely rapid since the Second World War and the consequences of this explosive growth are such that it must be viewed as overurbanization.

Further concern arises because in many West African countries a single city plays a dominant role and attracts a major share of national resources. An analytically separate problem is presented by a number of cities growing beyond what may be considered an optimal city size.

Finally, it is necessary to address the fact that the urban masses in West Africa live under extremely difficult and unhealthy conditions. Urban planners are only beginning to face the challenge of providing services for all with the extremely limited resources available.

The legacy of colonialism

The present pattern and conditions of urbanization in West Africa owe much to the colonial past. This is true not only of the atmosphere and location of towns but also with regard to the nature of the role these towns have played and are continuing to play in the economic development of the independent states.

The general pattern of distribution of towns and cities in modern West Africa is largely the result of events and conditions dating from the era of

26

coastal trade and the colonial period. Certainly, large towns and cities remain on indigenous sites; but in the coastal and central regions these bear the heavy imprint of colonial and modern European culture, and the remaining towns in the North have survived a process that dried up other population centers. Timbuktu, which today is part of landlocked Mali, provides a striking example. This place of trade and learning in previous centuries had shrunk to only about 7,000 inhabitants by the 1960s. Many of these older centers succumbed entirely to a second, economic desiccation of the Saharan region when the focus of trade shifted to the seaboard, where it has remained throughout the colonial period and on into statehood.

Today the majority of the towns of West Africa are located on the coast or close to it. Virtually all of them are so situated because at one time or another their sites served as important contact points for Africans and Europeans. The locations were determined by their accessibility from the sea and by the productivity of their hinterlands. The Portuguese in the sixteenth and seventeenth centuries were the first to establish settlements, which were generally only small forts, along the West African coast; these settlements included Rufisque, Senegal; Bissau, Guinea; Accra, Ghana; Porto-Novo, Benin; and Lagos, Nigeria. The Portuguese were followed in the seventeenth century by the French, Danish, Dutch, and British, who founded similar protective outposts, including those at Saint-Louis and Gorée in Senegal, at Sekondi in Ghana, and also at Accra. But many of West Africa's present cities did not come into being until after the Treaty of Berlin, when the colonial presence was more widely established: Bouaké (1896) and Abidjan (1903) in the Ivory Coast and Jos (1903), Maiduguri (1907), Enugu (1909), Port Harcourt (1912), and Kaduna (1913), all in Nigeria.

Not all the early forts grew into cities, nor have they all survived until the present day; but the ports and later European-initiated sites together constituted an organizing force for West African economies, directing attention and trade toward the coast, the colonial metropolis, and eventually the world economy. In turn, the pattern of urbanization proceeded to a very large extent according to the pull of trade toward the coast and foreign markets. Seaports grew in size and importance at disproportionate rates and became the seats of colonial administrations. In that period, whether or not interior settlements would be created or develop into towns was largely a function of the resources and accessibility of these areas to coastal ports. Of course, areas closest to the sea were generally the most accessible. Some rivers, such as the Niger and the Senegal, provided ready-made highways, but they were slow and inflexible arteries that were not fully navigable for a great part of the year. With the development of the railroads, and later of the automobile roadways, the rivers and the river ports that had sprung up beside them declined in importance, and new towns developed as old ones expanded along the new man-made routes. The construction of railroads that carried into the 1930s actually par-

28   *Urbanization and social change in West Africa*

allels the first phase of rapid urban growth in West Africa. We may say unequivocally that for West African towns, fortune rode the trains. Those that received terminals grew, but those that did not stagnated or declined, as did the many river ports.

The railroads opened interior sections to commerce and drastically reduced the cost of shipping mineral and agricultural materials to the coast. Access to the productive hinterlands also created the potential for new and expanded markets and towns at certain trackside points. William and Judith Hanna (1971, p. 16) point to the cases of Oshogbo (Nigeria), which was transformed "almost overnight" into an important trade center when the railroad and telegraph reached it in 1905, and Umuahia, to which the railroad virtually gave birth in 1913. Later, the development of roadways, delayed for a time by the heavy toll West Africa's terrain imposed on vehicle life, expanded access to new areas and amplified the impact of the railways in general.

New transport arteries had roughly the same effect on seaports that they had upon the river ports; that is, their number was reduced through functional obsolescence. The early railroad trunk lines provided reduced transport costs and thus gave advantage to certain already important seaports. The nature of the West African coastline reinforced the developing pattern of a few large ports absorbing the function of many smaller ones. H. P. White and M. B. Gleave observe that

the coast functions more as a barrier, separating land and sea by screens of surf and mangrove swamp, and by lack of natural harbors [there being] only two good natural harbors along the whole 2,400 miles of coast, . . . Dakar Roads and the Sierra Leone River. Elsewhere there are few opportunities for penetrating dune or estuarine bar, while lagoons are generally shallow. (1971, pp. 246f.)

The tendency was to improve the few largest ports because of the costs of the expanding overland transportation and of modern harbor installations. Smaller ports were thus robbed of their hinterlands as spreading networks of railroads and roadways swept up and funneled export commodities to those few larger coastal ports destined to become the focal points of national economies.[1]

Today, the most dense concentration of towns and the most rapid rates of urban growth are to be found within 100 to 150 miles of the coast. Here, where, in general, export cash cropping has developed furthest, the greatest demand has been created for goods and services and for the towns and markets to provide them. In Ghana for example, using a population figure of 5,000 as the lower cutoff for identifying a town, 91 out of 98 towns in 1960 (White and Gleave 1971, pp. 283ff.) and 113 out of 135 in 1970 were located either on the coast or below the northern limits of the forest belt, which extends only approximately 50 to 175 miles inland.[2] Further inland, the central administrative region of Ashanti was an area characterized by town life before the period of colonization and European administration. However, during that era, the system of Ashanti towns and their hinterlands underwent a substantial change as they were drawn into the colonial economy. The particular economic vehicle for rapid growth in this area was the development of cocoa cultivation for export. This crop was introduced near the turn of the century and triggered the building of the railroad and the expansion of road networks. But the area of growth was restricted to the broad coastal area. The export economy and the type of development it brought to Ashanti and to Ghana as a whole have led to a differentiation between the northern and southern regions. In the South, where towns and cities have proliferated, they are focused on the coast. During the period that saw remarkable urban growth in the South, the North remained virtually untouched by the trade, locally oriented, and stagnant (Berry 1962, pp. 56ff.). The contrast between the two exemplifies the general economic reorientation wrought on West Africa by European trade and colonial economy. The resultant pattern of urban growth held implications for the economic development of the independent states of the future.

In addition to the role played by Europe in determining the geographic location and the economic orientation of West African towns, the colonial era imparted a flavor or atmosphere to these places reflective of Portuguese, French, and British colonial styles. Writers generally remark on the formal parks, wide boulevards, open-air cafés, pastry shops, shuttered windows, and red-tiled roofs of the urban areas marked by the French presence. Where the British designed an addition to an existing urban center or created a new town, it, too, bore the imprint of the metropolitan country's urban style: the town plan includes a racetrack, golf course, and cricket field; the hotels still serve afternoon tea. In addition to the distinctive architectural styles of the colonial era, which are now being submerged beneath the skyline of the modern international style of architecture, the areas formerly dominated by the respective powers are heir to the more indelible characteristics of the planned grid of city streets like the language that binds together the inherited bureaucracy.

An even stronger contrast exists between the appearance of the colonial expatriate cities and the cities of indigenous origin. The Yoruba towns of Nigeria, such as the important centers of Ibadan, Oyo, and Abeokuta, are still in large part characterized by narrow, winding streets that obliterated the original town plans (see Chapter 1). But this describes only half of the typical Yoruba city currently facing modernization. It is the old half, characterized by the hodgepodge location of residences and manufacturing or service enterprises and the low profile of the corrugated metal roofs spilling into the distance. Today, some of these traditional towns of Yorubaland are important centers in a network of administration and trade. A new rationalization of land use has emerged. At times, attempts have been made to rezone the old areas, but the most typical manifestation of the economic and social reorganization is the establishment of a new city adjacent to the old. In the case of the Yoruba towns, one sector may overlap the other somewhat. In the Hausa towns of northern Nigeria, such as Kano and Zaria, the modern section is separated from the old area by a greenbelt. As Mabogunje (1968, p. 205) points out, the *sabon gari* ("new town") and the old area lead contrasting but related existences.

The colonial pattern is well described by Thomas Hodgkin (writing with reference to all Subsaharan Africa).

The colonial pattern of urbanization*

In parts of pre-European Africa (in the western Sudan in particular) urban communities existed. Jenne, Walata, Timbuktu, Gao, Kano, had many centuries of continuous history before the period of European colonization . . . What is new – a product essentially of the colonial epoch – is the great amorphous squalid *agglomération urbaine*: Dakar, Abidjan, Sekondi-Takoradi, Accra, Lagos, Douala, Brazzaville, Leopoldville, Kampala, Nairobi. These new African towns are as unlike Timbuktu as Stoke-on-Trent is unlike Chichester.

The comparison of these towns with the new industrial towns of northern England in the 1840s is one that immediately suggests itself – as regards not only their physical appearance and social conditions, but also the ideas which underlie their disorder . . . But in one essential respect at least mid-twentieth-century Dakar and Lagos differ from mid-nineteenth-century Leeds and Manchester: the cause of their existence, the basis of their economic life, is not factory industry but commerce. They have been brought into being to meet the needs of European trade. Their main function is to drain out of Africa its ground-nuts, palm-products, coffee, cocoa, cotton, minerals; and to pump into Africa European consumer goods – cloth, kerosene, bicycles, sewing-machines. Their focal points – substitutes for the cathedrals and guildhalls of mediaeval Europe, the mosques and bazaars of the Arab world – are the warehouses of the great European commercial houses . . . Hence the fact that so many of the new towns . . . are also seaports . . . Often the new towns were entirely European inventions – Abidjan, Leopoldville, Nairobi, for example: sometimes – like Lagos, Douala and Kampala – they were set alongside of, and eventually swallowed, the capital and trading-centre of a traditional African kingdom. Kano is something of a special case: an ancient walled Hausa city, whose pre-European prosperity was based upon the trans-Saharan trade, now transformed and inflated into a new town (within which the old survives) – with its main orientation reversed, so that it now looks south, down the railway to Lagos – a nerve-centre of the new system of air communications across Africa.

M. Richard-Molard (1954) brings out clearly the fundamentally commercial outlook of most African towns. Of Kaolack, a secondary port of Senegal, he says: "It is to ground-nuts that the town owes its whole existence; its entire cosmopolitan population – of middlemen and brokers, dealers in cloth, lorry-drivers, garage proprietors, hotel-keepers, *marabouts*, jobbers of all descriptions, officials, bank clerks, domestic servants, labourers and dockers: a town so concentrated upon ground-nuts that it forgets to think about itself, or even for the present to become a real town at all."

* Excerpts from Thomas Hodgkin, *Nationalism in Colonial Africa*, 1956, pp. 64–6 and 78, by permission of the author.

The spectacular growth of the new towns during the post-war period is connected with another fact: that the great commercial centre is also an administrative centre. Either – like Abidjan, Kumasi or Elisabethville – a regional capital; or – like Dakar, Lagos, Leopoldville – the capital of a colonial State. With the increasing complexity and expanding field of operations of the administrative machine, and the increase in Government spending, there has gone – particularly during the immediate post-war years – a building boom: a drive to erect new Government offices, schools, hospitals, post offices, telephone exchanges, airports, banks, commercial premises, hotels, etc. The new towns are thus partly the consequence of the demand for bigger bureaucracies, and more African labour to man the building industry. Moreover, the growing body of European officials, traders and technicians, and their families, seeking to reproduce the pattern of European life in Africa, and the developing African middle class (with their tendency to imitate European consumption habits), generate new demands for semi-luxury goods and services. The demand for more cars and cameras, cooked ham and chocolate éclairs, cafés, cinemas, chiropodists and circulating libraries, means an increase in specialised agencies to meet these demands . . .

The larger African towns, though relatively feeble as centres of production, are organized with far greater efficiency from the standpoint of consumption. There is little that cannot be bought – by those with money to buy.

Thus, the most common form of city that was inherited at Independence was a center of commercial exchange and government bureaucracy located on the territorial periphery of the new state. Import-substituting industries established in the 1950s and 1960s were drawn to the established major cities because they offered a local market, supporting services, a pool of experienced labor, and a culturally familiar and congenial setting for expatriate staff. There is little to attract industry beyond the security of the largest centers except the pull of mineral deposits.

With the advent of Independence, the political, administrative, and commercial functions of the colonial powers were transferred to the new nations. The political and administrative apparatuses swelled rapidly, but their location rarely changed; the national capitals were established at the former colonial headquarters.[3] What had been central locations of exchange and communication in the polity and economy of the colonial system were now eccentric locations in the new states. Today, the capital city of every West African country that touches the sea is located on the coast. West Africa continues to look down the railroad tracks toward these big coastal cities, nodes of exchange in a world trade system.[4]

As a consequence of their location on the geographic periphery of the new states, the young capitals of West Africa have acquired a political character that is more regional than national. Because of major ethnic and economic differences between the capital region and the rest of the nation, the geographically marginal capital comes to stand as a symbol of faction rather than national unity. Between 1950 and 1965, the average income in the south of the Ivory Coast, for instance, remained at about six times the level of the average income in the north; and in a 1967 report, the Ivory Coast Planning Ministry admitted that all the major new economic projects were located in the southern part of the country (Stryker 1971a, pp. 129ff.). Shifts of capital city sites have been undertaken elsewhere on the continent, but West African governments seem content to stay where they are.[5] When will the federal capital of Nigeria be moved to Kafanchan?[6]

Urban growth and overurbanization

Africa is the least urbanized of the world's major regions except Oceania (Table 2.1). Within the region, West Africa trails far behind South Africa and Northern Africa, but is ahead of other parts of Tropical Africa. In the world context, the level of urbanization of West Africa is close to that of Southeast Asia.

Table 2.1. *Total population and urban population for major world regions, 1970*

Region	Total population (thousands)	Urban population
Australia–New Zealand	15,280	84%
Northern America	228,766	75%
Europe	463,487	63%
USSR	244,125	62%
Latin America	281,934	54%
Asia	2,014,445	25%
Africa	352,568	22%
South Africa	20,044	50%
Northern Africa	85,095	35%
Western Africa[a]	111,890	20%
Middle and Southern Africa	38,297	15%
Eastern Africa	97,242	10%
Oceania	3,914	8%
World total	3,604,518[b]	38%

Note: These projections were made by the International Population and Urban Research Project, University of California, Berkeley, in 1968. They are based on official censuses, official estimates, and estimates by the project. Each country's own definition of urban areas was used.
[a] The definition of Western Africa used here differs from that of West Africa adopted in this volume in that it includes Saint Helena.
[b] Figures do not add because of rounding.
Source: Davis (1972, pp. 166, 170; n.d., pp. 57ff. pp. 111ff.).

Insofar as poor statistics permit conjecture, the rise in both the number and the size of urban centers in West Africa has been steady since the beginning of the colonial era. At the turn of the century, urban population was expanding moderately; it continued to do so until World War I, at which time a slight acceleration took place. Between the two world wars, urban populations and urban areas grew at a lively pace. From 1935, urban growth reflected the increased integration of West African economies into those of the colonial powers with the aid of improved transport and port facilities. World War II brought additional traffic in war supplies from Britain and America and the development of industries to replace foreign products that could no longer be imported. R. J. Harrison Church (1959, p. 20f.) has cited the example of Senegal, which, unable to export groundnuts to fallen France and unable to import sufficient fuel oil, brought in a Dunkirk firm that had been dispossessed by the war. It established a groundnut-crushing and oil-extraction plant, the product of which was substituted for diesel fuel oils in French North and West Africa. In addition to import substitution, the initial processing of export commodities contributed to industrial activity. Yet, even at the time of stepped-up industrial expansion in the late 1950s, the greatest number of employment opportunities opened up in the government bureaucracies and in service occupations. The cities promised new opportunities to those willing to come, and the response of erstwhile peasants and the resultant urban growth since World War II has proved overwhelming.

Thus, it is only since the mid-1930s or 1940s that West Africa has experienced the urban expansion that has given its cities and towns their present complexion. Although overall growth has been remarkable throughout the period, many observers have found the rate of urban growth since the 1950s downright alarming. Between 1950 and 1970, the urban population increased by a factor of 3.5, according to one estimate (see Table 2.2). West Africa thus holds the dubious distinction of having undergone the most rapid urban growth of any of the twenty-two world regions surveyed by Kingsley Davis (1972, p. 20). The estimated addition to the urban population of the region over the two decades is the equivalent of 6 to 7 percent annually, of which rural–urban migration must account for more than half.[7]

What are the consequences of present rates of urban growth for the economic development of the new states of West Africa? It has often been observed, and it is generally assumed, that economic development and urbanization are historically correlated in the experience of the developed world. The Industrial Revolution spawned the consumer base of Europe and North America through the division and rationalization of labor, which made the worker a dependent hybrid economic creature who consumed, not what he made, but what he could buy with his wages. In the industrialized world, employers and employees, no longer bound to the city by the economies of the great steam engine or the limits of early modes of transport, remained congregated in the urban marketplaces to which they had been drawn by the Industrial Revolution.

Close associations obtain between the level of per capita income and the level of urbanization in developing countries today (Kamerschen 1969). However, such findings do not provide sufficient evidence to sustain the argument that high rates of urban growth are a necessary condition for economic expansion. The rapid growth of urban populations is the consequence of the concentration of economic opportunities in the urban sector; it bears witness to severe urban–rural inequality. Well-equipped office complexes, comfortable apartment buildings, elegant shopping centers, broad avenues, and spacious parks tell us a great deal about the allocation of what, for these poor countries, are very substantial resources. The extent of urbanization and the form that it has taken may well be seen as indications of the level of production reached in a given country (i.e., that the country could have mobilized such resources). However, neither urban growth nor the dominance of modern architectural silhouettes on the skyline of a Third World city can be taken as evidence that these resources have been created in the urban sector, and there is no reason to assume a priori that such an allocation of resources is conducive to future increases in production.

There is controversy over whether West Africa is already overurbanized. Writers differ in their understanding of such a judgment (Sovani 1964), and data are fragmentary or impressionistic. We define overurbanization as urban growth that is inimical both in terms of economic growth in the narrow sense of increased economic production and in terms of economic development in the wide sense that includes an evaluation of the distribution of that production.

Two elements can be distinguished in urban growth: a natural population increase in the urban areas and rural–urban migration. There can be no doubt that a slowdown in present high rates of population increase would be desirable in economic terms, although the politics of antinatal policies are subject to argument. On economic grounds, the adoption of such policies would appear urgent, but the effects of such policies take considerable time to make themselves felt. Behavior changes that reduce fertility cannot be brought about overnight, and the present high birthrate has already produced a large population that will be of childbearing age a generation hence.

In considering short- and medium-term objectives, attention must therefore focus on rural–urban migration, now a major contributor to urban growth in West Africa. An economic evaluation of rural–urban migration involves a comparison between the rural and urban sectors in terms of both production and consumption. A comparison of the sum of private and public costs of consumption in rural and urban locations varies for different goods and services. Housing, transport, sewerage, provision of fuel, and distribution of staple foods stand out as five services that are expensive in urban agglomerations but cheap or altogether unnecessary in rural areas.[8] Whether the rural–urban migrant manages to pay for them, urban hosts provide them, or they are subsidized by public authorities, these costly services cut into, and in the aggregate probably more than offset, any savings that could be achieved in the provision of other services or goods, such as piped water, electricity, and medical care, that are cheaper to provide to urban population concentrations than to a dispersed rural population.

Rural emigration involves an opportunity cost because aggregate production remains lower than it otherwise would be. This proposition certainly holds in West Africa, where severe population pressure on land is still the exception. In every West African country, part of the migratory flow to the cities originates in areas where land is available to those who are willing to work it. Agricultural output is not realized because of the movement of rural labor to the cities.[9]

The urban picture is not so clear. Available statistics show that urban growth since Independence has far outstripped increases in the labor force employed in enumerated firms and government establishments. With the advent of Independence, manufacture, especially for import-substitution, received a boost, but job creation was limited because capital-intensive technologies were adopted. An increasing proportion of the urban population was left outside the sector in which wages are regulated by government, wage commissions, or collective bargaining, but many continue to try to enter it. Unemployment is accordingly substantial in all the major cities of West Africa.[10]

However, underemployment is probably an even more serious problem. When they first arrive in town, most migrants can count on the assistance of family, kin, or other people from their rural home. But as time goes by, a higher proportion of immigrants must fend for themselves. If they have not been able to secure employment, they are forced to look for casual work, to accept employment well below the legal minimum wage, or to engage in petty self-employment. Some get involved in crime and its attendant risks. Here is how Keith Hart describes one man's efforts to secure a livelihood for his family in Accra.

Atinga's bar in Nima, Accra*
The following case-history serves to illustrate the place of informal activities in the economic lives of Nima's labour force. Atinga was given a medical discharge from the army at Christmas 1965. He was 28 years old, had been in the South for nine years, and now lived in Nima with his wife and a brother's teenage son. He was without work and had not yet been paid any gratuity or pension; but he had £ 10 from his last pay packet.** At first he

* Excerpt from Keith Hart, "Informal Income Opportunities and Urban Unemployment in Ghana," 1973, pp. 79–81, by permission of the author and the *Journal of Modern African Studies*.
** The Ghanaian pound had 20 shillings and at that time was equivalent to U.S. $4.

thought of going home to farm, but the prospect of getting another job in Accra was more attractive. However, he had to finance the period of his unemployment and decided to set up as a retailer of *akpeteshi* or crude gin.

First he converted his room (rent £3 per month) into a bar-cum-living quarters by the simple expedient of hanging a cloth down the centre and piling his accumulated possessions on both sides – chairs and a table (bought for 15s.) occupied the 'bar' section. For next to nothing he got some small plastic glasses, an assortment of used bottles, and an old, rusting funnel, which were placed on the table. He then went to a nearby distiller and bought a 4-gallon drum of *akpeteshi* for £5. 10s. He handed over what was left (just under £4) to his wife for food, borrowed £4 elsewhere out of which to pay the month's rent, and opened his new business on 30 December.

The retail price of gin was fixed throughout Nima at 6s. a bottle, and smaller quantities *pro rata*; allowing for wastage, gross receipts from a drum came to £8 to £7. 10s. Profit margins could be varied by buying gin wholesale at prices ranging from £4 to £5. 10s. a drum, according to quality and method of payment (cash or credit). Atinga bought the best gin in order to attract a clientele, and because he knew that increased turnover compensated for reduced item profit.

His main problem related to the extension of credit; adequate turnover, given the improvidence of his customers, could only be maintained by generous credit facilities. But Atinga needed a high proportion of cash sales to replenish stock and to feed his family, as well as to pay other costs. His average daily expenditure was 7s. 6d. or £14–£15 per month, including rent. So he had to sell a lot of gin. He also tried to diversify; but his wife's sugar-lump sales business foundered under a saturation of competition in the neighbourhood, and his own attempts to sell Coca Cola were doomed without a refrigerator.

In the first three weeks Atinga ran into a crisis; he over-extended credit to the tune of £14 (a third of total sales) in order to keep up a turnover rate of one gallon a day and attract a clientele, some of whom were clearly out to take him for a ride. His stocks ran out before pay-day, leaving him with inadequate funds to replenish them. However, he weathered the crisis, borrowing in order to maintain supplies (otherwise his clients would take their custom, and their debts, away), and gaining repayment of enough credit to go on with. He now cracked down on credit facilities and, though this naturally slowed turnover, he built up a small regular clientele whom he trusted and who came to him whatever the quality of his gin; he was thus able to economise by buying gin at £4 a drum. The core of his regular customers consisted of young men from his home village.

By now Atinga saw that his bar was only viable as a sideline, supplementary to regular employment; moreover his wife was pregnant. For some time he tried persistently to get back into the army, while his wife looked after the bar. When things were bad, his landlord's wives helped out with meals and food supplies. Attempts to diversify in trade failed for lack of capital and expertise. Meanwhile his personal loans and debts were extended to roughly equal effect, a backlog of rent being the most significant item. After his narrow escape, turnover steadied out to around four or five drums a month, giving rise to a monthly income of between £10 and £12; moreover this was being realised (eventually) in cash, for his total outstanding credit in April 1966 was only £12 – a much smaller percentage of turnover – of which £5. 10s. had been written off as bad debts.

The remainder of 1966 saw a gradual decline in the fortunes of Atinga's bar, if not in his total income. For in September he got a job as a watchman at 8s. per day, leaving his wife to look after the customers. Turnover, however, slowed to a trickle and his wife consumed most of the gin. Occasionally he supplemented their income with a once-and-for-all enterprise, like the purchase of a stray dog for sale as meat and soup. At times like this, his bar did a roaring trade for a brief spell; but more often it was empty at night because he had no gin to sell, or his customers no money, or, more likely, both.

In December his wife gave birth to a son. In February 1967 the military bureaucracy got around to paying him £40 as an advance on his gratuity. The bar took on a new lease of life – £20 was spent on wood for a counter, partition, door, and shelves. Atinga even bought a gin-seller's licence; he did not, however, pay off any of his accumulated debts. For a few weeks he used the remainder of his capital to keep up an artificial rate of business, but he was soon back in the vicious circle of credit and turnover. In May he lost his job as a watchman, but was lucky to be accepted almost immediately for training as an escort policeman. In June he went off to Winneba and visited his wife and child at weekends. On one of these visits, in August 1967, he was thrown out of the house by his landlord, who accused him of being the informer behind a police raid on the premises. The room and all its wooden fittings were seized as part compensation for a debt of £32. 10s. owed to the landlord.

Atinga left the neighbourhood with his family, and the gin bar enterprise was at an end – his landlord's wife took it over, but was unsuccessful as she offered no credit whatsoever. Some 20 months of unemployment and intermittent formal employment had been negotiated satisfactorily by means of an informal operation which was always rickety, but which had been the main basis of his family's survival in the city. Atinga's story provides a case study of how informal employment may act as a buffer, for those who are 'out of work', against destitution or dependence on others.

How easy is it for someone who lacks alternative means of supporting himself to find work of this kind? The answer, of course, will vary according to the type of work. Nevertheless, despite the constraints on entry to informal occupations, the range of opportunities available outside the organised labour market is so wide that few of the 'unemployed' are totally without some form of income, however irregular. By any standards many of them are poor, but then so are large numbers of wage-earners.

Insofar as distinctions between levels of subsistence can be made in urban settings, the economic condition of the urban poor of West Africa is usually not so desperate as that of their counterparts in the infamous slums of Asia and Latin America. Many retain the option to return to a niche in the rural economy, a strategy that we will explore in Chapter 4. If they stay on at the margins of the urban economy, it is either because even there they are better off than they would be in agriculture or because they are prepared to endure hardship in the hope of ultimately obtaining employment in the regulated **urban sector**.

Individual incomes cannot be equated with a contribution to national production. The new arrival may be able to join the newspaper sellers who crowd the entrance to the post office and to secure a share of sales, but the number of newspapers sold is unlikely to increase. To the casual observer, the throngs of street vendors and shoe shiners in West African cities have long passed the point where an additional self-employed person enhances the quantity or quality of services rendered to customers.[11] In the language of economics, the marginal product in these occupations is zero. There is every reason to characterize recent urban growth in West Africa as overurbanization; still, rural–urban migrants continue to swell the ranks of the urban unemployed and underemployed.

Variations on a pattern

Although West Africa is one of the poorest and least urbanized regions of the world, significant variations do exist among the countries of the area (Table 2.2). Estimates of national income suffer from severe limitations, two of which stand out.[12] First, a major part of the production in West African countries is by peasants for their own consumption. National income statistics include no more than crude guesses at the value of this subsistence production. Second, international comparisons fail to deal with differences in price levels among countries; they use official exchange rates to convert figures to a common denominator. The problem was highlighted in the case of Ghana when the cedi (the national currency) was devalued; national income statistics showed a drop in gross domestic product (GDP) per capita from $289 in 1966 to $230 in 1967 mainly because of the devaluation (United Nations 1970, p. 9).

Reservations concerning estimates of the level of urbanization are also in order. West Africa shares the problem of comparability of population figures found elsewhere in the developing world. That is, censuses are not so up-to-date as one would like, they have been taken in different years for different countries, and errors in enumeration and even deliberate misenumeration have been alleged.[13] Especially important for our purposes, countries vary in their criteria for designating an urban area, and delays in adjusting administrative boundaries as urban agglomerations expand are the rule. Lagos had a population of 665,000 according to the 1963 census, but over 1 million people were already living in the metropolitan area at that time. The figures presented here are intended to convey only major differences; the reader is cautioned against placing too much trust in them as absolute values.

Four countries, Liberia, the Ivory Coast, Senegal, and Ghana, stand apart from the rest of the region, with a quarter to a third of the population in the urban sector and GDP per capita estimated to be between $200 and $350 in 1970.[14] Intuitively, it might appear that an output of this magnitude requires a correspondingly enlarged urban sector, but only Senegal (where Dakar was

Table 2.2. *Total population, urban population, and gross domestic product per capita for West African countries, 1950–70*

Country	Total population (thousands) 1974	Urban population (thousands)			Annual growth in urban population		Urban population 1970	GDP per capita 1970
		1950	1960	1970	1950–60	1960–70		
Mauritania	1,290	15	22	28[a]	4%	2%[a]	2%[a]	$165
Senegal	4,869	415	730	1,081	6%	4%	25%	216
The Gambia	506	19	25	37	3%	4%	8%	101
Mali	5,560	141	247	429	6%	6%	8%	54
Guinea-Bissau[b]	810	61	84	119	3%	4%	15%	n.a.
Guinea	5,390	119	240	451	7%	7%	9%	82
Sierra Leone	2,911	175	250	362	4%	4%	14%	167
Liberia	1,500	42	128	344	12%	10%	26%	268
Ivory Coast	6,387	197	511	1,244	10%	9%	23%	347
Upper Volta	5,760	98	154	253[a]	5%	5%[a]	5%[a]	59
Ghana	9,610	689	1,551	2,990	8%	7%	34%	257
Togo	2,176	59	139	305	9%	8%	16%	134
Benin	3,027	135	244	438	6%	6%	16%	82
Niger	4,480	48	76	118[a]	5%	4%[a]	3%[a]	90
Nigeria	73,044	4,000	7,700	13,826	7%	6%	21%	145
West Africa	127,320	6,213	12,102[c]	22,025	6.9%	6.2%	19%	

Note: Urban population figures are based on official censuses, official estimates, and estimates and interpolations by the International Population and Urban Research Project, University of California, Berkeley, for 1950 and 1960; projections for 1970 were made by the project in 1968. Each country's own definition of urban areas has been used.

n.a. = not available

[a] The urban population projected for 1970 in Mauritania, Upper Volta, and Niger would appear on the low side (World Bank 1976b, p. 511), the annual growth in urban population 1960–70 and the proportion of the population urban in 1970 understated to that extent. [b] Guinea-Bissau includes the Cape Verde Islands. [c] Figures do not add because of rounding.

Sources: First column from World Bank (1976a, p. 12); columns 2–4 from Davis (n.d., pp. 58ff.); columns 5 and 6 calculated from columns 2–4; column 7 calculated from column 4 and extrapolation of column 1 to 1970 according to population growth rates reported by the World Bank (1976a, p. 12); last column from United Nations (1976d, pp. 3f.).

the earliest center of industrial activity in West Africa) and Ghana have significantly higher levels of industrialization than other countries in the region; and in both, the proportion of GDP accounted for by manufacturing is still quite low: 11 percent in Ghana in 1970–2 (United Nations 1976c, p. 498) and probably little more in Senegal.

We need to consider an alternative interpretation: that countries with greater economic resources tend to channel them into the urban sector, especially into the bureaucratic apparatus and public works. The relative wealth of Liberia, the Ivory Coast, Senegal, and Ghana is not manufactured in the urban areas; it is derived from the labor of peasants growing cocoa, coffee, and peanuts, the production of the rubber plantations, and the extraction of iron ore and phosphates.

The remaining ten West African countries that were independent in 1970, with GDP per capita estimated at about $50 to about $170, are among the poorest countries of the world. This acute poverty has been further exacerbated in Mauritania, Mali, Upper Volta, and Niger, where conditions have fallen below the subsistence level for many as the great desert has apparently once again taken a giant stride over its old boundaries. Hundreds of thousands have died during six years of drought.

The hubris of capital cities

Most national capitals of West Africa have grown at a breathtaking pace (Table 2.3).[15] In two thirds of the countries the population of the capital city more than quadrupled over the last two decades. The capital is the largest city in almost every country of the region; the only exception is Benin, where Porto-Novo trails Cotonou, the chief port. In Nigeria, Lagos bypassed Ibadan only in the sixties. Three other countries approach the rank-size rule (i.e., the largest city is about twice the size of the second city). However, two thirds of the countries display a strong tendency toward urban primacy (i.e., a pattern in which the first city is much larger than the second). A comparison with earlier data (Clarke 1972b, p. 450) shows that the pattern has become more pronounced in almost all these countries over the last decade. In recent years urban primacy has reached extremes in Guinea, Senegal, Liberia, and Togo: In Guinea the capital is apparently nearly nine times, in each of the other three countries it is nearly seven times bigger than the next-largest town. An expression once used to highlight the pernicious consequences of the dominant position of Paris in relation to the rest of France is now echoed in West Africa: *"Dakar et le désert sénégalais."*

The growth of the national capital and its ever more impressive skyline are a source of pride to some. But anyone who ventures beyond to the vast expanses of West Africa is stunned by the disparity between the concentration of resources in the capital cities and the neglect that is the fate of much of their

Table 2.3. *Population of West African capital cities, 1920–76*

City	1920s year/source[a]/population (thousands)	1930s year/source[a]/population (thousands)	1940s year/source[a]/population (thousands)	1950s year/source[a]/population (thousands)	1960s year/source[a]/population (thousands)	1970s year/source[a]/population (thousands)	Average annual growth 1950s to 1970s	Two-city index[b] year/ratio
Nouakchott					1961 C 6	1972 E 55[c]		
Dakar	1921 V 34	1931 V 54	1945 V 132[c]	1955 C 231[c]	1961 S 375[c]	1976 C 799	6%	1972 2.3
Banjul	1921 C 9	1931 C 14	1944 C 21	1951 C 20	1963 C 28	1973 C 39	3%	1976 6.8
Bamako	1926 C 16	1936 E 21	1945 E 36	1958 C 76	1965/6 C 168	1972 E 225	8%	1973 4.2
Bissau				1950 C 18	1960 L 22	1970 C 71	7%	1969 5.6
Conakry	1921 L 9	1934 L 9	1943 L 26	1958 C 76[c]	1960 C 112[c]	1972 C 526[c]	15%	1972 9.2
Freetown	1921 C 44	1931 C 55	1944 C 99[c]		1963 C 160[c]	1974 C 274	5%[d]	1972 8.8
Monrovia	1920 G 5	1934 G 10	1945 G 18	1956 C 42	1962 C 81	1974 C 164	8%	1974 3.6
Abidjan	1921 L 5	1931 L 10	1942 L 36	1955 C 126	1963 S 242	1974 C 555	10%	1974 6.6
Ouagadougou	1926 V 12	1933 V 12	1945 V 18	1957 V 47	1961/2 C 59[c]	1970 E 170	8%	1970 4.8
Accra	1921 C 44	1931 C 61	1948 C 124		1960 C 388[c]	1970 C 636[c]	8%[e]	1975 1.5
Lomé	1923 C 6	1931 C 7	1944 C 38	1958 C 69	1964 S 116	1970 C 193	8%	1970 1.8
Porto-Novo	1921 L 20	1938 A 24	1943 L 29	1950 C 41	1961 S 64	1970 E 87	4%	1973 1.1[f]
Niamey	1926 L 3	1931 A 2	1943 L 6	1950 L 9	1960 A 79	1972 S 108	12%	1973 3.7
Lagos	1921 C 100	1931 A 126		1952 C 333[c]	1963 C 1,090[c]	1976 E 2,500[c]	9%	1971 1.3

[a] Abbreviations indicate the following types of data: administrative census (A), census enumeration (C), calculated estimate (E), guesstimate (G), secondary source (L), sample survey (S), evaluated secondary source (V).

[b] The two-city index of urban primacy is based on the ratio of the populations of the largest and second largest city.

[c] Population in the urban agglomeration.

[d] Average annual growth for Freetown is for 1963 to 1974.

[e] Average annual growth for Accra is for 1948 to 1970.

[f] The largest city in Benin is Cotonou, not the capital city.

Source: Peter K. Mitchell, director of the Demographic Documentation Project, Centre of West African Studies, University of Birmingham; column 7 calculated from columns 4 and 6, unless indicated otherwise.

hinterlands. There may be reasons of economic efficiency for locating new industry in the country's biggest city, but to paraphrase Colin Clark (1967, p. 323), it is easy to distinguish additional factors that have made for the primacy of Dakar, Bamako, Conakry, Freetown, Monrovia, Abidjan, Lomé, and Niamey: the concentration of so much political, administrative, educational, and cultural authority there and the uses to which that authority has been put. The hubris of capital cities in West Africa is rooted in the political and social structure of these countries, which tends to appropriate to the capital.[16] As we proceed, we will propose an inventory of the forces at work; but at this juncture, an illustration may suffice.

The Ivory Coast provides a striking example of the singular magnetism of the capital. Michael A. Cohen (1974a, p. 229; 1973, p. 238) reports that 499 of the country's 617 industrial enterprises are located in Abidjan and that 60 percent of the jobs in the modern sector of the economy are found there.[17] In 1968, the eight-story, 500-bed Centre Hospitalier Universitaire, one of the largest and most modern hospitals in Africa, was built in the luxurious Cocody quarter, home of high government officials, but the funds given by France were originally intended for twelve regional hospitals (Michael A. Cohen 1974b, p. 229).[18] With this consistent bias in favor of Abidjan, it is not surprising that the city's population increased more than fourfold over a period of fifteen years, passing the half million mark in the late 1960s.

The political dimension underlying the concentration of resources in the capital of the Ivory Coast is well documented by Richard E. Stryker (1971b, pp. 96f.). No elections have followed those held in 1956 for any of the existing nine municipal councils (they were scheduled for 1959 and 1965), and council memberships have been seriously depleted through deaths and changes in residence. The municipal council in Daloa was disbanded in 1960 and never reconstituted. The status of *commune de plein exercise* was withdrawn in 1965 from Grand Bassam, ostensibly for financial but at least in part for political reasons. In fact, 66 of the 100 deputies "elected" to the National Assembly in 1970 live and work full time in Abidjan (Michael A. Cohen 1974a, p. 176).

A shift toward the development of secondary urban centers is desirable for reasons of equity, and it might also have positive effects for economic growth. First, regional growth poles would reduce the severe imbalance among different regions in terms of access to urban facilities (e.g., postprimary education and health care) and urban opportunities, especially employment. Second, new rural opportunities arising from the requirements of the urban population and from processing centers would be distributed more widely. Third, the lines of communication would be shortened for the many urbanites who maintain close ties with their rural areas of origin; this would be particularly important for those who have to leave their wives and/or children behind.

It has been argued that concentrating employment opportunities in the national capital allows people from many different backgrounds to meet, that they thus come to know each other, that barriers are surmounted, that a sense of national unity emerges. However, as we will see, the majority of urban dwellers maintain strong bonds with areas of origin, ethnic identities continue to be salient, and ethnic loyalties frequently affect decisions that are crucial to the man in the street, such as recruitment into jobs, allocation of trade licenses, and access to housing. Offering the different regions the prospect of strengthening the position of their own urban centers, on the other hand, is a prescription that may have serious consequences in the long term for ethnic peace within national boundaries. An optimal strategy would seem to involve the promotion of economic development in the different regions, based on a division of labor among a number of growth poles that would provide for sustained national integration through regional economic interdependence.

The emergence of the metropolis

The population of metropolitan Lagos, the federal capital and primary port of Nigeria, reached the 1 million mark in the early 1960s; an estimate for 1976 puts it at 2.5 million. Ibadan, the Yoruba metropole until 1976, and, capital of Western State, a region more populous and with a greater GDP than any West African country other than Nigeria, attained an estimated three-quarters of a million in the early 1970s. Accra, the capital of Ghana, a country ranking second in West Africa in terms of both population and GDP, reached 500,000 in the mid-1960s. Dakar, Abidjan, and, apparently, Conakry, the capital cities of rather small nations, followed closely, propelled by their primate position. These new and nascent metropolises confront us with the issue of optimal city size.[19]

Any attempt to determine an optimal city size or, more realistically, an optimal size range, is highly suspect. Joseph J. Spengler (1967, p. 59) emphasizes the difficulty of assessing the performance of cities (i.e., of identifying, measuring, and appropriately aggregating all costs and all benefits, both private and public) and correlating changes therein with changes in size; multiple variables have to be taken into account, information on these variables is frequently nonexistent, and such data as are available are subject to wide margins of error. Harry W. Richardson (1973, p. 121) has recently charged that those who offer judgments on optimal city size base their observations on value judgments, implicit but untestable weighting systems, and arbitrary selection of a limited set of criteria. Finally, what little research has been done concerns highly industrialized, affluent countries; the exception is a detailed study in northern India (Stanford Research Institute, et al. 1968).

Still, the issue has to be faced. Decisions affecting the future size of cities are taken (or not taken) daily by public authorites, private investors, and individual migrants. The limited literature suggests a U-shaped curve for many variables; that is, with more people, per capita costs fall, then rise again. A range of 100,000 to 200,000 appears optimal in many respects; however, the optimal size for a given city will vary according to the functions it performs.

Nevertheless, none of the few studies to date has suggested a size exceeding 500,000 as optimal, even where manufacturing is fully developed.

Spengler (1967, p. 72) concludes his discussion of the African case by suggesting that the advantages associated with increases in city size are usually exhausted before a city's population exceeds 100,000. Above that level, he cites the consequences of rising capital and service costs, pollution of air and water, impediments to beautification, congestion, loss of time and living space, and waste of capital and labor inputs as control becomes more difficult for larger private and public administrative units. We would emphasize the severe diseconomies of scale that arise for housing and/or transport. High-density multistory housing mandates more stringent structural standards and more expensive materials than the majority of the urban population can afford; low residential densities increase commuting distance unless housing is allocated close to the place of work.

One more argument in support of keeping city size down has been completely neglected. In small towns, a greater proportion of the work force can live in peri-urban areas. Here customary obstacles to the transfer of land are fast disappearing, and urban workers can acquire land, build houses to standards they can afford, and engage in part-time farming. Such peri-urban agriculture offers wife and husband an opportunity to supplement his wages and thus the prospect of more substantial income than can be obtained from petty trade. As long as urban earning opportunities for women remain severely limited, this is for many the only alternative to the familiar pattern of separation that leaves the wife on the farm.

The study of optimal city size is as yet inconclusive, and we may want to give the benefit of the doubt to city sizes of up to 500,000 in population. However, six cities in West Africa have already gone well beyond that point and are continuing to expand at a fast pace. The case of Dakar is particularly striking. When Dakar's status was reduced from capital of French West Africa to capital of Senegal, a hinterland of little economic promise with small population, migration continued to add new residents in unprecedented volume.

Lest it be assumed that metropolitan growth is simply the outcome of attempts to locate investment optimally in terms dictated by the national economy, several factors have to be recognized that affect those economic variables in turn or interfere directly with investment decisions. First, government and public administration expanded considerably immediately prior to Independence and also subsequently, but it remained heavily concentrated in the national capitals. Second, this political and administrative apparatus, in turn, has drawn economic activities to the capitals. Third, national decision makers appear greatly concerned that the national capital project a "modern" image to foreigners; therefore, what may well be called "conspicuous investments" are made in airports, four-lane highways to whisk visiting dignitaries to magnificent conference halls, and skyscrapers to house the offices of the bureaucracy. Fourth, the showy consumption of the elite who are assembled in the capital city provides further impetus to economic activity there. The subsidized housing built for the elite and the domestic help it employs are two important elements. Fifth, the centralization of political and administrative machinery in the national capitals has made ready access to decision makers an important externality for private investors. Sixth, although private investors are attracted by the externalities that bigger agglomerations offer, these investors do not bear the costs generated by their decision to locate there to the extent that these costs are public costs or, when translated into private costs, appear as average rather than marginal costs. Seventh, capital cities have thus become ever more attractive to the managerial elite as places in which to live. Who would want to miss the comforts of the Hôtel Ivoire, the chance to gamble at its Casino Elephant d'Or, the pleasures of the Riviera resort complex planned near Abidjan?

The plight of the urban masses

Like cities everywhere, those of West Africa harbor a range of conditions and living standards and styles. Of course, the cities boast modern buildings and facilities occupied and utilized by national and expatriate elites, but they also contain the range of places of residence and work of the rest of the urban population. A major proportion of this large remainder of homes and businesses accommodating unemployed migrants, factory workers, clerks, and even skilled workers consists of overcrowded tenements and shacks. These are the slums and shantytowns found throughout the Third World.

The contrast between the mansions of the rich and the tenements and shacks impresses itself on the most superficial observer. The plight of low-income earners is compounded by the fact that the national elite imposes minimum standards for new urban housing and other amenities that are imported from more affluent countries. The masses thus are forced to live in severe overcrowding and/or in shantytowns beyond the reach of administrative controls.

Overcrowding is a serious problem. A 1964 survey of households of married persons in Lagos municipality found an average 4.1 persons per room (Ohadike 1968, p. 85). Among a sample of factory workers interviewed in Accra in 1966, 18 percent were living more than 3.5 persons to a room, and 37 percent more than 2.5 persons, counting children under age five as half-persons (Peil 1972, p. 165). A 1961 survey in Dakar found an average 2.8 persons per room (Mersadier 1968, p. 262).

A second concern is "spontaneous housing" (dwellings erected without any control by public authorities).[20] Up to 30 percent of the population of Dakar and about one-third of the population of Abidjan are thought to live in unauthorized buildings (World Bank 1972, p. 82; Haeringer 1972, p. 629).[21] San Pedro, the new port city of the Ivory Coast, had an unauthorized settlement of 8,000 to 10,000 people before the port was even completed; the construction workers and the traders and artisans they attracted had nowhere else to go, and present plans make no provision for housing that this population could afford (Haeringer 1972, pp. 642ff.). What the poor can do for themselves is illegal by definition. Standards that cannot be met by the majority of the urban population lead to construction that is totally uncontrolled. Houses on difficult terrain, preemption of alternative land uses, poor settlement layout, and inadequate house design are the results; as are populous settlements that lack roads, water, sewerage, and electricity. Rehabilitation is vastly more expensive than an initial investment in planning and a modicum of services would have been (United Nations 1968).

From the point of view of authority or the public, the poorer sections constitute an embarrassment of substandard living. However, these areas have come about as a product of economic conditions and actually represent an adaptation to the low income of the urban masses. Peter Marris indicates the emergence of conflict between city and nation, on one side, and community, on the other. The case he describes is the one of the Central Lagos Slum Clearance Scheme initiated in the 1950s, but the situation is similar in Dakar, Freetown, or Abidjan.

With the approach of independence, the people of Nigeria began to look more critically at their Federal Capital, and saw in its congested lanes of ramshackle houses a poor reflection of their aspirations. As the Minister of Lagos Affairs remarked, "it is the mirror through which foreigners make their initial appraisal of Nigeria and many regard it as an index of the progress and prosperity of Nigeria." The condition of Central Lagos, he said was "humiliating to any person with a sense of national pride." (1961, vii)

But the people of the area, many of whom were self-employed traders and craftsmen, were largely dependent on being at the center of commerce for their livelihood; they attracted a group of regular customers who lived or worked nearby and to whom they were readily available. The people of the "slum," as the physically run-down area was called, were involved in a delicate economic and, not incidentally, kinship network. The economic viability of the family, supported by the availability of occasional credit and the wife's petty trade in the familiar social milieu of the neighborhood, was precariously balanced. The need in terms of shelter was for low-cost houses with many rooms that could be built cheaply to provide a family home and space for trade. Whether or not national pride can afford to allow the poor to mar its showcase, the poor cannot afford the showcase.[22] Marris has further articulated the dilemma.

The problem of slum clearance in Lagos*
The fundamental problem raised by the Lagos slum clearance scheme is this: how can a neighbourhood be physically destroyed, without destroying

* Excerpt from Peter Marris, *Family and social change in an African city: A study of rehousing in Lagos*, 1961, pp. 129–31, by permission of the author, the Institute of Community Studies, Routledge & Kegan Paul, and Northwestern University Press.

at the same time the livelihood and way of life of the people who have settled there? If these are disrupted, the clearance of slums is likely to do them
more harm than good.

It seems that if compulsory rehousing is to be just, and a benefit to those
rehoused, it must fulfil two conditions.

(1)   The people must be able to afford it. In Africa, this must mean
that it will cost them no more to live in their new houses than
their old, since very few people have money enough to pay for
better housing. Those who can afford it and want to spend their
money in this way will have already provided for themselves. If
people are forced to pay for housing they cannot afford, their
poverty will oblige them to restrict their participation in social
life. Above all, it will withdraw them from their family, and this,
in Africa especially, can cause great unhappiness.

(2)   They must be able to re-establish their pattern of life in the new
surroundings. They must not be too far distant from their kin,
nor their work, and the same range of economic activities must
be open to them. And their new homes must be so designed that
they can be adapted to their way of life. That is to say, if they
have depended for their livelihood on being at the centre of
trade, they must be rehoused where they have the same chances
of custom, or where there are alternative ways of earning a
living open to them.

These two conditions are likely to be very difficult to fulfil in practice.
The second condition can most easily be realised by rehousing the people
on the site which has been cleared, but if they are to be less crowded than
before, the buildings will have to be of several storeys. In Lagos, at least,
this would have been very expensive indeed, and the cost could not have
been recovered in rents. To rebuild in the suburbs, as in Lagos, brings down
the cost of housing to government only to increase the cost in fares and
living expenses to the people themselves, and makes it very much more difficult to prevent the disruption of family groups and economic relationships.
New markets must be developed, new opportunities of employment provided; and the new estate must be able to absorb not only those removed
from the slums, but relatives who wish to settle with them or near them.

Lastly, however the problem is tackled, it is likely to cost a lot of public
money. The people to be rehoused may be expected to bear some of the
cost themselves, on the grounds that they are, after all, enjoying a higher
standard of housing, and the scheme is for their benefit. But many will not
be able to afford to raise their standards, without sacrifices they would not
make from choice. If their interests only are to be considered, it would be
better not to rehouse them at all, but to use the available resources in a general improvement of health services and public amenities. The worst housing can meanwhile be gradually improved and rebuilt as national resources
and personal incomes rise. But if, for reasons of prestige, neighbourhoods
are redeveloped to a standard in advance of the general growth of prosperity, the whole cost is a fair charge on the public purse. And the cost will
include not only the buildings themselves, but substantial subsidies to the
people who are to live in them.

This illustrates a dilemma which the newly independent nations of Africa
will often have to face. They are urgently reaching out towards the prosperity of much richer countries, impatient of the limits set by their present

wealth. For the time being, they have to make an uncomfortable choice: if they spread their resources evenly in overall development, the progress must fall disappointingly short of their aspirations. But if they attempt, here and there, to reach a standard not yet generally possible, they may overburden groups in their society with a standard of living beyond their power to sustain. In Lagos, it is beyond the means of the Federal Government to house the whole population to the standards of space and amenities that they would accept as minimal. That is not surprising, when even in London, Moscow and New York there are still congested and insanitary slums. But if one neighbourhood of Lagos is selected as a start, where standards will not be compromised, the people themselves cannot live up to them. Their way of life is suited to the social and economic pattern of Nigeria as it is, not as it may hope to be, and they do not earn enough to adapt themselves. The cost of unbalanced development is social disruption: even if rents are subsidised, economic opportunities restored at government expense, and compensation for hardship freely given, an artificial pattern of life is still being imposed. It is therefore doubly expensive to anticipate progress: not only does the selected project claim a disproportionate share of resources, it causes hardships which have to be put right by an expensive programme of rehabilitation. Only the elite can overleap the obstacles in the way of their country's development, and fine houses for Ministers, suburban estates for senior civil servants, hotels for diplomats, add an air of prosperity to Lagos which the occupants can afford to enjoy. But there is a danger, too, in allocating so much of the nation's resources to benefit the already rich. Unless these problems are understood, the symbols of progress will be achieved only at the price of growing injustice.

Slum clearance is a good example of what has been called "partial planning" (Madavo 1971). Another example is low-cost housing projects that are invariably built to standards that make them much too expensive for the majority of the urban population. They typically end up being occupied by middle-income earners. Where such projects do house low-income families, they are either severely overcrowded or have to be heavily subsidized, thus making it impossible to provide shelter for any but a small minority of the low-income group.

The need to deal with the housing problem of the urban population at large and a recognition of the extremely limited resources available to any West African country have led to the development of the site and services approach. In recent years, the International Bank for Reconstruction and Development (World Bank) has committed itself to support for and evaluation of such projects. The first scheme has been launched in Dakar. A formerly unoccupied area is being leveled, divided into evenly laid-out lots, and given some limited access to water and electricity. Public facility buildings are to be provided. The utilization of local labor is emphasized. Lots are to be sold on installment and building costs substantially reduced, as each family will construct its own dwelling and make such improvements as it can over time. Many more low-income families will thus be able to afford their own legally held plots. Still, half of Dakar's population is too poor to qualify for the project (World Bank 1975, p. 70f.).

Clearly, the site and services approach is a step in the right direction. Nevertheless, any project that remains out of reach for so many constitutes a less than satisfactory solution to the problem it addresses.[23] Furthermore, the Dakar scheme appears to be one more instance of partial plannings. It perpetuates the bias in favor of the capital city over the country's six regional centers. Fourteen thousand units are now being laid out in Dakar, but only one regional center is included (Thiès, with 1,600 plots). The pull of the primate capital–port city for migrants is thus reinforced, and an opportunity to make the regional centers more attractive in comparison with Dakar is lost.

More than a decade after Independence, urbanization in West Africa is characterized by severe inequalities. There is an imbalance in economic opportunities between the urban and the rural sectors. Among cities, the extremely limited resources available are concentrated in the capitals. Within cities, there is the huge economic disparity between the urban masses and a tiny elite.[24]

The inequalities created by present patterns of urbanization in West Africa are all too obvious. The economic inefficiency inherent in these patterns is a more controversial matter. We have used two approaches to suggest that the allocation of economic resources is far from optimal for economic growth. First, we have argued that economic resources are wasted in urban unemployment and underemployment, in metropolitan growth, and in uncontrolled urban settlement. Second, we have questioned the assumption that recent patterns of urbanization are the outcome of an optimizing allocation of resources by exploring factors that affect the economic variables or interfere directly with investment decisions. We have begun to direct attention to the political process that appears consistently biased toward the interests and concerns of a small group of decision makers.

If the future of the cities of West Africa is to be other than an exaggeration of the present, comprehensive planning is called for. Urban planning has to face the challenge of providing amenities for all urban dwellers. Regional planning has to focus on the development of intermediary urban centers. National planning has to effect improved living conditions for the rural masses.

It is difficult to envisage the adoption and implementation of the sweeping measures required in order to reverse present trends. But it is even more difficult to picture any effective solution to the problems faced by the governments and city dwellers of West Africa at some time in the future. The picture conjured up by a projection of present trends is manifestly clear.

3   Rural—urban migration

A la queue leu leu,
Ils vont, ils vont . . .
A la queue leu leu,
A la queue leu leu
Le baluchon sur le dos
A la queue leu leu
Les pieds poudreux dans leurs sandalettes
A la queue leu leu
Leurs sandalettes de fortune en peau de vache
A la queue leu leu.

A. Serpos Tidjani (1960, p. 509)

Tell the world that the unemployed are in real want. I have nothing to eat, no house and no clothes. This life is punishment for me.

Letter to a Lagos newspaper, cited by Peter C. W. Gutkind (1968, p. 355)

Africans used to walk hundreds of miles from their rural homes to areas of employment; today, fast means of transport are generally available. Employers and colonial governments once complained about shortages of unskilled labor; today, crowds are waiting outside factory gates. Independent governments worry that the unemployed threaten the political stability required for economic development; radical critics hail them as potential supporters in the revolution to throw off the shackles of a neocolonial order. Rural–urban migration in West Africa has been much researched and is now attracting renewed attention as the concern over urban unemployment and underemployment mounts. There can be no doubt that the scourge of Calcutta and Rio de Janeiro has come to Dakar and Abidjan, to Accra and Lagos.

Population movements have always been a major feature in African history. Peoples have sought better hunting grounds, new grazing lands for their cattle, or better soils for farming. They have fled before the onslaught of stronger neighbors or the tsetse fly. Men, women, and children have been carried off from their homes into slavery. But with the development of the money economy and the opening up of employment opportunities, a new pattern was introduced.

The demand for labor by colonial administrations, traders, and plantations frequently exceeded the supply; and after the abolition of slavery, various forms of forced labor were resorted to. In the early days of colonial rule, this was sometimes the only proved means of meeting labor requirements because in some areas the money economy had not yet made much of an

50

impact. In these places, people did not aspire to the goods that money could buy. Generally, however, forced labor was the tool of a cheap-labor policy. Money was attractive enough, but the wages offered were too low and working conditions too harsh to draw sufficient numbers of workers (Anthony G. Hopkins 1973, pp. 229ff.). During World War II both the British and the French made use of forced labor. Only in 1946 was the practice abolished in French West Africa; as late as 1959 forced labor was noted as one of the major causes of population movements in Guinea-Bissau (Carreira and Meireles 1960).

The imposition of taxes provided a more subtle means of coercion. Unless people were prepared to part with their cattle or to grow cash crops, they had to earn wages in order to obtain the necessary cash for taxes. In the days of rudimentary administration there were flat taxes on huts, persons, or livestock or excise duties on one or the other of the few goods that were in general demand. However, there were limitations on the extent to which it was possible to rely on taxation as an effective spur to economic activity. Unless taxes were kept low enough to be payable without much difficulty by the less prosperous, these people either endured serious hardships or moved to another part of the country or across the frontier. If arrangements had to be made for many full or partial exemptions, a heavy additional administrative burden was created. Furthermore, rises in taxes were often used as a lever for securing higher wages. So although taxation sent people into the labor market, its effect was limited; it could not rival the impact of the spreading demand for the goods money can buy (Powesland 1957, pp. 13ff.).

The economic imperative

Once the contact with outside cultures had been established, the contagion of new aspirations in West Africa was spectacular.[1] As the first migrants returned with their riches, a self-reinforcing process was set into motion. Elliott P. Skinner (1965, p. 69) gives a vivid account of the Mossi migrant's triumphant homecoming: He offers presents to his relatives, his friends, and the chief; in his new clothes, he tours the markets, accompanied by minstrels who sing his praises and those of his ancestors.

Most societies rapidly accepted major changes in order to gain access to the new goods.[2] Modifications in the division of labor were frequent. In many of the societies, much or all farm work had been considered demeaning to the dignity of the free man. Nevertheless, men took it upon themselves to work new cash crops while the women continued to raise the food crops. Thus, the men were frequently able to obtain control over the cash income from agriculture. When employment opportunities appeared as the means of participating in the money economy, they were eagerly taken up by the men.

The predominant cause of rural–urban migration in West Africa has been economic. The substantial literature on migration is quite consistent on this issue (for a comprehensive review see Hutton 1973, pp. 89ff.). The same conclusion is reached whether migration flows or the migrants' self-images are explored (Beals, Levy, and Moses 1967; Caldwell 1969).[3] Given felt cash needs, the peasant's decision to seek employment for wages can be analyzed in terms of a comparison of economic opportunities as perceived by him in his rural home and in employment; that is he considers the rural–urban balance of economic opportunities.[4]

The adaptation of the normative system to economic change is remarkable. Jean Rouch (1956, p.194) observed that seasonal migration to Ghana had become a status-enhancing tradition in many parts of the Sudanic belt. J. Clyde Mitchell (1959, p. 30) went so far as to argue that the normative system of the society is one of the axes along which the motivation of labor migration operates. However, where the advantage in the rural–urban balance of economic opportunities shifts over time, changes in response follow quickly.

The relationship between economic and noneconomic factors

Although it is generally agreed that the search for economic betterment plays a major role in rural–urban migration, the impact of what are frequently identified as social and psychological factors is less clearly defined. There is the individual whose position in the rural community has become difficult or untenable (e.g., he is accused of murder or adultery). Formerly, he would have moved to another rural community; today, the town offers a ready refuge.

In his study of Freetown, Michael Banton (1957, pp. 48ff.) obtained information both in the city and in those parts of northern Sierra Leone from which emigration was heaviest. Freedom from the control of the older generation appeared to be an important motivation. The young men maintained that their principal reasons for coming to the towns were that money was so easily obtained there and that so many fine things could be bought with it. However, they further emphasized that in Freetown they were liberated. In the chiefdoms they were subject to oppression and extortion; the chiefs sided with the rich men and the old, they prevented ambitious young men from rising, they demanded more communal labor than the six days sanctioned by law, and they penalized protesters. "Make I go Freetown, make I go free" was the attitude of many.

The migration of independent women can be understood in similar terms. Women who have not been able to bear children are particularly prone to desert the rural community because without children they are frequently in a weak economic and social position. Similarly, marital instability, be it traditional or a product of new forces, pushes women into the city. Often, young girls who have obtained some education are dissatisfied with the prospects that marriage in the rural community offers. With a pronounced sex imbalance in most West African towns, many of these independent women are drawn into informal relationships that range from relatively durable unions to prostitution. However, the curiosity that they have aroused among scholars and the attention that they have been accorded is disproportionate, because, in fact, many more women come to town as dependents.

Cash needs are more strongly felt by certain age-groups than by others. The need to obtain cash for bridewealth is a recurrent theme. Whereas goods, often cattle, had formerly circulated within the intermarrying group, the money economy has opened the system in this respect, too. Once labor migrants have returned with goods or cash, other prospective bridegrooms are thereby encouraged to do likewise. A considerable part of the increased bridewealth is consumed, and the system becomes dependent on the continued inflow of resources. The older generation thus enforces its claim to a share in the new wealth.

Obviously, the rural–urban balance of economic opportunities varies for different people. There is often a degree of equality at the rural end: in the social structure of the rural community, through systems of ultimately communal control over land, and because of cooperation within the extended family. However, certain categories may find themselves in an unfavorable position for long periods. For instance, unmarried sons frequently have no land of their own. But on the urban scene, a premium is put on youth and strength wherever openings for unskilled labor occur.

Attempts to integrate the multiple causes of labor migration into a single framework have been made by Gulliver and Mitchell. Phillip H. Gulliver (1955) christened and dismissed the "bright lights theory," the notion that people are lured into migration by the excitement that the city promises, and instead emphasized that the main factor pushing men to seek work is economic. Other factors – a final quarrel with a brother or yet another dispute with a neighbor, some real or supposed injustice suffered at the hands of the chief, or an adverse court decision – appeared to be no more than precipitating reasons,

. . . relatively unimportant and . . . generally of the "last straw" type – i.e., difficulties which affect individuals in their family and social life and which go to tip the balance and induce a man to leave home for a spell at a particular time. Even for particular individuals the prime factor of economic necessity is almost always the real cause. (1955, p. 32)

A review of part of the considerable literature on the causes of labor migration also led Mitchell (1959) to emphasize the importance of economic factors. He proposed what would seem to be two theoretical approaches. The first is based on the distinction between necessary and sufficient conditions of labor migration.

In logical terms, economic factors appear to be a necessary condition, but they may not in themselves be a sufficient condition. In other words if the economic drives to labour migration are not present it is unlikely that it will occur, but if the economic conditions are present the actual migration may not occur until some event in the personal life of the individual precipitates events and triggers off his decision to go. (1959, p. 32)

This interpretation does not fit the available data; in fact, the very reports discussed by Mitchell suggest a different emphasis. For many peoples, economic factors provide a sufficient condition. Gulliver (1955, p. 28), when first introducing the concept of last-straw causes in his study of the Ngoni, noted that they almost all felt the economic pinch at home. Some went immediately to where money was most readily obtainable; others continued to manage until some further event precipitated their departure. He specifically stated that in practice those who continued to manage for a while constituted the smaller category. Nor are economic factors always a necessary condition. This is obvious at the individual level, but it also applies to societies in which economic factors do not favor labor migration.

Mitchell's second approach identifies a familiar methodological difficulty: How much store can be put in what the migrants themselves say are their motives? Audrey I. Richards (1954, p. 65f.), in particular, has stressed that memories are blurred, but a concrete objective or a dramatic event stand out in the migrant's narrative, rather than the cumulative effects of hopes and fears that constitute the imperatives. He may be quite unable to describe the gradual deterioration of local conditions that finally resulted in an unbearable situation. Thus, a particularly angry scene with his local chief may have become dramatized in his mind for all time and may continue to overshadow any consciousness of a long sequence of economic frustrations and hardships. Motives adduced by migrants may therefore hide rather than reveal underlying causes.

Mitchell proceeds to propose an approach based on a distinction between the rate and the incidence of labor migration:

One of the advantages of separating out economic and personal factors in this way is that it enables us to distinguish between the incidence and the rate of labour migration (Parsons 1937, pp. 344 ff.).[5] When we talk about the incidence of labour migration we refer to the set of unique circumstances which induces a particular emigrant to leave his rural area. It implies therefore a complete appreciation of the conditions underlying the migration both economic and personal.

The personal factors of the type that have been mentioned as "causes" of labour migration are of the type that operate independently of the underlying conditions. Tensions arise between kinsmen, regardless of changes in economic condition, the desire to experience town life and to savour the adventures of travelling, are probably constantly present. Therefore, as Durkheim [(1897) 1951, pp. 145–51] cogently argued concerning the operation of similar factors in causing suicide, these factors cannot explain the size and trends of the *rate* of labour migration. The rate of labour migration, it appears, is determined mainly by economic factors. (1959, p. 32)

The merit of this approach – its stress on the importance of economic factors – is also its weakness because it appears to allow for only one collective force and subsumes all others under a residual category of "personal factors." This accounts well enough for much of the empirical data because of the predominance of economic factors. However, in the case of societies that have no emigration for economic reasons, it is inadequate because the different rates of emigration from such societies have to be related to collective non-economic factors, such as the frequency of certain crimes and types of punishment. In some cases, the rate of emigration from a given society may vary significantly over time irrespective of economic factors (e.g., because of insecurity in rural areas).

But it is at the analytic level that Mitchell's approach is most unsatisfactory. The rate of rural–urban migration has to be seen as the result of the aggregate of economic, social, and political conditions. The incidence of migration (i.e., why one man rather than another migrates) appears, then, determined by the differential impact that these collective forces have on individuals.

That a certain characteristic should lead to departure, whether through death by suicide or through emigration to town, is socially determined. However, that an individual has such a characteristic is a matter of personal history. For example, he is born a first son, his character or the characters of those who educate him push him in a certain direction, or an illness or an accident handicaps him physically. It is in this sense that we can speak of personal factors. Of course, they may well be economic (e.g., whether a man has inherited riches or rags, whether his wife has borne him many children or few to support).

The assumption that individuals take the decision to migrate is usually implicit in this discussion of rural–urban migration. However, where more or less extended families continue to be well integrated, they constitute the decision-making unit. In West Africa today, the imbalance between rural and urban economic opportunities is the prime determinant of the rate of rural–urban migration. Again, economic factors largely determine the incidence of rural–urban migration in terms of the family units that are induced to release one or more of their members to the urban scene. Further, the incidence in terms of the particular individuals who make the move is a function of their personal characteristics, with their economic implications a major consideration (i.e., the comparative earning power of potential migrants). Finally, to take up Gulliver's point again, particular events may influence the timing of departure; and although these are frequently not economic in nature, they can very well be so (e.g., the date when a tax has to be paid).

The myth of the backward-sloping labor supply function

A major issue facing policy makers and economists alike has been the proposition that the labor supply function in West Africa is backward sloping. That argument is based on the idea that migrants are target workers; that is to say, they come to earn a certain amount of cash to satisfy specific wants. As Elliott J. Berg describes it,

wage-earners in newly-developing countries are alleged to have relatively low want schedules or high preference for leisure as against income, so that they work less at higher wage rates and more at lower ones. In the underdeveloped world, and notably in Africa, this has been the almost universal opinion of foreign employers of native labour, an opinion shared by outside observers . . . It was no less common a view in eighteenth century England, where a typical complaint was that "If a person can get sufficient in four days to support himself for seven days, he will keep holiday the other three; that is, he will live in riot and debauchery." (1961, p. 468)

Berg (1961, pp. 470ff.) has pointed out that most contemporary nonindustrial societies are in varying degrees of transition. They have been in contact, however sporadic and tangential, with the goods and ideas of the outside world for at least two or three generations. They have consequently undergone changes that have made them responsive to the money economy outside the villages. Moreover, analysis in terms of a target income is short term; over longer periods, rising wages open up new consumption possibilities and so increase the propensity to work outside by raising income goals.

Even where the individual labor supply function is backward sloping, it does not follow that the aggregate supply function is backward sloping as well. The latter would be correct only on the assumption that the size of the labor force is some constant proportion of the total population. For many peasant families, however, labor migration is not the only possible source of cash; they have the alternative of producing for the market, and hence the wage level (compared with the prices for rural produce) influences the number who chose employment over the raising of cash crops.

It follows that a rise in wages for the classic type of target workers has two opposite effects on the supply of labor. First, the target worker will reduce the time spent in employment. Second, more men will seek employment. Which would be the dominant factor cannot be said a priori. However, there can be little doubt that the targets have been quite flexible in much of West Africa for a long time. Furthermore, a considerable proportion of labor has been mobile enough for decades to move between self-employment in the rural economy and urban or rural employment.

In those cases where, indeed, the aggregate labor supply function was backward sloping in the past for an overall labor market, the regional character of labor migration in colonial Africa has to be taken into account. Individual countries formed parts of what constituted regional labor markets for the unskilled. Labor migrants were rapidly informed of changes in wages and working conditions and acted accordingly. Any given country could augment its labor supply by increasing wages; the argument applies a fortiori to any given industry or firm (Berg 1961, pp. 489ff.). The proposition that the labor supply function in West Africa was backward sloping bore little relationship to reality; rather, it was a myth that provided the ideological underpinning for a cheap-labor policy.

Friedrich Mühlenberg (1967, p. 219) agrees with Berg that once wages rise above the subsistence minimum, the supply can be expected to be price elastic under present-day conditions through the mobilization of additional workers. He adds, though, that with increases in wage rates, supply will become less elastic and probably even "inverse elastic" well before the total active male population has entered the labor market. This is so not so much because of the relation between leisure and income preferences or because of the necessity to maintain the traditional economic and social basis; rather, the decisive fact is that the migrants perceive the rural areas as home, as the locus of meaningful consumption and investment in the long run. The argument rests on the assumption that all workers will remain committed to rural communities. Yet, further rises in wage levels and social security measures would make it feasible in economic terms for a growing number of migrants to settle in town permanently. Supply could then be expected to be highly elastic as rising wages make this alternative increasingly attractive.

The rural–urban balance of life chances

The impact of the money economy on the societies of West Africa has been so effective that shortages of unskilled labor are long past. Instead, those in the urban areas face substantial unemployment. By now, the money economy has reached into the farthest corners of West Africa, and aspirations have risen to a level at which they can no longer be satisfied by one or a few short spells of labor migration.

Some people have little choice but to leave an agriculture that no longer provides them with even bare subsistence. In a number of areas, population pressure on land has become severe. Rural famine has been a common experience in the Senegal River valley for a long time (Diop 1965, p. 58f.). The last few years have witnessed mass starvation throughout the Sahel from Mauritania to Niger.

In other parts of West Africa, plantations and commercial farms have been established over the last eighty years; and with them, a rural landless proletariat has emerged whose wages and working conditions vary greatly. Frequently, these are quite unattractive, and the opportunity cost of migrating to urban centers is accordingly low.

For the peasant, the opportunity cost of migration depends on the institutional setting (Stiglitz 1970; Knight 1972). At present, an intermediate situation appears to constitute the prevalent pattern in West Africa. Much land is still held communally, but migrants settle in town for long periods of time because the difficulty of finding employment discourages voluntary job separation. Now the family often follows the migrant to town, and the land they labored on reverts to the rural community without compensation. Here, then, the opportunity cost of migrating approximates average family product, insofar as the communal system is quite egalitarian. The distinction of this pattern from other institutional settings in which the opportunity cost of migration is limited to the marginal product becomes more important as arable land becomes scarcer and the difference between the marginal and the average product of rural labor increases. However, such a tendency may be reversed by the adoption of more labor-intensive techniques (see A. D. Goddard 1974 on the Kano area).

The rural–urban income gap is much talked about, but information for West Africa is rudimentary at best. For Ghana, the evidence yielded by household income and expenditure surveys suggests that, on average, urban incomes exceed rural incomes to a small extent. On one measure the differential was as high as 50 percent; on another it was only 9 percent; indeed, on a couple of measures it was actually negative. In most cases the urban advantage was found to survive an adjustment for differences in the cost of living. There was strong evidence that the urban–rural income differential varied considerably over time. The real earnings of African employees rose by 50 percent between 1952 and 1960, but by 1966 nearly all this gain had been eroded by inflation. Government minimum wages followed a similar pattern but fared less well, the real value of the minimum wage in 1966 being 73 percent of the 1952 level. In agriculture the trends were very different for food and cocoa farmers. The value of food production was static throughout the 1950s, but by 1966, it had risen to 136 percent of the 1952 level. In contrast, cocoa income per rural household showed a cyclical pattern. It repeatedly declined, then recovered to the 1952 level; but in 1966, it stood at only 37 percent of that level (Knight 1972).

For Nigeria, most rural–urban comparisons reveal a substantial and widening income differential, with rural incomes less than half of urban incomes. However, the usual basis of comparison is between some index of urban wage rates and a crude index of agricultural incomes, such as prices received by farmers for export crops. More rigorous measures of rural incomes revealed that those in northern Nigeria were about 80 percent of the government's unskilled wage rate (Byerlee 1973, p. 16).

Clearly, we do not have the data to compare the incomes of marginal rural categories with the wages that the urban economy may seem to promise, let alone to estimate the size of these categories. But if information on rural–urban income gaps is less conclusive than is commonly assumed, it is quite obvious that the more important urban centers in particular offer the better opportunities for education and training. Furthermore, a whole range of amenities not available in rural areas is found in the towns, especially in the capital cities; and such amenities as public housing, piped water, electricity, and medical care are typically heavily subsidized.

Life expectancy is one indicator of well-being that is universally highly valued. Unfortunately, rural and urban mortality rates are difficult to compare because of the different age structures of the respective populations. Still, infant and early child mortality are fairly generally recognized to be lower in towns than in rural areas, in spite of poor living conditions and a high incidence of tuberculosis (Clarke 1972a, p. 68). For Senegal, mortality during the first month of life has been estimated at 3.6 percent in urban centers but 10.9 percent for rural areas in 1960–1 (Baylet, Benyoussef, and Cantrelle 1972). In Liberia, the infant mortality rate has been reported to be almost twice as high in rural as in urban areas (International Labour Office 1972, p. 71). The crux of the matter is that the new nations of West Africa have given priority to their urban populations. We have already elaborated on this fact in Chapter 2, and we will return to it in Chapter 9, where we discuss stratification and social mobility.

Migrating to urban centers of unemployment

Continued rapid urban growth throughout West Africa indicates that many rural dwellers find it advantageous to move to the cities. Given the relative sizes of the rural and the urban sectors, considerable potential for rural–urban migration remains in every country. The migratory flow appears to swell whenever urban employment opportunities look up. The entire body of aspirants for urban employment may be visualized as an iceberg. A few show as urban unemployed; the bulk remain hidden as they wait in the rural areas. But why does migration continue in the face of widespread urban unemployment? Why do so many unemployed stay on in town instead of returning to rural areas where they have claims to land or opportunities for work?

Some authors, while accepting that migrants are primarily motivated by economic considerations, suggest that they fail to appreciate how difficult it has become to secure urban employment (Anthony G. Hopkins 1973, p. 241f.). Such an interpretation would also have to assume that these migrants, when faced with the disappointing realities of the urban scene, have reason not to return to their rural homes. Bruce T. Grindal (1973), in his account of a group of northern Ghanaian immigrants in Accra, suggests that they had indeed been misled by stories they had heard from returned migrants who described the South as a land of great wealth, where the buildings are many stories high, where the people ride either in cars or on bicycles, where the "social life" abounds, and where one can earn money for things such as bicycles, clothing, and finery. Such myths were perpetuated by returned migrants who wished to convey to others a positive image of themselves and their experiences. They talked much less about the problems they had encountered in the cities of the South. In contrast with the expectations thus raised, the successor migrants' first contact with southern urban life was an unexpected and often shattering experience. Many were then forced by pride to remain in the South in order to spare themselves the humiliation of returning home in poverty.

Studies that are not limited to a small ethnic group tell a different story. John C. Caldwell's (1969, pp.120ff.) survey in predominantly immigrant areas of Accra-Tema, Sekondi-Takoradi, Cape Coast, and Kumasi gives little support to the contention that rural–urban migrants come with false expectations. Nearly two-thirds of the immigrants interviewed stated that life in the town was just what they thought it would be. Among those who found their impressions markedly astray, almost half had been too apprehensive about urban conditions. Those who had been disappointed numbered only about one-sixth of all interviewed. The unexpected deficiencies of the town divided almost evenly into lesser economic opportunity than anticipated and greater social problems or insufficient facilities to cope with problems of urban living. That potential migrants act in accordance with accurate information can be further demonstrated in cases where conditions in alternate employment areas are substantially altered. Thus, in the 1960s, migrants from Upper Volta increasingly gave preference to the Ivory Coast over Ghana as the economic fortunes of the two countries changed (Songre, Sawadogo, and Sanogoh 1974).

Formal education has generally been thought to constitute a particular problem. Pupils, it has been suggested, were not equipped for agricultural pursuits and, worse, were made averse to farming. Indeed, the more educated are likelier to move in search of urban employment, a fact that can be explained in terms of a rational economic calculation: The return realized for an additional year of education is usually higher in the towns than in the rural areas, and the probability of being selected for any given job increases with the level of education. Those who have completed primary school have taken up agriculture where it offered a standard of living comparable to that in the urban economy. But when urban opportunities are perceived to be significantly better than those in rural areas (given a certain level of education), no change in school syllabi will inculcate a commitment to agriculture. Thus, it can be expected that peasants will continue to resist attempts to "ruralize" the education of their children as long as rural prospects remain severely limited and opportunities are so obviously located in urban areas.

We hold that most migrants have a pretty accurate idea of what to expect and that their migration decisions are rational in economic terms. By joining the urban unemployed, they participate in a lottery; they try their luck at the urban economy game (Gugler 1969b). It is a lottery because so much of the hiring is haphazard. And it is a very serious gamble. Rural income is forgone, costs are incurred in migration, and severe hardships are experienced because of unemployment. But new migrants keep joining in the West African equivalent of the American frontier, seeking new opportunities in the city.[6]

Migrants have to survive until they find employment. The extent to which not only relatives but also friends provide assistance is impressive, but as time goes by, an increasing proportion of immigrants have to fend for themselves. If they have not been able to secure employment, they are forced to look for casual work, to accept employment well below the legal minimum wage, or to engage in petty self-employment.[7] Job seekers who survive in these ways appear to be most prevalent among street vendors and domestic servants. For obvious reasons, there is little information about those unemployed who get involved in illegal activities and take the attendant risks.

Peter Kilby (1969, pp. 275ff.) has suggested that every increase in the wage rates determined by government, wage commissions, and collective bargaining will tend to depress the ruling wage in the sector not so regulated and to increase unemployment. These consequences follow because employment in the regulated sector becomes more attractive for the potential migrant and because his move is facilitated as the capacity of those employed in that sector to support him increases. In Nigeria, Kilby reports, the real wage rate rose by 50 percent between 1953 and 1964 in the regulated sector and fell in the unregulated sector.

The migrant may well accept a standard of living below what he had in the rural economy in the hope that he will be better off in the future. As long as the unregulated urban sector allows the barest survival, the earnings in this sector are ever more widely spread among a growing army of underemployed. As Dan R. Aronson reports for Yoruba from the Ijebu region:

Individuals coming to the cities have reasonable expectations that they are *not* necessarily going to find work, yet they come anyway, in order to put themselves into positions in which they perceive they will be able to take advantage of any opportunity which does come their way. Ijebu – and many other Nigerians – are, in my estimation, much more willing under these conditions than Americans to defer the self-admission that they are doing their life's work. Instead, they engage in activities which will enable them to be self-supporting while for several years they may look for, or wait for, what they feel will satisfy their occupational aspirations. The process of getting a start in the city, therefore, involves finding a legitimate "pursuit" rather than a job which might turn out to be permanent. (1970, p. 169)

Although migrants are able to secure minimal earnings that allow them to subsist while they hope for better days, the aggregate of goods and services provided does not increase significantly. The unregulated urban sector acts as a sponge, disguising unemployment while depressing the incomes of a major sector of the urban population. Pride in the rapid growth of West African cities is ill conceived when increasing numbers of unemployed and underemployed constitute a major element in that growth. Their contribution to the economy will frequently be less than it would have been had they continued to work in the rural sector; the cost of providing them with a subsistence minimum in town is definitely higher. The hope that sustains the unemployed and underemployed, the hope of finding a full place in the urban economy, is bound to end in disillusionment for most, and there can be little doubt that they incur heavy social costs in the meantime.

We can now establish the aggregate supply function of unskilled labor (see Figure 3.1). There is a limited supply of labor from two sources at subsistence wages: a small group that leaves the traditional sector for noneconomic reasons (e.g., those who take refuge in town) and a group, greatly varying in size according to harvests and produce prices, that is forced to migrate by actual hardship in the rural economy (Mühlenberg 1967, pp. 218f.). Beyond that, supply can be expected to be price elastic under present-day conditions through the mobilization of additional workers. Actually, wages in the regulated sector call forth a supply well in excess of demand. Some of this excess supply is found in the urban-sector unemployed and underemployed. More are waiting in the rural areas, to be rapidly mobilized by the first sign of an improvement in the employment scene.

This reserve army of aspirants to the regulated employment sector does not depress wage levels in that sector, but it does stabilize the labor force; workers

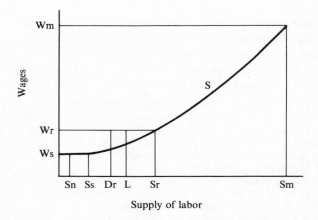

Figure 3.1. Demand and supply of unskilled labor in West Africa

    S = supply of labor
   Ws = wage providing worker's subsistence minimum
   Wr = wage in regulated sector
   Wm = wage securing maximum supply of labor
   Sn = supply for noneconomic reasons
   Ss = Sn plus supply of those who cannot subsist in rural economy
   Dr = demand for labor at regulated wages
   Sr = Sn plus supply of labor at regulated wages
   Sm = maximum supply
    L = labor force available in town
 L - Dr = urban unemployed and underemployed
 Sr - L = potential migrants at regulated wages

have to decide whether they want to keep their working place or abandon it with little hope of finding employment again later. Hence, the choice for any one migrant to limit his individual contribution to the total supply of labor has been severely restricted. Today, most urban workers stick to their lathes; they have settled down for a working life in town. Short-term and intermittent labor migration has become the exception, and the target worker has all but vanished. West Africa thus boasts a fully committed labor force; labor turnover and absenteeism in the major firms is lower than in industrialized countries.

What trends can we anticipate in the future? In West Africa as a whole, something like 80 percent of the population lives in rural areas. The absolute size of this reservoir of potential migrants is growing because the rural areas continue to absorb a major part of the natural population growth, estimated at about 2.6 percent a year for the region (United Nations 1976a, p. 139). More importantly, absorption of even part of this population increase is becoming more difficult in many rural areas. At the same time, frequently precisely because of severe population pressure on the land, the dissolution of communal control over land is spreading, land is commercialized, and the rural landless are becoming a more common feature.

Policy makers are faced with a dilemma: They want to increase urban wages, both for political reasons (to reduce the gap between low- and high-income groups in urban areas) and for social reasons (to provide the minimum income required to maintain a family in town). But any change in urban conditions that improves the lot of the urban unemployed and underemployed will also enhance the promise of the urban alternative for the swelling reservoir of potential migrants.

A long-range policy to stem the tide of rural–urban migration and the rise in urban unemployment and underemployment to which it contributes must pursue both a more equal rural–urban balance of life chances and a reversal of present trends toward the marginalization of parts of the rural population and entire regions.

4 Townsman and absentee villager

This expansion of the horizons of the community, in terms of the physical distribution of those who claim membership of a socially defined aggregate such as a lineage, makes it no longer easy to dichotomise, at least spatially, the traditional and the modern or even the rural and the urban in Frafra life today. The world of the migrant and that of his homeland are not separable entities – they are both part of a wider society, a society which has reached a high level of instant internal communications and is defined by nationwide institutions.

Keith Hart (1971, p. 26)

Many of the urban residents of West Africa maintain strong ties with the rural area that they consider to be their home. They participate in the urban economy while remaining loyal to a rural community; they operate in geographically separate but culturally and economically integrated systems. "Rural" and "urban" styles and standards, modes of production in the city and its hinterland, are synthetic products of the exchange between these systems, which in fact are no longer so distinct. Here is how the pattern appeared to us in 1961–2 in what was then Eastern Nigeria:

A striking experience when talking to Eastern Nigerians in urban centers is that they will invariably stress that they are strangers in town. Irrespective of his birthplace every Eastern Nigerian can point without hesitation to a community in which his forefathers lived and which he considers his "home place." It will be a rural community except for the few who descend from families long-established in Onitsha or one of the minor centers on the coast. The home community conversely refers to them as "our sons abroad." They are expected to maintain contact and to return eventually. In fact only a few break contact completely, and the hope that they will return ultimately is not given up until their death . . . These same people are fully committed to earning their living in town. Nearly all expect to spend their entire working life away from their home place. Losing their employment or their trade is the worst calamity that could befall them . . . Even on retirement many will make an attempt to find other sources of urban income. (Gugler 1971, p. 405)

Extent of urban–rural ties

The link between sons abroad and their home community is expressed in many ways. The migrant visits his home; he welcomes visitors from the village; he helps new arrivals to get started in the city. He returns to his home area to find a bride. Messages flow to and fro. Money and goods are taken to the village or sent there through trusted intermediaries; presents are received in turn. The urbanite builds a house in the village; he plans to retire there; he wants to be buried in his home. This is a widespread pattern.

64

Data on urban–rural ties are now available from a number of surveys (Table 4.1). They are not strictly comparable because in each the definition of the population studied, the sampling procedure employed, and the formulation of questions differ. Still, they give some measure of the strength of urban–rural ties in five quite different settings.

It is less hazardous to make comparisons within a survey. The Enugu data allow us to compare three occupational groups. The railway workers find it difficult to support a wife and children in town, but even one out of every five senior civil servants has one or several of his children living in the rural home. The incidence of house building back home is highest among market traders. The proportion of those who intend to retire to the rural areas is lowest among senior civil servants, but two-thirds of those civil servants still plan to do so. In fact, it is the similarities among the three groups that are most striking. Everyone claims land rights back home; great majorities visit at least once a year; nearly everybody, including 84 percent of the senior civil servants, wants to be buried at home.

In addition to the evidence of urban–rural ties maintained by individuals, there are various accounts of urban-based organizations involved in village affairs. Here are some observations on the situation in Eastern Nigeria:

Decisions on village affairs are taken not so much by the village residents as by co-villagers living in towns.[1] If many an ethnic association calls itself "Improvement Union" this refers not to the improvement of urban living conditions, but to the development of its members' home area. Such associations transmit new ideas and aspirations; they constitute an urban lobby for village interests; they provide counsel and finance for village developments: the building of roads and bridges, schools, maternity clinics and dispensaries, in a few instances even secondary schools, hospitals or water supply systems; they offer scholarships, at times with the specific object of providing local staff for the institutions they are establishing; they direct the role the local area plays in the wider polity.[2]

In some villages an institution called "Mass Rally" has come into existence. All "sons abroad" are urged to return at the same time. The regular intervals between these meetings vary from two to five years. They usually take place at Christmas time as this provides the longest stretch of public holidays. Return on these occasions is not strongly enforced, though it is said to be compulsory.

During Christmas 1961 we witnessed such a Mass Rally in Ukpo village. Mass Rallies had been held here every three years since 1952. In 1961 the entertainments included a ballroom dance – an electric plant had been hired for the occasion – and the display of traditional dances and masquerades. A sewing machine, a bicycle and a radio were the first prizes in a raffle.

According to our survey 87 per cent of those living "abroad" had returned for the occasion. For a few days the village was transformed into an attractive center of social activity. New patterns from the town were introduced to the villagers. The entertainments were expected to yield a profit to be used for development projects in the community. People living throughout the year in different parts of the country met again – and came to know each other's children born in town. The Ukpo Improvement Union used the opportunity to publicize its activities, in particular to

Table 4.1. *Survey data on urban–rural ties in Senegal, Ghana, and Nigeria*

Dimensions of relationships with rural "homes"	188 industrial workers in Senegal, 1964–5	500 urban households containing at least 1 rural–urban migrant in Ghana, 1963	460 immigrated industrial workers in Ibadan and Lagos, 1963–4	Immigrant household heads, 1971–2		Eastern Nigerians in Enugu, 1961		
				600 in Ife	437 in Oshogbo	49 railway workers	49 market traders	58 senior civil servants
Have wife at home			⎰ 29% [a]			39% [b]	9% [b]	2% [b]
Have children at home			⎱			54% [c]	18% [c]	19% [c]
Have more good friends at home		54%						
Visit home at least once a year	71%	69%	52%	91%	95%	87%	92%	88%
Send money home	34% [a]	63%		62%	54%			
Take presents home		88%						
Take money home		78%						
Claim land rights						100%	100%	100%
Have built house at home		23%				16%	35%	23%
Now building house at home		6%						
Intend retirement at home	35%	92%				92%	98%	66%
Actually retired at home		79% [e]						
Desire burial at home						98%	96%	84%

the villagers, and to gather support by drawing up a development plan and convening a "General Meeting" of all men. (Gugler 1971, pp. 412f., edited)

Aronson (1970, pp. 296ff.) surveyed forty-seven associations of Yoruba from the Ijebu region in 1966–7. Over the preceding fifteen years, they had embarked upon sixty-four different projects involving financial aid to their hometowns, and they had made at least thirty-three petitions to the government of what was then Western Nigeria. There had been regular patterns in the projects attempted, and most of them had been public works operations that closely paralleled or preceded government involvement in the same activities. Almost all had been oriented toward the provision of social and economic infrastructure. Aronson emphasizes that few economically productive enterprises had been established in spite of the urgent demand for job opportunities. He further notes the lack of guidance concerning general feasibility and optimal detail, the competition and conflict among neighboring areas that tended to discourage cooperative efforts, and the fact that some projects had little to recommend them to people at home. We might add that the overhead cost of fund collection is considerable at times, and cases of embezzlement are not unheard of. Still, conspicuous investment in village developments has its merits over conspicuous consumption.[3]

Motivations in urban–rural relationships

Economic factors play a major role in tying urban dwellers to their rural areas of origin. For some, rural income constitutes a necessary complement to urban earnings; for others, it is a welcome supplement. It is land that holds the assurance of security for most.

Some urban workers have no choice but to leave their wives and children in their rural home areas. Even if they have found jobs in the regulated sector, where wage legislation is enforced, the minimum wage is invariably below what is considered the basic requirement to support a family in town (the lack of family housing is only one aspect of this). Moreover, urban earning oppor-

---

Notes to Table 4.1

[a] Percent of married men with wife and/or children at home.
[b] Percent of married men only.
[c] Percent of fathers only.
[d] Percent sending money home regularly.
[e] Data from a survey of 1,782 rural households: percent of long-term migrants over age 64 who had returned permanently.

Sources: Col. 1: Pfefferman (1968, pp. 296 f., 299 and 307); col. 2: Caldwell (1969, pp. 141, 146, 152, 162, 185f. and 196); col. 3: Hans Dieter Seibel (1968, pp. 313f.); col. 4: Adepoju (1974, pp. 386f.); the Enugu data in col. 5 have not been published in this form before, but see Gugler (1971) for related data and discussion.

tunities for women are severely limited. Some women are able to secure employment; others are engaged in crafts; and although many are active in trade, most of these earn only a pittance. Therefore, many wives stay in the rural areas, where they can engage in farming and where shelter is cheap. The separation of home and workplace engendered by the Industrial Revolution has been drastically magnified in West Africa.

Urban workers who are able to support a family in town still find that the way to maximize their income is not to forgo the income and savings they enjoy as long as their wives and children stay in the village. Not only is life cheaper there, but once they leave the farm, their rights to its proceeds lapse; the family hand becomes a family mouth. Furthermore, land usually cannot be sold; abandoning it means surrendering part of the family income without compensation. At the urban end, much depends on the earning opportunities for women, a point well illustrated by the contrast between the Enugu railway workers, 39 percent of whom had a wife living at home most of the time, and the market traders, for whom this was the case for only 9 percent (Table 4.1). We will return to this issue in Chapter 8.

Many families do establish themselves in town. Some are fortunate in that wives have secured urban earnings that compensate for the higher cost of living and for rural income forgone. Other families have decided that a reduction in standard of living is preferable to separation. Many seek better educational opportunities for their children in town. But a family that has sufficient revenues to support itself in town today has no guarantee that it will enjoy such revenues in the future. Urban unemployment and underemployment are widespread, and unemployment compensation remains virtually unknown. Social security systems covering disablement and old age are still in their infancy.[4] For the majority of urban dwellers, the only social security, meager but reliable, is provided by the solidarity of the village.[5] Maintaining ties with people back home ensures a refuge in hard times; being recognized as "our son abroad" translates into an effective claim to partake of the communally held land on return.[6]

We have seen that the proportion who intended to return to their rural areas of origin on retirement was considerably lower among the senior civil servants in Enugu than among the railway workers and the market traders. And, indeed, these senior civil servants had European-pattern pension rights, and none expected ever to be reduced to making a living from agriculture.[7] In fact, high-income earners who maintain the village link generally incur an economic loss; gifts to relatives, contributions to village developments, and the cost of rural houses are disproportionate to the value of the limited land rights they thus retain. For a few elite members, the village provides a political base, some find a ready-made clientele for their businesses, others may anticipate a time when land will become more easily transferable and their standing in the community will give them an advantage in establishing a commercial farm,[8] but the majority are clearly losers in economic terms.[9]

A substantial proportion of high-income earners maintain ties with their rural areas of origin in spite of the considerable economic cost. The social attraction of the rural home that explains their continuing commitment is felt in all income groups. It springs from the fact that the majority of adult urban dwellers in West Africa are rural born and bred. They are attached and often indebted to their parents and members of their extended families; they remain close to other villagers they have known intimately; they continue to conceive of themselves as members of the rural community. Kofi A. Busia, writing of Ghana, expressed this attitude:

A person's membership of his lineage binds him forever to the village where the lineage is localized. Wherever he may go, however long he may be away, he belongs to his lineage town or village. The economic and social obligations of kinship such as those connected with funerals, marriages and divorce, as well as political allegiance and jural rights and status which are also tied up with kinship, keep alive his attachment to his native town or village. (1960, p. 73)

Most urban residents value the prestige they enjoy in the eyes of people back home. Many a man who has had a measure of success in town will demonstrate it by building a house in the village to bear witness to his continuing commitment. This rural monument to his achievement in the city will perhaps be most important on the day he is brought home to be buried in his compound according to custom. David Brokensha recounts an incident in Larteh, a small town of about 6,000 inhabitants:[10]

Recently a lawyer died and was brought from Accra to Larteh, his home town, for burial. He had built houses for himself in Accra, where he had his practice, but not in Larteh, thereby ignoring the convention that successful men should build houses in their home town. When his body was lying in state it was reviled, some women cursing him for neglecting his own town by not building there. The scene created a vivid impression on bystanders, who, while deploring the violent words, which contravened values of propriety, yet secretly agreed that the lawyer should have built a house. His brother, also an Accra lawyer, shortly afterwards did build a house at Larteh. (1966, p. 202)

Whether economic advantage or social attraction is the dominant motive for nourishing strong ties with a given rural area, the commitment is usually articulated in an ideology of loyalty to home. The deviant is confronted by people from his area of origin proclaiming this ideology and bringing pressures to bear on him to recognize his responsibilities. The man who has not returned to his home for some time is urged to do so by other migrants from his village; he may even be visited by a delegation from the village, who entreat him to return. Destitute women have been known to be repatriated against their will.

It is difficult to distinguish commitment to the village community from participation in an extended family network partly located there (a topic on which we will focus in Chapter 7). Contributions made to enhance the general welfare of the village will assist those members of the extended family now living there or likely to return in the future. In fact, improvements in the village make it a more comfortable place for the benefactor to visit and ultimately retire to. In Eastern Nigeria, many senior civil servants spent most of their vacations in their home villages in spite of discomfort, but they rapidly built substantial houses there and were preoccupied with plans to establish services that were as yet the prerogative of urban areas. Village development was thus seen as directly relevant to themselves; they expected to enjoy the fruits of their efforts.

Whatever the motivations, the urban–rural flow of resources is remarkable in many parts of West Africa. Regular and intermittent transfers, large and small, of cash and goods, channeled home from the large cities through extended family ties or ethnic associations, provide a means of mitigating the serious inequalities that exist between urban and rural areas. The compilation of hard data on the aggregate volume of these transfers is difficult, but speculative calculations have led Caldwell (1967, p. 143) to suggest that from Accra alone, about £5 million per year, or roughly 10 percent of all income earned in that city, flowed out as remittances, savings, or goods, most of which found their way to rural Ghana. Although these transfers certainly cannot by themselves come near to equalizing income and life chances between the urban and the rural sectors, the investment of money, energy, and advocacy on behalf of the rural area by urban dwellers has prompted the conclusion that the Ijebu Yoruba "do far more now in self-help than the Nigerian government can hope to do for many years to come in the way of social and economic development" in their home area (Aronson 1970, pp. 289f.).

Variations and prospects

The data required to trace variations in the strength of urban–rural ties in West Africa are lacking,[11] but our analysis suggests a number of important variables. We will explore them in terms of both the variations they suggest and the future they portend.

The economic rationale, whether it be sheer necessity, just advantage, or anticipation of future need, is founded in the control that the village community exerts over access to land. Where land is not communally held, but instead controlled by a local elite, we would expect allegiance to focus more directly on it. Alternatively, where land is becoming the property of individuals, there will be less dependency on the rural community.

Control over land is only one facet of a more general issue: the structure of the rural society. Settlement in Eastern Nigeria is in compact villages in which political control was traditionally limited to the village group. The members of the village claim a common ancestor; as a rule, all agnates reside within the village, and most affines live close by. Status differentials are recognized, but mobility is high. The returned migrant can convert urban achievement into rural status by taking on the substantial expense that will gain him admission to a title society. As Peter C. Lloyd suggested:

A man who can return home after years in the urban areas and take his place as a lineage elder, claiming his rights to land and political office, is more likely to maintain his links with his home area and to plan to spend his retirement there.

Conversely, he is less likely to maintain such close links with the home community, where prestige is determined by political offices gained through a lifetime of service; where land rights may be forfeited by absence; where the returning migrant finds that men junior to him in age have surpassed him in rank or where status in a community is determined largely by a network of patron–client relationships. (1966a, p. 32)

In terms of the social attraction exerted by the rural community and an extended family located there, a question arises: How much of a relationship will the second generation (those who grew up in the city and whose siblings are also there) maintain with the home of their parents? In Eastern Nigeria, many children of city parents experienced a major part of their early socialization in the village. However, Jean-Marie Gibbal (1974, pp. 288f. and 309ff.), in his Abidjan study, came to the conclusion that nearly all second-generation urbanites had definitely cut loose from the rural base. In his survey of two residential areas he differentiated two income groups and distinguished between those born in their home area (either in the village or in a town within the ethnic area) and those born in towns elsewhere. Among the second generation, only one out of every ten identified a village as his home, none visited such a village more than once a year, and none had built a house in a village. The differences in anticipated place of retirement are instructive (see Table 4.2). In terms of income, plans for retirement varied somewhat in the expected direction. The contrast within the middle-income group was more striking. Close to two-thirds of those born within their ethnic home area anticipated retiring to a home village, but in the second generation away from the ethnic home area, none recognized a home village to which he expected to retire, nor did any anticipate retiring to a small town close to such a home village. It will be interesting to get comparative data from elsewhere in West Africa. If, indeed, the growing proportion of the urban population that is urban born and bred has broken the connection with the rural sector, that has important implications. Whatever the evidence on second-generation urbanites will turn out to be, though, the majority of the urban population is at present made up of first-generation immigrants, and their proportion will remain substantial as long as rural–urban migration continues at a fast pace.

Rural development reduces the gap the urbanite has to bridge in order to reintegrate himself with the village. Communication is easier with villagers who have some experience of the same type of education. A stay in a village equipped with basic amenities is less strenuous; retirement there a more attractive prospect. Rural development and the maintenance of urban–rural ties can thus become mutually reinforcing. If rural development encourages emigrants to maintain ties, they, in turn, further village development through their advice and the transfer of economic resources. In addition, the more developed a village is, the better equipped are its sons to succeed in the urban

Table 4.2. *Retirement plans in two residential areas in Abidjan, about 1967*

Place of retirement	65 men born in ethnic home area, low income	138 men born in ethnic home area, middle income	39 men born in town out-side ethnic home, middle income[a]
Home village	72%	64%	0%
Small town close to home village	0%	12%	0%
Small town outside Ivory Coast where born	0%	0%	8%
Other town in the Ivory Coast or outside	6%	0%	28%
Abidjan	6%	13%	41%
Don't know	15%	11%	23%
Total[b]	100%	100%	100%

Note: Respondents answered the question: "Quand vous aurez fini de travailler, où habiterez-vous? et pourquoi?"
[a] Apparently, some men who came to the village in early childhood and were reared there were excluded from this category and others who left the village in early childhood were included. (Gibbal 1974, pp. 129ff. and 289).
[b] Because of rounding, percent do not necessarily add up to 100.
Source: Gibbal (1974, pp. 131f. and 314ff.)

environment. There is thus a powerful mechanism for the relative development of villages to be reflected in the position of their sons abroad. The more affluent urbanites can usually look forward to returning to relatively developed villages, but emigrants from the poorer rural areas tend not to have much of a stake in the city, either.

Distance between the town of residence and the area of origin was over-come in the past, when it presented a formidable obstacle. Since then, trans-port and communication have improved immeasurably, and the cost of travel has decreased relative to incomes. Today, the battered truck, called the "mammy wagon" because women traders – mammies – use it extensively, plies everywhere. Furthermore, physical distances between place of origin and workplace have been reduced because restrictions on foreign workers have curtailed long-distance migration and forced more migrants to concen-trate their search for employment within the boundaries of their own country. However, distance still affects visiting patterns, especially among low-income earners.

The level and security of urban income weigh heavily in the economic cal-culus and affect urban–rural ties, as both the Enugu and the Abidjan studies demonstrate. It remains to be seen what happens to wage trends and to urban earning opportunities for women and what deal agricultural producers get. Security of urban income is fostered by recent social security legislation and, more importantly, by increased opportunities for deriving regular income from urban property, especially real estate. In a survey in Mushin, an outlying part of Lagos, half of the men and two-thirds of the women who considered themselves permanent residents of Lagos were landlords (Sandra T. Barnes 1974, p. 79).

The ideology of loyalty to home is proclaimed in many immigrant groups today. Will it continue to mandate close urban–rural ties when the majority of migrants are no longer tied to the village by considerations of economic advantage? Normative support for rural–urban migration disappeared quickly where the economic imperative changed. Is the norm of loyalty to home similarly dependent upon many perceiving it to coincide with their economic interests? Or is there something special about *home*?

5 Social relationships in the urban setting

> Tribal movements may be created and instigated to action by the new men of power in furtherance of their own special interests which are, time and again, the constitutive interests of emerging social classes. Tribalism then becomes a mask for class privilege. To borrow a worn metaphor, there is often a non-traditional wolf under the tribal sheepskin.
>
> Richard L. Sklar (1967, p. 6)

Most persons in the towns of West Africa live in a dual system: They are urban residents loyal to a rural home, part both of the towns they live in and of the villages they have come from. Consequently, the demands they make on the urban system are limited. Their ultimate economic security remains in rural areas, and their identity and emotional satisfaction are to some degree derived from there. A less than complete adaptation to the urban environment is thus required.[1]

Making friends

The majority of adult urban dwellers in West Africa are first-generation townsmen. They spent their early childhood in an ethnically homogeneous milieu; they and their schoolmates shared the same background. Local languages are used in the first years of schooling in Nigeria, Ghana, Sierra Leone, and the Gambia; many secondary schools are dominated by one ethnic group. Childhood friends are thus usually drawn from a single small ethnic category.[2]

Rural–urban migrants usually make their first move to a town where they can expect to be received by a relative or at least a covillager. Only between 8 and 13 percent of factory workers interviewed in Accra, Kumasi, and Takoradi, Ghana, reported knowing no one in town before they came; about two-thirds stayed with a kinsman upon arrival (Peil 1972, pp.145 and 164).[3]

Stemming from this pattern of initial urban association, there follows a tendency for persons of the same or similar origin to form residential clusters.[4] Such trends are checked somewhat where the choice of residence is restricted by housing shortages. More severe constraints arise where public authorities and/or employers closely control a major part of, or even virtually all, housing. They typically discourage ethnically homogeneous neighborhoods. However, in preindustrial towns, the division between the old town and new residential areas for strangers – the *sabon gari* ("new town") in Nigeria, *zongo* ("strangers' quarters") in Ghana – usually received administrative sanction.

Where ethnic clusters exist, organizations established on a neighborhood basis will underpin ethnicity. Aristide R. Zolberg [(1964) 1969, pp. 116 and 357] reported that neighborhoods in the smaller towns in the Ivory Coast were ethnically homogeneous and that ward committees of the Parti Démocratique de Côte d'Ivoire (PDCI) were in effect ethnic communities as well. Party life thus contributed to the maintenance and even the reinforcement of affiliations based on ethnic ties.

Whether residentially dispersed or not, recent immigrants will tend to make friends within their ethnic group as they conceive it. Here there is the reassurance of associating with people known from back home, the pleasure of sharing familiar customs, the ease of conversing in one's own tongue. As the lament (Mitchell 1956, p.7) in a Kalela song on the Zambian Copperbelt goes:

> You mothers who speak Tonga,
> You who speak Soli, mothers,
> Teach me Lenje.
> How shall I go and sing?
> This song I am going to dance in the Lenje country,
> I do not know how I am going to speak Lenje.
> Soli I do not know,
> Tonga I do not know,
> Lozi I do not know.
> Mbwela is difficult,
> Kaonde is difficult.

The attraction of categorical similarity is reinforced to the extent that immigrants are drawn together by their ties to a common home area. We should not be surprised when 50 percent of the workers in a survey in Ibadan and Lagos state that their best friend is from the same village or town, when 86 percent say their best friend belongs to the same "tribe" (Hans Dieter Seibel 1968, p. 201).[5]

According to place of origin, a whole series of potential social identities are available to the immigrant arriving in town; depending upon current situational factors, he or she will look to the extended family, home village, village group to which it belongs, "subtribe," "tribe," "supertribe," nation, race. Some are traditional contexts of ethnicity, some are newly expanded. The number of people from his family, village, village group, and so on that he can find in town will determine how far he has to reach out to make friends. The new experiences and problems encountered in the city will affect which groups he identifies with. A set of concentric circles provides a graphic model of the more narrowly or more largely defined ethnic groups that the individual identifies with, recruits his friends from, joins in unions, and supports in formal organizations (see Gugler 1975, p. 304). When the urban immigrant begins to establish social relationships outside his or her ethnic group, the neighborhood, the workplace, and the church are the three key environments where the contacts with strangers are fostered.

Neighbors can come to know each other over time,[6] or they may unite abruptly over a common grievance (e.g., the residents of a public housing project in opposition to the authorities). Neighbors play a particularly important role in the effective social network of low-income earners who have limited access to transport. Where choice of residence is restricted, the neighborhood imposes a set of potential friends and acquaintances on the urban dweller. Residential patterns thus become a factor in their own right in shaping social relationships.[7] Here is how Sandra T. Barnes describes neighborhood activities in Mushin, an outlying part of Lagos built up since World War II.

Social and economic ties among neighbors in Mushin, Lagos*

The word "neighborhood" is taken from the Yoruba *àdúgbò* which refers to ward or quarter in older towns and cities and delineates geographic, political, and social space. Like traditional neighborhoods, those of Mushin also are spatially, politically, and socially delimited, but the extent and criteria vary according to the perceptions of each resident.

In a formal sense, neighborhoods are given boundaries for administrative purposes. They encompass five square blocks or more, depending upon the geography of the area, its population density, and its historical development. Landlords generally perceive their neighborhoods as extending throughout the fullest bounded limits because they are involved in ward organizations and social activities that bring them into association with residents from the entire area. Tenants, by contrast, are more likely to envision residential neighborhoods in an informal sense, as small units consisting of only a few streets. In whichever way they are perceived most individuals do delimit a social area which they equate with residence and which can be called neighborhood.

Despite the variety of available social outlets, neighborhoods are not the primary sphere of activity for all residents. Familial and other associational meetings take place anywhere in the city and draw residents out of their neighborhoods quite regularly. Employment takes men, but less frequently women, outside their neighborhoods in the majority of cases. And those residents who have been in the city for a relatively short period are more likely to have ties that fan out into the city to whichever friends, townsmen, or kinsmen can be found, than to have had the opportunity to develop neighborhood social ties.

Those who have spent a few years in Lagos have had the time to develop more social ties with neighbors. But the fact that an individual has a high level of social participation within his neighborhood does not preclude social participation outside it. The longer a resident has been in the city and the firmer his commitment to remain there, the more likely he is to have a high density of contacts and activities radiating throughout the whole of the city as well as within his neighborhood of residence.

Neighbors know each other well. Inside one's house it is impossible to retain anonymity due to the proximity and small size of rooms, the sharing of cooking, washing, and sanitary facilities, and the lack of recreational space within individual living quarters. The amount of knowledge one tenant has of another is relative to ethnic group and time spent in the lodgings, but it is extensive.

* Excerpt from Sandra T. Barnes, *Becoming a Lagosian*, 1974, pp. 61–8, edited, by permission of the author. Based on research in 1971–72.

Outside the confines of the house there is a high level of informal interaction between neighbors. More than four-fifths of adult women in Asala spend virtually all of their time in their neighborhoods.** Most of them, particularly Yoruba women, do not remain inside their houses but engage in petty trade at small street-side stands in front of or near their houses. A relatively small percentage trade in markets. The closeness of the trading stalls facilitates contacts between women who work and converse in clusters throughout the day; even those who do not trade are brought into the social lives of those who do.

In contrast only about a fifth of the adult men remain in their residential neighborhoods during the work day, while slightly fewer work within one to two miles of their residences. The majority is scattered throughout all sectors of the city in pursuit of a livelihood. Except for the few who are unemployed or retired, men who remain in the neighborhood also are engaged in trade or in crafts or other services. As with the women, their days are interspersed with visits among co-workers and neighbors. Because most shops and trading stands open onto the streets workers are easily familiarized with each other's movements.

When workers return to their houses after a day's work, streets and shops teem with activity. Gaming establishments and bars are found on nearly every block and local residents begin to fill the empty chairs and benches around five o'clock each afternoon. Informal games of ping-pong and draughts and the weekly lotteries also draw neighborhood groups together regularly. As the evening passes music fills the air from amplifiers at record shops and bars, hawkers call out their wares in an attempt to make last sales, food sellers enjoy their most brisk activity of the day, and social calls reach a peak. This is the time when verandahs are full of relaxing housemates and friends. Men may go farther afield to seek out companions while women prefer to socialize nearby.

Neighborhood business is abundant. It has been observed before that in the center of Lagos individuals rely heavily on their neighborhoods for economic purposes whether or not they are primarily employed there (Marris 1961, 81). In this outlying area, where commerce is not excessive compared to other areas of the city, a total of 1,247 street-side businesses can be found in a space less than three city blocks wide and eight blocks long. This number does not include hawkers who solicit business on foot, middlemen who operate supply depots from their rooms, or those who specialize only in early morning or late evening trade. At least half of the petty traders specialize in small quantities of manufactured or consumable commodities which they display on small tables or stalls. Others, working in house-front shops, tend to sell bulkier provisions, such as beer and soft drinks, or to specialize in lotteries and other games of chance. There are food sellers, tailors, seamstresses, craftsmen (e.g., mechanics, electricians, carpenters, goldsmiths, cobblers), building-materials purveyors, hairdressers, and barbers – all present in great force.

Nearly all residents must rely occasionally on credit for food and goods. And as with other business dealings in the city, obtaining credit from local traders is contingent upon being known. A newcomer initially purchases items on a cash basis with a few neighborhood dealers. He becomes acquainted with the traders in the process, and lets them know where he

---

* * Asala is the pseudonym Sandra T. Barnes gave to the section of Mushin on which her research focused.

resides. Once a trader is sure of a face, a residence, and the type of company a customer keeps, she is prepared to extend or deny credit on a monthly basis. So substantial are credit transactions that a trader maintains a credit book, carefully noting each purchase that requires future payment.

The trader in turn is dependent upon occasional credit in order to obtain merchandise from middlemen suppliers during slack periods of a month when income from sales is low. While she is developing a trustworthy clientele, she must establish a similar reputation with her own creditors. Ultimately the trader is dependent upon the neighborhood's knowledge of herself and her fair business dealings for the success of her business. Gaining a known clientele and finding middlemen-creditors are achievements which tend to stabilize residence, particularly for women. A man whose wife is a successful trader is less likely to move than is the man who has few economic ties to his residential area. For the men and women who work near their residences and for their families, it is literally profitable to be well known and trusted within the neighborhood.

Local recognition has another advantage. For the resident who has marital discord, arguments with co-tenants, or other problems which require advice, being well known to others increases the prospects of support. As one neighborhood elder puts it:

"The action of a man cannot be hidden. If you are living in the neighborhood and you are bad, before you speak your neighbors will know what kind of man or woman you are. If you are good, or poor, people of the neighborhood who watch you will know your condition. If you go to them for help, they will pity you and help you. They may help you settle a quarrel. They may help you get a job. They may give you money. It is not very hard to know a man who is hungry. A man who is hungry and a man who is angry – they are two faces which are the same."

When problems arise residents prefer to turn to those nearby such as landlords, friends, or relatives rather than seek the advice of persons living farther away in the city.

Another activity that tends to be neighborhood-centered is religion. Most individuals belong to religious groups that meet within the immediate vicinity of their residences. In fact, this type of associational life coincides with residence more frequently than any other (except for those organizations that are recruited exclusively on the basis of neighborhood, such as landlords' associations). For example a majority of religiously active residents belong to prayer groups or congregations in the same neighborhood in which they reside; a few are active within a mile of their residences; about a third belong to groups elsewhere in Lagos. Religious groups are among the first organizations sought out by migrants after they arrive in the city. While they ordinarily wait several years to join other types of voluntary associations, they usually find their religious groups within the first year (Barnes 1975, 83f.).

Finally, neighborhoods have provided an important focus for political activity. Before the military government was instituted in 1966, ward associations became politicized and in some cases functioned as political party units on the lowest level of the organizational hierarchy. Although some of these groups still exist they now have no partisan functions. They do attempt to serve community needs, however, and to act as non-partisan units in a localized chieftaincy system.

Neighborhoods have a second political attribute in that they are stratified

on two levels: those of landlords and tenants. Property own
on landlords the right to participate in ward association activ
right is not extended to tenants. This means that tenants
excluded from neighborhood-level political groups and as
enjoy the same local status as do real estate owners. They, far more than
their tenants, are looked to for advice and solutions to a wide range of
problems. In their neighborhoods landlords act as community elders or
patrons, and tenants frequently become their clients.

Neighborhoods in which houses have been privately built are frequently
characterized by a certain socioeconomic diversity. Apart from the widespread
pattern of landlords and their tenants living side by side, the very rapid growth
of many cities has pushed more affluent groups into previously marginal residential areas. Public housing projects, on the other hand, tend to be rather
homogeneous in terms of social stratification. In the colonial situation, Europeans typically lived segregated de facto if not de jure from the Africans they
ruled.[8] The Africans, who, upon Independence, took over their positions
usually also succeeded them in their housing. The groundwork for fairly rigid
class segregation has thus been laid. Residential patterns have been further
differentiated by public low-income housing projects ultimately occupied by
middle-income groups. The situation is different in places where the colonial
influence was not felt or where it encountered preindustrial urban patterns.
Thus, Merran Fraenkel (1964, pp. 52ff.) reported from Monrovia that there
was a correlation between neighborhood and social status but that no area
was exclusive; poor, illiterate families could be found living next-door to (or
more often behind) wealthy, "civilized" families.

A number of important characteristics interact with the ethnic and socioeconomic composition of a neighborhood: economic activity within the neighborhood, the pattern of house ownership, and household makeup and size. No
West African studies are available to allow comparison with the pioneering
work carried out by Valdo Pons (1969, pp. 102ff.) in Kisangani, Zaïre, in the
1950s. He described a neighborhood close to the town center as a crowded
and lively area of great diversity and contrasted it with two much quieter
outlying neighborhoods that attracted other categories of immigrants and
absorbed the new arrivals in different ways.

More generally than is the case with neighbors, workmates are imposed, not
chosen. But work groups or cliques within the work group encourage links
with strangers, and occasion for the defense of common interest against management arises easily. There appears to be little opposition to working with
strangers. In the same survey of workers in Ibadan and Lagos in which 86
percent reported that their best friend belonged to the same "tribe," 80 percent
said they preferred working with people from different "tribes"; this position
correlated positively with level of education. However, there was considerable
variation according to firm; in the one firm that was ethnically homogeneous,
57 percent of the workers interviewed indicated a preference for working with

people of their own "tribe" (Hans Dieter Seibel 1968, pp. 195ff. and 389f.). In the parallel survey of women workers conducted by Helga Seibel (1969, p. 58) in some of the same factories, including the ethnically homogeneous one, two-thirds stated a preference for working in an interethnic context.

Strangers in town may be drawn together through common religious belief and practice. In the largely immigrant section of Ibadan, different Yoruba groups were represented in each of the four congregations (one Anglican, three belonging to independent churches) studied by J.D.Y. Peel (1968, p. 194). They thus transcended intra-Yoruba divisions. However, there were only a handful of non-Yoruba, and they were difficult to accommodate to the extent that the congregations used the Yoruba language.

Relatively recent is the growth in appreciation of an important innovation in urban research. The approach goes beyond specific associational contexts such as neighborhood and workplace in an attempt to develop a clearer overall picture of relationship and change. Generally called the "social network approach," this method avoids analysis of attitudes and actions of individuals in terms of specific bounded groups, acknowledging instead that individuals are enmeshed in a web of social relationships that lie within and without several organization and categorical boundaries.[9] The analytic importance of explicitly recognizing this somewhat elementary idea is suggested by Mitchell:

The essential idea behind a social network . . . is that the variations in the behaviour of people in any one role relationship may be traced to the effects of the behaviour of other people, to whom they are linked in one, two or more steps, in some other quite different role relationship. A man may quarrel with a kinsman because the latter is linked through a workmate to an adamant political opponent of the former. (1969, p. 46)

Understanding the social context of urbanites in West Africa requires the application of social network methodology and analysis. The largely rural-born populations of nontraditional West African cities are participants in the social life of their place of origin, either through periodic visits or at least through economic support and plans for retirement; at the same time, they are resident participants in urban life. In other words, the social field of typical urbanites stretches across geographic and organizational frameworks; given widespread migration and the element of cultural discontinuity between home and town, they may be placed most intelligibly in terms of their social network. By associating in town primarily with people from the same homeplace or region, they create a social environment that is neither of the town nor of the homeplace. In addition to its communities of permanent residents and cosmopolitans, the social fabric of town and city life may be conceived of as a mosaic of these various social networks based on place of origin and ethnic group, all overlapping in institutional and geographic nexuses of employment, religion, residence, and so on that, in turn, each provide the arena for the formation of other networks of association.

Participation in unions

The vitality of voluntary associations on the urban scene in West Africa has been much commented upon. However, an understanding of the role they play requires that different types be distinguished. Three patterns stand out: the society limited to a specific function, the small union with diffuse functions, the large-scale organization.

Societies performing a specific function are widespread and important for the services they render. Funeral benefit societies and savings clubs are ubiquitous. Specificity may reach extremes; some saving clubs never meet as a group, and all the members are known only to the organizer (Banton 1957, p. 188). We will focus on unions in this section, and then we will examine large-scale organizations.

The most common basis for a union is ethnicity. Persons who recognize a shared origin may be residentially dispersed, they are usually surrounded by strangers at work and they may transcend ethnic boundaries in church, but they can and usually do get together during their leisure time. In addition to their informal reunions, "home people" frequently institute regular meetings, attempt to have all from home join in, and establish a measure of formal organization. Such unions are multipurpose and elicit intensive participation.[10] Chukuka Okonjo's account of meetings among Western Ibo in Ibadan introduces us to the range of their concerns and communicates some of the flavor.[11]

Town, village, and clan improvement associations of Western Ibo in Ibadan*

> *Madu agbazi akali ebo?*
> 'Can one grow greater than his clan?'
>
> (Western Ibo saying)

The rhetorical question asked above is indicative of the central position of the town union in the affairs of the Western Ibo migrants in Ibadan. This type of association has been ably described by Ottenberg [1955] for the Ibo from the Afikpo area. As a general rule, all migrants from each locality in Western Ibo have a village, town or clan union. Where the number of migrants from a locality is too small to warrant the formation of such a union, they tend to associate themselves with the town or village union of their mother's home. Where pride or politics in the Western Ibo area do not allow of this, the migrant regards himself as a distant member of the nearest existing union of his town or village. Union rules generally make provision for the inclusion of distant members.

Town and village unions are considered to be branches of an all-Nigeria

---

* Excerpt from Chukuka Okonjo: "The Western Ibo," in the collection *The City of Ibadan*, 1967, pp. 108–13, by permission of the author, Cambridge University Press, and the Institute of African Studies, University of Ibadan. Footnotes have been renumbered.

union whose headquarters is generally situated in the home town or village. Sometimes, however, where good leadership is not available at home, the headquarters of the union might be sited in a centre where vigorous leadership is available. The general aim of such unions is, to quote the rules and regulations of one town union:

> i to work for the upliftment of the town's society, spiritually, culturally and materially and
> ii to encourage the evolution of a new spirit of unity and co-operative effort.

The same theme of improving the home town and encouraging co-operative effort among migrants from a particular locality runs through the constitution of all the unions that we have investigated in Ibadan. Membership is mandatory for all migrants from a locality, although registration and attendance at meetings is not compulsory, especially in the larger unions, provided the member concerned pays his dues.

One meeting is held every month, and emergency meetings can be called at very short notice. Meetings usually take place in the compound where the president or the oldest member of the community, the *diokpa* (always referred to in English as the patron), lives.[1] Large unions make use of nearby schools. Meetings are usually held on Sunday afternoons and are conducted in Ibo. However, minutes are often written not in Ibo but in English. As the time for the opening of the meeting approaches, members arrive, in twos and threes. The officers of the union – usually a president, secretary, financial secretary and treasurer – take up seats around a table facing the rest of the members. There is a provost to maintain order. Older members of the community take up the more comfortable seats, and where no seat is available a younger member rises in traditional respect and offers his seat to the older member. When the president sees that a quorum is formed he declares the meeting open by asking the oldest member of the community to pray. Kola nuts, provided by the person in whose compound the meeting is being held, are broken while wishes and prayers for the wellbeing of the association, the progress and welfare of the members and the home town are offered.[2] The kola nuts are then served and the meeting can proceed.

First, all new members are introduced and rigorously examined as to

1 Traditionally town, village or clan union meetings have been presided over by the oldest member of the community who was referred to as the president of the union, the other offices being filled by a general consensus of opinion of members, age and achievement being the main criteria for the selection of officers. In the last twenty years there has been a change in union organization, whereby age no longer serves as a criterion for office-holding. As a consequence of this change, officers are now elected and the oldest member of the community no longer holds executive power but has become the patron of the union. Where the physical facilities permit, meetings are held in the compound where he lives.

2 The youngest member of the union takes the kola nuts on a plate to the *diokpa* who then announces: *Ibe anyi oji abiakwanu*. The ceremony then proceeds as follows: *Diokpa, wa nu: 'Anyi ga di o', 'Ise.' 'Ife onye chota oga enwea.' 'Ise.' 'Ego, umu, ahudimma.' 'Ise.' 'Onye ni kwene na nke anyi ga aga, nkea ama ga.' 'Ise.'* Translated: 'Comrades, kola nuts have been offered us.' Members then ask him to break the kola nuts. He then continues whilst breaking the nuts: 'We will live long. What we have come here to seek we will find – money, children, health. He who does not want us to progress will not himself progress.' To each of these wishes members reply with *Ise*, meaning 'so be it'. After this kola nuts are served according to age.

whether they have paid up all their dues in their former branch unions. If they have come straight from home they are registered, even though they might not have belonged to the home branch of the union. Each new member has a sponsor who gives a short background of the man being introduced, of his parents, his occupation and, where he has no work, his needs. Minutes are then read and passed as being correct, after any necessary amendment. The business of the day is then dealt with. This usually involves the settling of disputes between members, the giving and recovering of loans, information about events at home and correspondence with other branch unions, petitions for help by indigent members, and any other business which may crop up. After this the secretary reads aloud the names of members, who then pay their dues while the financial secretary records payments. At this stage fines are also paid, as well as loan repayments. After all have paid, the money is counted and the total collected is announced. The meeting is then closed with the traditional blessing, given by the oldest member present.

The union is the centre of activities for migrants from a locality. Where the number of migrants is small, men and women sit together in one meeting. Otherwise, meetings for men and married women are held separately. Unmarried women sit with the men and have an equal say with men in the proceedings of a meeting. Only in a few instances have unmarried women been allowed to sit in on meetings of married women. In the few cases where this has taken place, the women concerned have been relatively highly educated and respected members of the community, holding positions like that of a secondary school teacher. Such persons often act as secretary or in another official capacity, where their knowledge could be of use to the women's wing of the branch union.

The union thus acts both as a meeting place and as a court of appeal for the immediate family circle in the case of quarrels between members. It also gives to the new migrant a sense of belonging to a community.[3] It must be remarked that very few Western Ibo migrants consider themselves in any way as being citizens of Ibadan. They may have lived for nearly forty years in Ibadan and have returned home in this length of time only once; their children may have been born and brought up in Ibadan; still the belief dies hard – they are in no way citizens of Ibadan.[4] It is extremely interesting to

3 Most unions have rules stipulating that members must first refer any disputes between them, which might be actionable at law, to the union for settlement. Permission is rarely granted for cases between members to go to the law courts. Unions adjudicate, for example, in cases of fighting, disrespect and insult shown to an elder by a younger, infringement of marital rights, rivalry in a place of employment, family disputes, suspected spell-casting, poisoning or witchcraft.

4 This does not imply a total rejection of a sense of belonging to Ibadan in all social sectors, but rather in a majority of sectors. There are in fact cases of partial rejection in a sector. In the religious sector of Western Ibo society, for example, while Anglican Protestants belong to the Ibo Anglican Church in Ibadan they feel that they also belong to the Diocese of the Niger, not to the Ibadan Diocese; Western Ibo Catholics, on the other hand, feel that they are a part of the Ibadan Catholic community. The same holds true for the other splinter Christian sects – there is an Ibadan community spirit. It is interesting in this connexion to note the behaviour of traditional religionists when questioned as to their religion. Quite a number do not acknowledge their religion on first inquiry but give themselves out as Christians. Closer questioning then elicits the fact that they are not Christians. No Muslim was discovered in the sample of migrants interviewed.

follow up the effects of this belief amongst second-generation Western Ibo in Ibadan. Born and bred in Ibadan, they are all bilingual, speaking Yoruba without an accent. Their playmates are Yoruba. The very young ones, in fact, after their first visit to their parents' home town come back to deride it as being backward, with no electricity and no water supplies. It is only later in life that the prejudices begin to take root. Stereotyped ideas of their hosts develop and the majority end up by marrying not one of their Yoruba play-mates but rather one either from the Western Ibo group in Ibadan or from elsewhere.

The unions are seen operating most efficiently in cases where there is an emergency – a need to collect money for an approved project or for a funeral or a feast. We will take the case of collection of money for an approved project . . . Worthy projects are generally approved in the annual general meetings of all branch unions held in the home town or village, to which the branch union sends one or more delegates. Such projects are usu-ally construction projects – the building of a school or hospital – or a land case. A flat levy for all persons from the town living anywhere in Nigeria is made. The rates for married women are lower than that of men and unmar-ried women. Groups to collect these levies are formed, and authorized by the union to use whatever force is necessary and sufficient to collect the dues.

Most people on being visited pay up their levy immediately, or borrow money to pay up at once, for the penalties for not paying are great. Any durable goods in the defaulter's rooms can be seized, only to be redeemed later by a payment much higher than the original levy. If the defaulter attempts to resist the removal of his property, he might be beaten up by the collectors. Attempts to report such fights to the police invariably end in the case not being taken up, since the police are loath to take up what they con-sider are family quarrels. If the police are, however, 'misguided' enough to take up such a case, and members of the union are fined in a court for what has happened, the defaulter will be promptly excommunicated from his union. Letters are written about the incident to the traditional authorities at home and to all branch unions, and the defaulter is boycotted by every member of his town. Very few people ever allow matters to reach such a stage. In fact, if the defaulter is prepared to do this, his immediate relatives will pay his levy and fine for him and any other expenses to which the union has been put. For should any disaster befall the individual during the period of his excommunication, no one would come to his aid.

Feasts are another occasion for active participation in union affairs. Everyone enjoys a feast and all strive to be present. Procedure is similar to a normal meeting with the feast being the only business transacted. As the festivities warm up, palm wine is served, and singing and dancing com-mence. There is a stock of songs for such occasions, although special ones might be composed for the feast. Two songs deserve mention. The first runs:

Onye nyem na onu
Onye nyem o
Onye nyem na onu
Onye nyem o

Refrain:
Nnemu nyem na onu

Nnemu nyem o
Nnemu nyem na onu
Nnem nyem o.[5]

The other song is used to attack people who are felt to be mean and do not entertain their townsmen in the right manner when visited. It runs as follows:

Onye na ala manya ma odi enuta.

Refrain:
Ola manya ma onuo
Ola manya ma onuo
Ola manya ma onuo.[6]

In the next stanza the name of the person being attacked is substituted for '*Onye*' in the first line.

Church congregations can also elicit intensive participation and assume multiple functions beyond the realm of religion. Such a pattern is particularly prominent among independent churches.[12] The independent church was, for one thing, a response to the colonial situation, to use Georges Balandier's [(1955) 1971. pp. 34ff.] classic term. It meant emancipation from a foreign clergy and a challenge to the colonial society by reference to a supernatural power beyond that society's control. Political secession was impossible and economic dependence difficult to escape, but the new creed had a chance of survival, even though it usually met with opposition from the colonial society. That opposition, in turn, frequently strengthened the independent church's appeal to the masses. Once Independence had been granted, the independent church either redefined its role within a new polity that was now accepted or became a focus of opposition to this polity and, in particular, the group in power [Balandier (1955) 1971, pp. 481f.]. Here, our concern will be with the local congregation and its characteristics as a union.[13]

Unions make possible a high degree of participation. At work and in the broader political sphere, only a privileged minority enjoys a similar degree of participation. Peel (1968, pp. 179ff.) found that virtually all regular members of both Anglican and independent churches in Ibadan belonged to church societies. These societies could take a great deal of a person's time and social energy and were a major field for the individual's social battles. Fraenkel (1964, p. 165) reported that Pentecostal services in Monrovia allowed a great deal of participation by ordinary members of the congregation. Offices proliferated; rather more than one in three of the Pentecostalists she surveyed were choristers, deacons, elders, preachers, treasurers, or had some other church

5 Who was it who fed me? Who was it? Who was it who fed me? Who was it?
It was my mother who fed me. It was my mother. It was my mother who fed me. It was my mother.
6 Who is it that drinks palm wine without ever buying?
The drinker who never buys. The drinker who never buys. The drinker who never buys.

title. Banton (1957, pp. 171f.), in his account of Temne friendly societies in Freetown, emphasized that they were organized in such a way as to permit the maximum number of persons to hold office; one branch had at least forty-five offices, although the membership was no more than ninety. Status is thus provided in a subsystem that has a degree of independence from the system of social stratification.

Members of a union have a broad basis of shared values and norms, either derived from a common origin or established in a new creed. They are in communion; they can partake fully; they relax from the constraints of a foreign urban environment. Fraenkel (1964, p. 164) noted as the most obvious point about the services and religious celebrations of Pentecostal churches that people enjoyed them. As an advertisement for a celebration of the Church of the Lord read, "Come and enjoy yourselves spiritually."

But the role of unions is not limited to the provision of enjoyment in the company of those of like mind. Unions can at times deal effectively with the problems confronting the immigrant. He or she is helped to find shelter and employment, attended if ill, given economic and moral support in bereavement, assisted when in trouble with the law. Reciprocity is thus strengthened by the establishment of institutional controls.

Unions are strongly placed to exert a socializing function. Their leadership articulates responses to the juxtaposition of old and new that characterizes the urban scene in West Africa. Secessionist churches propagate new rules on polygamy and on the relationship between husband and wife in general. Ethnic associations explicitly introduce a new immigrant to the rules of life in the urban setting. To anticipate terms that we will explore in Chapter 6, unions are active agents in historical change, and at the same time, they are intermediating situational change.

Much of the socialization is latent. The member who is made to pay a standard fine for arriving late at a meeting, for failing to attend without a valid excuse, or for disorderly behavior during the meeting may see the sanction as an expression of the authority of the association and of its leadership in particular, but he is also thus introduced to the rhythm and formalization of present-day urban life.

Unions are concerned with their public standing. Their control is extended beyond their own activities. Members are taken to task for actions that run counter to the norms of the union or damage the reputation of its membership with the public. Typically, attempts are made to settle disputes among members by arbitration within the union, outside the courts.

The position of stranger group warrants particular circumspection in a foreign country. Suzanne Bernus (1969, pp. 152f. and 168ff.) relates how in Niamey the union of Yoruba originating from Shaki and Ighobo, Nigeria, took sanctions against dishonest merchants and drug pushers in its ranks and discouraged participation in local politics. The union made substantial donations to the ruling party and contributed to the building of a mosque in Niamey and of another mosque back home in Shaki. The usual forms of assistance were provided to members in difficulty and undesirables were re-patriated to their hometown.

Members interact not only within the framework of union functions but tend to associate in extraunion activities as well. One important consequence of this is the increased probability of inmarriage, which weaves the web of association within the union more tightly. The development of multiplex relationships among members in turn inhibits the emergence of crosscutting loyalties in the urban setting because the membership becomes a somewhat autonomous island of association in the city.

Where unions also fully control the structural relationships of their members at work, they may approach the model of the total institution. Rouch (1956, p. 153) found such a pattern among Zabrama immigrants in Accra. All emigrants from the village of Gothey, Niger, went to Accra, where they worked exclusively in the timber market.[14] The traveling costs of a first-time migrant were borne by a master who controlled about sixty unskilled workers. The new arrival received food, clothes, and accommodation from his master; he was also given some clothes when he returned to Gothey at the beginning of the planting season. For his second stay in Accra, the master entrusted him with £40 or £50 ($112 or $140), telling him to shift for himself. If he had not made a profit at the end of the season, he was sent home for the growing season at the master's expense. For his third stay, the apprentice was told to get half of his capital elsewhere; if he was unsuccessful again, he was abandoned by his master. Thus, the people from Gothey had their own housing, their market, their lorries; at the time of Rouch's study, they wanted to organize a permanent shuttle service between Gothey and Accra. It is because of this "splendid isolation" that such immigrants were, in one sense, "super-tribalized," more conscious and proud of their ethnic identity than they had been at home (Rouch 1956, pp. 163f. and 193 footnote).

Although ethnic unions may at times be referred to as "voluntary" associations, they are usually quite indispensable to the immigrant's survival in town both in economic and in psychological terms. Furthermore, strong norms, underpinned by sanctions, may make membership quasi-compulsory. In a survey in Enugu in 1961, 82 percent of the unskilled workers and petty traders interviewed, and 57 percent of a sample of senior civil servants, professionals, and contractors reported that they were regularly attending and contributing to an ethnic union (Gugler 1971, p. 410). W. T. Morrill [(1963) 1967, p. 175] observed in Calabar that the absorption of new Ibo immigrants into their respective ethnic unions was such a natural and inevitable thing that informants were simply unable to conceive of anything else.

The member, in turn, is given unquestioning support. In Chinua Achebe's novel *No Longer at Ease,* the Umuofia Progressive Union pays for the services of a lawyer for Obi, even though Obi has repeatedly acted against the wishes of the union and only recently shown great disrespect. After Obi has been condemned to a prison sentence, the union continues to back him: "They had no illusions about Obi. He was, without doubt, a very foolish and self-willed young man. But this was not the time to go into that. The fox must be chased away first; after that the hen might be warned against wandering into the bush" (1960, p. 5).

The assistance given individual members by the union may be analytically distinguished from the common interests it pursues, although frequently they coincide. In Achebe's novel, the unconditional support the hero receives from the union is seen by the members to be in their own best interest as well as that of the Eastern Nigerian village they represent in Lagos.

The active membership of a union as a rule falls within a limited range, say fifteen to ninety people. The lower limit can be understood in terms of a minimum of resources, both financial and in leadership personnel, required to run a formal organization. We would suggest that the upper limit is set by what we have outlined as the characteristics of the union: That is, members spend a considerable part of their leisure time within its framework and are subject to its social control; they participate actively; the more ambitious hold offices.

A union with a growing membership sooner or later faces a split. An ethnic union will be succeeded by unions with a lower common ethnic denominator, even while the context of ethnicity (i.e., the body of people identified as coethnic) is expanding at another level. A conflict over dogma or ritual may provide the rationale for the split of an independent church. Or perhaps the membership of the successors to the ethnic union or the independent church is not delineated in terms of differences of origin or religion respectively, but of residential propinquity.

Organization and power

The relatively small size of a union severely limits its capability to act as a pressure group. Ethnic unions that want to lobby for rural interests or, more precisely, for the interest urban dwellers hold in the development of their home areas, need to reach higher administrative echelons than those accessible to the clamor of a small organization. Hence, they are induced to combine and establish formal organizations at higher levels of integration. Eastern Nigerians usually defined such second-level organizations in terms of rural administrative units. A subtle interplay could then be observed. Administrative boundaries had commonly been designed to follow traditional divisions, but where they did not coincide, a new identity, in terms of shared interests in the administrative unit, competed with traditional identity; more important, larger administrative units nurtured a wider consciousness and common identification as the population made demands on the administration.[15]

Howard Wolpe (1974, pp. 73ff., 145ff., and 213ff.) illustrates the nontraditional character of many ethnic identities and ethnic organizations in his study of the political history of Port Harcourt. He uses the term "geo-ethnic" to designate ethnic groups borne from artificial administrative units. Wolpe describes the impact of ethnic identities on urban politics in Port Harcourt in the 1960s in this way:[16]

Given the primacy of communal identities for the vast majority of Port Harcourt residents, the absence of communally segregated residential areas limited the extent to which residentially defined electoral wards developed meaningful political identities. Municipal councillors, though technically serving as ward representatives, were seldom guided in their political behavior by considerations of ward interest. Interest in self and in kinship and wider communities of origin appeared more often to be the dominant points of reference for the local politician as they were for the average citizens. As kinsmen and townspeople were distributed throughout the municipality, political service did not consist of battles for urban amenities (more water taps, better roads, improved conservancy service), for such amenities were "indivisible benefits" that could not be divided among geographically dispersed individuals. Rather political service normally consisted of the provision of personal patronage in the form of contracts, jobs, and political office . . . The absence of communally segregated residential areas meant, in effect, the absence of a significant neighborhood stimulus to community development. (1974, p. 29)

Effective political action in the urban and national arenas requires the support of a major segment of the population. This consideration provides the incentive to establish formal organizations at even higher levels, still on ethnic lines but usually encompassing peoples who did not recognize a shared identity in the traditional context.[17] Such an extension of ethnic identity, the emergence of the "supertribe," usually finds its main strength in the urban setting. Here, the ethnic organizations represent not only the interests of rural areas but also those of a category of people of the same origin in town.[18]

Intricate organizational structures are thus established. For one thing, an ethnic association is joined in a federation with associations representing its own home area in other towns; together, they may establish a headquarters in the home area. At the same time, within the town, the association is integrated into a pyramid of organizations representing increasingly larger areas of origin.[19] Eastern Nigerians typically had a three-tier structure: ethnic unions, delegates of ethnic unions working in the second-level organizations that represented major administrative units, these, in turn, sending delegates to a third-level organization such as the Ibo State Union or the Ibibio State Union.

Not surprisingly, third-level organizations of Eastern Nigerians were little heard of in towns where the majority of residents would have come under the jurisdiction of one such organization, but they played an important role where they represented a vocal minority. Thus, in Northern Nigeria, Ibo always felt threatened, and they formed the Ibo Northern Regional Union to speak and act for all of them. Severely handicapped in access to educational facilities, Ibo, through the Ibo Northern Regional Union, ran two primary and two secondary schools in Northern Nigeria. In Calabar, Eastern Nigeria, the Ibo Federal Union provided social welfare services unavailable there through any other mechanism and employed funds to ensure that Ibo were not discriminated against politically in this area, where they were strangers [Morrill (1963) 1967, p. 176].

Although third-level organizations were defined in ethnic terms by Eastern Nigerians, they did not represent traditional political units. However, the new structural alignments followed lines of cultural affinity. When a group of Yoruba students and professional men founded Egbe Omo Oduduwa, a Pan-Yoruba cultural society in London in 1945, they were similarly motivated by interests that were political as well as cultural. Leaders of Egbe Omo Oduduwa were the principal organizers of the Action Group when it was launched in 1950; it became one of the three major Nigerian parties until the early 1960s, when it dissolved into factions in which ethnic origin (i.e., distinctions between Yoruba subgroups) strongly reinforced ideological and party-political differences (Sklar 1963, pp. 67 and 102; Aronson 1970, pp. 216ff.).

In terms of expansion of the ethnic context, language is a key element in determining the boundaries of cultural affinity.[20] A common language or related languages foster the recognition of shared identity in ethnically heterogeneous situations and facilitate communication. Whether Ibo, Ibibio, or Yoruba, the new broader ethnic entity is circumscribed in terms of language in every case.

A common language or related languages unite the members of traditionally distinct polities, cementing the "supertribe." Thus, they are defined in opposition to speakers of another language or language group. Language has accordingly come to be seen as a major issue in the building of the new nations. In no West African state does the majority of the population share one mother tongue. Everywhere, a European language has been adopted as national language. However, English, French, and Portuguese have invariably remained foreign to the masses.

The various dialects of the Ibo were clearly different from the languages of their neighbors. Yet, there was such variation within Ibo that some dialects were barely mutually intelligible. Significantly, then, major efforts were made to evolve one standard Ibo speech and script. In addition, certain elements of traditional culture, such as music and dance, were reaffirmed, and a new pride in Ibo identity was fostered.[21] Thus, new structural alignments, in turn, suscitate new cultural contents.

Religion provides a common cultural denominator for northern Ghanaians living in the cities of southern Ghana. The immigrant comes to perceive himself as a Northerner as he encounters the ethnic prejudice of Southerners and gains awareness of the relative affluence of the South. Adopting Islam, he underscores his enlarged ethnic identity, at the same time improving his status by moving from a "backward" traditional religion to a world religion (Grindal 1973).

Thus, a common cultural superstructure emerges for an group. It relates more or less tenuously to the cultural heritage constituent parts of that group. An ethnic renaissance, a selecti and popular reassertion of tradition and expansion of the boundai belonging, creates a new cultural collectivity. Underlying it are ꓳal changes establishing new ethnic identities.

Even where the boundaries of the ethnic entity have not changed, the perceived coincidence of ethnic difference and economic opposition may lead to a reaffirmation of cultural distinctiveness and culminate in an ethnic renaissance. Abner Cohen describes this process among the Hausa in Ibadan.[22]

Political ethnicity in contemporary African towns*

Sabo developed in conjunction with the growth and organization of Hausa monopoly in long-distance trade in kola and cattle between northern and southern Nigeria.** The Hausa have been able to overcome the technical problems which are involved in this trade by the development of an ethnic monopoly over the major stages of the trade. This has involved the development of a network of Hausa migrant communities in the Western Region of Nigeria. Sabo thus came into being as a base for control over parts of the southern end of the chain of the trade.

But in the process of achieving such control, the Hausa have come face to face with increasing rivalry, competition, and opposition from various Yoruba individuals and groups. From the very beginning, economic competition led to political encounters with members of the host society. The Hausa, confronting mounting pressure from the Yoruba majority, were forced to organize themselves for political action. With the growth of the trade, the increase in the number of settlers in the Quarter, and the expansion of the host city, Hausa political organization became more complex and more elaborate, in two different, but closely related, spheres. First, the Hausa developed and maintained their tribal exclusiveness. Second, they built an internal organization of political functions: communication, decision-making, authority, administration, and sanctions, and also political myths, symbols, slogans, and ideology. The principal aims of the whole system are (a) to prevent the encroachment of men from other ethnic groups into the trade, (b) to co-ordinate the activities of the members of the community in maintaining and developing their economico-political organization, and (c) to maintain mechanisms for co-operation with other Hausa communities in both the South and the North, for the common cause.

During the period of Indirect Rule by the British many of these functions were officially recognized and constituted part of the formal organization of power which had been set up by colonial rule. The Hausa were recognized

* Excerpts from the concluding chapter of Abner Cohen, *Custom and politics in urban Africa: A study of Hausa migrants in Yoruba towns,* 1969, pp. 183–7, 190, and 193–4, by permission of the author, Routledge & Kegan Paul, and the University of California Press. Based on research in 1962–3.

** Sabo, an abbreviation of *sabon gari,* means "new town" in Hausa. In Ibadan, it was established as a special quarter for the Hausa in 1916. At the time of the study, it was nearly exclusively inhabited by Hausa, constituting the bulk of Ibadan's Hausa population.

as a distinct 'tribal' group and were given a well-defined residential base and a recognized 'tribal' chief. The authority of the chief was ultimately supported by the power of the Administration.

This formal recognition of Hausa political organization enabled the people of Sabo, not only to consolidate their gains in the control of trade, but also to capture more economic fields, and the actual Quarter itself, with its buildings, sites and strategic position within the city, became a vast vested interest for the community.

With the coming of party politics in the 1950's, as the Nigerian nationalist movement arose and later with independence, the whole formal basis of Hausa distinctiveness was undermined. Sabo was no longer officially recognized as an exclusive 'tribal' grouping and the support which had been given by the power of the government to the authority of its Chief was withdrawn. The weakening position of the Chief affected not only the organization of the functions of communication, decision making and co-ordination of action, but also the very distinctiveness of the Quarter because it was no longer possible for the Chief to force individuals to act in conformity with the corporate interests of the community.

In the meantime, the ethnic exclusiveness of Sabo was being threatened by increasing social interaction between Hausa and Yoruba in two major social fields: in party political activities and in joint Islamic ritual and ceremonial. Interaction of this kind was likely to result in the creation of primary, moral relations between Hausa and Yoruba, under new values, norms, and symbols.

The adoption of the Tijaniyya by the Quarter brought about processes which halted the disintegration of the bases of the exclusiveness and identity of Sabo.† The reorganization of the Quarter's religion was at the same time a reorganization of the Quarter's political organization. A new myth of distinctiveness for the Quarter was found. The Quarter was now a superior, puritanical, ritual community, a religious brotherhood, distinct from the masses of Yoruba Moslems in the city, complete with its separate Friday Mosque, Friday congregation, and with a separate cemetery.

The localization of ritual in the Quarter inhibited the development of much social interaction with the Yoruba.[1] On the other hand, the intensification and collectivisation of ritual increased the informal social interaction within the Quarter, under Hausa traditional values, norms, and customs.

The principle of intercession which the Tijaniyya introduced, and the concentration of all the mystical forces of the universe in Allah, vested a great deal of ritual power in the malams. The malams became the sole mediators between laymen and the supernatural powers of Allah. Through their services as teachers, interpreters of the dogma, ritual masters, diviners, magicians, spiritual healers, and officiants in rites of passage, the malams developed multiple relations of power over laymen and, through the hierarchy of ritual authority instituted by the Tijaniyya, this power is finally concentrated in the hands of the Big Malams.

Through their manifold relationships with the business landlords and the Chief, the Big Malams have become part of the 'Establishment'. They act as

---

† The Tijaniyya order is an Islamic sect that was joined by the overwhelming part of the Hausa of Sabo in 1951–2.

1 Some Yoruba became Tijanis, but because of the localization of ritual under local Mukaddams no interaction with Tijani Hausa could take place.

advisors to the landlords and to the Chief and they formally participate in the formulation of problems, in deliberation, and decision-making, and in the co-ordination of action in matters of general policy. They also play significant roles in the processes of communication and co-ordination in the course of the routine administration of the Quarter.

The Hausa of Sabo are today more socially exclusive, or less assimilated into the host society, than at any other time in the past. They thus seem to have completed a full cycle of 'retribalization'. They speak their own language even in their dealings with the Yoruba, and they dress differently and eat differently from their hosts. Hausa customs, norms, values, and beliefs are upheld by a web of multiplex social relationships resulting from the increasingly intense interaction within the Quarter. On the other hand, the absence of inter-marriage with the Yoruba, and the ritual exclusiveness brought about by the Tijaniyya, have insulated the Hausa from much social interaction with the Yoruba and thus inhibited the development of moral ties and loyalties across the lines of tribal separateness. Finally, with the withdrawal of the British from Nigeria, the two ethnic groupings came into a sharp confrontation and the cleavage between them became deeper and more bitter.

Sabo has acquired more social and cultural distinctiveness as a result of marked social and cultural changes among the Yoruba in Ibadan. During the past few decades the Yoruba have developed cash crops, trade in European goods, and some light industry. They have adopted a relatively great measure of Western education and developed a fair degree of occupational differentiation and specialization in their society. The adoption of the city as capital of the Western Region, and its development as an administrative centre, together with the building of a large university[2] and a university hospital in it,[3] have brought further differentiation within its population. The formation of different kinds of voluntary associations,[4] the intensified activities of political parties, the emergence of a Western oriented elite[5] and of a new economically privileged class in it, have created a web of links and cleavages crosscutting one another, and have thus changed the structure of Yoruba society.

In sharp contrast with all this change among the Yoruba of Ibadan, Sabo society and culture remain basically unaffected, like an island of continuity in a sea of change. Its economy remains stable and is today not much more sophisticated in its organization than it was twenty years ago. Its education remains purely 'Arabic' almost untouched by Western education.[6] The ambition of a Sabo man is success in trade, higher Islamic learning, and, as the crowning of success in both endeavours, pilgrimage to Mecca. While many of the Yoruba are culturally oriented towards European or American civilization, the Hausa of Sabo remain oriented towards the North and the North East, towards the interior of Africa and the civilization of Islam . . .

The Hausa in Ibadan are more 'retribalized' than the 'Western Ibos', not

2 It was initially established as University College associated with the University of London, and was meant to cater for the whole of British West Africa. It was converted into an independent university in 1963.
3 Nearly half of the doctors of Nigeria were concentrated in Ibadan.
4 Ibadan has been prolific in the formation of numerous types of voluntary associations, particularly since the Second World War.
5 See Barbara B. Lloyd (1966) and Peter C. Lloyd (1966a).
6 Except for the small group of men who learnt English privately.

because of their conservatism, as LeVine suggests, and not because of special elements in their traditional culture, as Rouch and others contend, but because their ethnicity articulates a Hausa political organization which is used as a weapon in the struggle to keep the Hausa in control of the trade. Ethnicity is thus basically a political and not a cultural phenomenon, and it operates within contemporary political contexts and is not an archaic survival arrangement carried over into the present by conservative people . . .

If status cleavages will cut across ethnic divisions, then the manifestations of ethnic identity and exclusiveness will tend to be inhibited by the emerging countervailing alignments of power. The less privileged from one ethnic group will co-operate with the less privileged from other ethnic groups against the privileged from the same ethnic groups. The privileged groups will, for their part, also close their ranks to protect their interests. If the situation continues to develop in this way, tribal differences will be weakened and will eventually disappear and the people will become politically detribalized. In time, class division will be so deep that a new sub-culture, with different styles of life, different norms, values and ideologies, will emerge and a situation may develop which is similar to that of 'the two nations' of Victorian Britain.

However, the situation will be entirely different if the new class cleavages will overlap with tribal groupings, so that within the new system the privileged will tend to be identified with one ethnic group and the under-privileged with another ethnic group. In this situation cultural differences between the two groups will become entrenched, consolidated, and strengthened in order to express the struggle between the two interest groups across the new class lines. Old customs will tend to persist, but within the newly emerging social system they will assume new values and new social significance. A great deal of social change will take place, but it will tend to be effected through the rearrangement of traditional cultural items, rather than through the development of new cultural items, or, more significantly, rather than the borrowing of cultural items from the other tribal groups. Thus to the casual observer it will look as if there is here stagnation, conservatism, or a return to the past, when in fact we are confronted with a new social system in which men articulate their *new roles* in terms of traditional ethnic idioms.

In parts of West Africa, organizational structures on ethnic lines were sufficiently effective in controlling most urban immigrants to have functions of public administration delegated to them by colonial authorities. In a number of countries, they were entrusted with the collection of personal taxes. Official devolution of administrative and judicial powers to the leaders of immigrant groups went particularly far in Freetown (Banton 1957, pp. 11f., 25ff., and 142ff.; Kilson 1966, pp. 259ff.).[23]

When party politics started, ethnic organizational structures became obvious channels of communication to urban voters and, through them, to the rural masses.[24] Recruitment of members for the parties frequently followed these same lines. In fact, when the National Council of Nigeria and the Cameroons (NCNC) was founded in 1944, membership was organizational, and the overwhelming majority of the organizations was made up of ethnic associations

(Coleman 1958, pp. 264f.). K. W. J. Post (1963, p. 382) notes how the *West African Pilot,* the organ of the NCNC, continually published affirmations of loyalty by Ibo clan, town, and village unions for several months preceding the federal election of 1959. The Ibo State Union also backed the NCNC, as it had done since its founding in 1948.

The initial ties of the Sierra Leone People's Party (SLPP) were also with voluntary associations such as the Mende Tribal Committee and the Temne Tribal Union in Freetown. However, the ties were not based on organizational membership, rather, they were provided by interlocking leaderships. These links were more important than the party branches in communicating the party's aims and policies to the urban population. Conversely, the association gave the articulate supporters of the SLPP much more opportunity to initiate lines of action and policy for the party than the party branches did. At election time and on other occasions, the ties between the SLPP and voluntary associations were a crucial factor in the popular backing the party received (Kilson 1966, pp. 241f. and 259).

We have already noted how in the smaller towns of the Ivory Coast ward committees of the PDCI were in effect ethnic communities. In Abidjan, where neighborhoods were heterogeneous, the two major party branches were organized on the basis of ethnic subcommittees. Party leaders expressed concern about this state of affairs, but proposals to alter it were not implemented for over a decade [Aristide R. Zolberg (1964) 1969, pp. 116 and 319f.]. Only after the political crisis of 1969 and the appearance and recognition of cross-ethnic interest groups in Abidjan was the establishment of PDCI subcommittees based on neighborhood wards initiated (Michael A. Cohen, 1974b).

Ethnic organizations provided a training ground for leadership. The experience of running an organization and negotiating with other parties, the ready clientele of rank and file, and the connections established with other leaders furnished the basis for the career of many a politician. All the thirty councillors in Aba and all the regional and national politicians who returned to the city after the January 1966 coup held responsible positions in ethnic organizations (Callaway 1970, p. 139).[25]

The quest for Independence united Africans in each country against the ruling power. With Independence and little progress toward Pan-African unity, internal divisions became more important. The fact that popular support for the nationalist movement had been organized on ethnic lines now thwarted efforts at nation building. Nearly everywhere in West Africa, ethnicity came to constitute a dominant theme in politics.[26] Appeals were made to ethnic identities; interaction among the rank and file of political groupings followed ethnic lines; the leadership found itself dependent on ethnically circumscribed support. That handful of leaders who in the early days of the nationalist movement had worked on the territorial level, or even created interterritorial alliances, had to fall back on their areas of origin in order to be recognized as sons of the soil and get elected. In such a climate, factions that developed over the allocation of the extremely scarce resources were all too readily perceived to coincide with ethnic cleavages.

Ethnic categories monopolizing specific economic opportunities are a recurrent reality in West Africa. Two processes are responsible. First, during colonial rule, some ethnic groups built up a considerable lead because of better access to education, because they were recruited into certain occupations (most importantly the army), because their land offered exceptional opportunities (e.g., the growing of cocoa), or because they dominated the distribution of important commodities (e.g., Hausa control of the long-distance trade in cattle). Second, once an ethnic group was established in a privileged position, it wielded considerable influence over the opportunities open to others; patronage tended to go to kinsmen, covillagers, or any "brother."

In West Africa, ethnic groups that occupy privileged positions do not constitute social classes. For one thing, ethnic groups rarely have exclusive control over political power and never monopolize upper-class positions of wealth, income, and status. Furthermore, a wide range of differentiation in power, income and wealth, and status is found within the ethnic group.[27] It is more accurately thought of as a vertical than as a horizontal cross section of society. Each ethnic group occupies many tiers in the stratification system, but with disproportionate representation at some levels. This has not resulted in the development of social classes. In fact, as we will see in Chapter 9, identification, association, and organization along ethnic lines impede the recognition of shared political, economic, and social positions across ethnic lines that would signal the emergence of class consciousness among the masses.

As we have seen in the case of the Ibadan Hausa, the position of such privileged groups became vulnerable once the protective umbrella of colonial rule was removed. When Independence approached and universal suffrage was introduced, they risked being outvoted because they constituted numerical minorities. At present, voters in most countries are no longer in a position to effect political change. However, those in power. whether they carry the card of the one party or wear an army uniform, face the constant threat that some underprivileged groups will close ranks and effect a coup to redress the balance.

Tens of thousands of Ibo were killed in the 1966 pogroms in Northern Nigeria once their leadership lost the major share they had held in political power at the federal level.[28] The officers had taken over from the politicians, but ethnic divisions were more exacerbated than ever. The army men were unable to effect a political solution and resorted to what they had been trained to do. Ethnic conflict was driven to its devastating conclusion in a civil war that lasted two and a half years, destroyed major economic assets, and took untold lives of combatants and civilians.

6 Three types of change

Cultural learning . . . is a function of opportunity, not generations.
                                    Melville J. Herskovits (1954, p. 63)

A separate chapter on change does not suggest that the remainder of this study of West Africa adopts a static perspective, as the reader is well aware by now. We have presented historical stages of urbanization in West Africa. We have discussed the relationship of urbanization to economic development. We have observed the sequence of forced labor, migrant labor, and permanent labor. We have asked what the future of urban–rural ties will be. In Chapters 7 and 8, we focus on changes in the family and in the position of women; and in Chapter 9, we analyze the emerging class structure.

The rationale for a separate chapter on change, then, is not that we fail to deal with it elsewhere, but that the study and interpretation of change itself has been a central concern of urban research in Subsaharan Africa. In this debate, the conceptualization of the changes occurring in the cities of Africa has shifted several times. We propose to examine this intellectual development and to offer an interpretation of change, by identifying three analytically distinct realms of change: historical, situational, and biographic.

Historical change

Change is most commonly discussed at the cultural and social-structural level – that is, in terms of a given society changing over time. It is the model implicit in much of the discussion of change elsewhere in this study. Following Mitchell's (1962, p. 128) terminology, we will refer to such overall changes in a societal system as "historical change." It is important to recognize that historical change does not occur simultaneously in different parts of a given society. In West Africa, it has most commonly flowed from the cities to the rural areas that have lagged behind. This was the case not only when historical change was introduced from the outside but also where it evolved endogenously.

We have already glimpsed the trans-Saharan trade that flourished over many centuries and heard echos of the rise and fall of great empires. We can conjure up images of the wealth accumulating in the cities, as merchants and rulers developed their trade, of artisans producing for these cities and for faraway trading partners, of the learned men interpreting the scriptures and dispensing justice. We imagine the rural masses drawn into these exchanges, made to pay tribute to distant rulers, or enslaved to till the land for the urban powerful, to work for them in the cities, or to be sold to distant lands.

The establishment of trading relationships and the expansion of Islam appear to have gone hand in hand. The soldiers and teachers of the Prophet conquered the Sahara as early as the ninth century. Islam was implanted in Timbuktu from the time the city was established early in the twelfth century. The new faith gradually and with some use of force spread across vast lands and to diverse peoples as the now Islamized cities relayed it to their own hinterlands and beyond. When the borders of Bornu expanded in the late sixteenth century, Koranic law was extended over all parts of the empire, and brick mosques appeared in a number of places (Mabogunje 1968, p. 50). Most existing indigenous African cultures gave way to the world religion. We are fortunate to have testimony of the world view of one people, the Dogon, who sought refuge in the cliffs and saved their cultural heritage (Griaule 1948; Griaule and Dieterlen 1965).

European ships integrated the West African coast into new trade routes across the Atlantic. For several centuries, the most important element in this trade was the commerce in humans. Again, knots of urbanization emerged to administer the trade. Also, indigenous tendencies for urban living were reinforced as people were driven to live within the walls that protected them from raids and sheltered them somewhat from the wars that provided another source of slaves.

After the abolition of that inhuman enterprise, European commercial involvement in West Africa expanded rather than diminished. Industrial growth in Europe created rising demand for oils and fats; palm oil and later palm kernels and groundnuts became the staple exports of West Africa. Palm products and groundnuts could be produced efficiently and on a small scale by households possessing little capital, employing family labor, and using traditional tools (Anthony G. Hopkins 1973, pp. 125ff.). An economic transformation in major parts of the coastal hinterland set in that took them from subsistence to cash crop production by independent agriculturists.[1]

The growing demand of overseas markets fostered the building of railways and the development of road transport that would make it possible to tap more distant hinterlands. The Senegal railway was begun in 1881, and Dakar was finally joined to Bamako, 720 miles away, in 1923. In Nigeria, the principal line was begun at Lagos in 1896 and reached Kano, a distance of 711 miles, in 1911 (Anthony G. Hopkins 1973, pp. 194ff.). The expansion of commerce led to the growth in number and size of towns at key railway and road points. They reached ever deeper into formerly isolated areas of West Africa. In addition to the demand of foreign markets, the food requirements of the growing urban populations became increasingly important in the twentieth century.

The missionaries followed the merchants. The protagonists of the new religion offered "civilized" status and training in the emerging lingua franca and its script. Being able to speak, read, and write a European language became the key to success both in commerce and in the gradually established and expanding colonial administrations.[2] Obtaining an education, therefore, was highly instrumental, but mission school and mission church combined to destroy much of the cultural heritage, sometimes enlisting the assistance of the colonial authorities. Europe thus managed to establish control over many aspects of indigenous culture. The major area of resistance to European belief and custom is circumscribed by the penetration of Islam, another world religion backed up by a written code.

The loss of much of the indigenous cultural heritage of West Africa stands in striking contrast with the situation in Asia. We have testimony of traditional excellence in the fine arts. African sculpture, "discovered" by avant-garde artists at the beginning of this century, now has gained world renown. But most of the artifacts produced in West Africa were short-lived because of the materials used and, especially in the forest zone, the climatic conditions. We are fortunate to know the sixteenth-century bronzes of Ife and Benin (the present-day Benin City, not the People's Republic of Benin). The presumably much more widespread wood carving of those days has disappeared long since. Unfortunately, our ignorance about the nonmaterial aspects of these cultures is even more profound. Their beliefs were not enshrined in scriptures, and we have to rely on what oral tradition will communicate.

Whereas most Asian societies developed durable institutions and social structures that withstood the onslaught of alien technology, culture, and way of life, the societies of Subsaharan Africa were fragile, often collapsing from the shock waves of Western conquest. Whenever indigenous institutions and structures were replaced by modern ones, the modern institutions tended, in Africa much more than in Asia, to resemble Western models (Ghai 1972, p. 258). Five differences between the two settings suggest elements of an explanation. Culture areas in Subsaharan Africa were more limited in space and population. They lacked the support of a technology of writing, the most effective way of communicating over space and time. Severe debilitation resulted from the slave trade and the devastating raids and warfare that accompanied it. Then, there is the time factor. The relatively short duration of colonialism meant that changes were telescoped for most of Africa into a span of fifty to eighty years; whereas the impact of the West upon Asian societies took place over a period of two to three centuries. Finally, colonial administrations were more supportive of cultural penetration in the "Dark Continent" than they were in areas where a world religion was firmly established, whether it be in Asia or in the Muslim belt in West Africa.

The European powers delineated spheres of interest in Africa at the 1884–5 Berlin Conference and proceeded to establish political and economic control throughout the continent. Effective opposition was sporadic because African societies could not match the economic and technological resources of the imperialist forces. Liberia, the apparent exception, was established as an independent state in 1847. But Liberia's dependency was such that when confronted with the Back to Africa movement in the United States, the official choice was to join the governments of Britain, France, and the United States in opposing Garvey's plans. A diplomatic note sent to the United States government declared that the Negro republic was "irrevocably opposed in principle and fact to the incendiary policy of the Universal Negro Improvement Association, led by Marcus Garvey" (Cronon 1955, p. 129). By the latter part of the nineteenth century, Liberians had lost control of the republic's trade to German and British firms, and American rubber interests came to play a dominant role in the economy after 1926 (Fraenkel 1964, pp. 16ff.). Following World War II, Liberia attracted foreign investment from diversified sources, and iron ore came to take the place of rubber as the most important export commodity. But the development of rubber plantations and iron mining proceeded within enclave situations; even today there is little interdependence between the foreign concessions and o.her sectors of the economy. The Northwestern University economic survey team that worked there from 1961 to 1962 characterized Liberia as a case of growth without development. That is, enormous growth in primary commodities produced by foreign concessions for export was not accompanied either by structural changes to induce complementary economic growth or by institutional changes to diffuse gains in real income among all sectors of the population (Clower et al. 1966, pp. vi and 23ff.).

Liberians did continue to hold the political positions and to staff the government administration. Elsewhere, Africans lost positions both in commerce and in government. European merchant houses moved in and displaced the more prominent African middlemen, and colonial administrations recruited greater numbers of Europeans once the causes of malaria were understood and the death rate among Europeans dropped drastically. In 1850, when what was then the Gold Coast was granted its own government, independent of Sierra Leone, it was not regarded as anything out of the ordinary that a number of Africans should be appointed to key official posts. Of 43 higher posts, nine were filled by Africans as late as 1883, including 7 District Commissioners. However, by the turn of the century, opportunity for Africans in senior government service had all but vanished. The handful of Africans who were already in senior posts gradually dropped out, and no effort was made to find others to replace them. By 1908, only 5 out of 274 officers listed in the senior civil service were Africans. In 1948, just nine years before Independence, Africans held only 98 of a total of over 1,300 senior appointments (Kimble 1963, pp. 65, 94, 98ff., and 123). The African District Commissioner had been gone from the scene for close to two generations.

There was thus a gross structural contradiction. As the numbers of educated

Africans increased, occupational opportunities that had been open to their fathers and grandfathers were shut off. From the frustrations of this tiny elite arose the nationalist movement that was to provide the impetus for the most dramatic change to occur in West Africa in this century: the advent of Independence. In the context of a changed international constellation after World War II, twelve West African countries joined Liberia in Independence between 1957 and 1961. The Gambia followed in 1965. In the only remaining colony, Guinea-Bissau, an armed struggle was launched in 1963 that brought Liberation finally in 1974. Here is how Coleman, in his classic study of nationalism in Nigeria, summarizes the forces underlying this historic movement:

Nationalism in Nigeria*
Nationalism was the end product of three major developments or conditions. The first was the "social mobilization," to use Karl Deutsch's phrase, of substantial numbers of Nigerians as a result of a policy of determined Europeanization by Christian missionaries, a literary educational curriculum, and the growth of an urbanized wage-labor force whose members were haunted by a sense of economic and psychological insecurity. The second was the accumulation of conscious economic grievances among the mobilized groups, derived from the presence and the practices of large-scale European enterprise and what was believed to be government indifference regarding economic development. The third, and decisive, development was the emergence of a Western-educated minority whose members were employed as clerks, artisans, and subalterns in the government and in the firms, and who suffered most acutely from the inequalities and the frustrations of colonial rule. At the top of the new social structure was an exceedingly small group of European- or American-educated professional men (lawyers, doctors, journalists, teachers) who had become saturated with Western ideas, particularly the ideas of democracy, large-scale political organization, national self-determination, and rapid economic development. Under the system of indirect rule these Western-educated elements were largely excluded from any meaningful role in the government of the country. As a consequence many were attracted to nationalism in a mood having certain striking characteristics: a profound distrust and suspicion of the European; a deep bitterness regarding racial discrimination; a passionate belief in the idea of progress and the power of technology which convinced them that they, the enlightened few, were not only destined by right to rule, but also that by an act of will they could create an independent Nigerian nation which would allow them, in the words of their prophet Nnamdi Azikiwe, to walk "majestically with the other races of mankind."

The external influences that helped to shape the ideas and awaken the aspirations of what was at first a very small claimant minority came from India, the United Kingdom, America, and Soviet Russia. Nigerian students in America were compelled to partake of the color consciousness, as well as the hopeful expectancy, of the American Negro. Soviet Russia offered an example of the capacity of man to transform his environment and liquidate the stigma of backwardness within a single generation. Most of the nation-

* Excerpt from James S. Coleman, *Nigeria: Background to Nationalism*, 1958, p. 410–12, by permission of the author and the University of California Press.

alist leaders came from the small group of Nigerians who had studied in American and British universities. While abroad their sense of distinctness was sharpened by the cruder forms of color discrimination they were compelled to suffer. Their detachment from their traditional culture, their bitterness over their exclusion from white culture, their resentment of the inferiority implications in the European allegation that they had no history and no culture, and their critical observation of the shortcomings of Western culture, all combined to stimulate among these students a deeper appreciation of their own culture and history, or a determination to create a neo-African culture.

Most Nigerian nationalists are not cultural nativists; they are eclectics, desiring to keep what is useful and attractive in the old and fuse it with the new. From the West they have absorbed the scientific attitude and the idea of progress. These distinctly exotic notions have inspired their conviction that man can manipulate nature and creatively shape his own destiny. A factor of even greater importance has been the nationalists' desire to liquidate the stigma of inferiority and backwardness; and they are convinced that the only way to accomplish this is to utilize modern forms and techniques. However, it is their belief that modernity and progress are the standards by which they have been judged and will continue to be judged. Indeed, they are the standards by which they tend to judge themselves. Nigeria has not had a Gandhi.

Most nationalist leaders, as well as their active supporters, are members of the second or third generation since culture contact. This is borne out by the initiative taken by educated "native foreigners" in early nationalist activity. The changing perspectives of each succeeding generation have been succinctly described by Premier Awolowo: "Our grandfathers, with unbounded gratitude adored the British. . . . Our immediate fathers simply toed the line. We of to-day are critical, unappreciative, and do not feel that we owe any debt of gratitude to the British. The younger elements in our group are extremely cynical, and cannot understand why Britain is in Nigeria."

The cultural impact of Europe appears to have been similar in British and French colonies. There has been a tendency to characterize French educational policy in Africa as assimilationist and to contrast it with a British practice that emphasized the notion of cultural adaptation. The French were said to aim at the creation of "black Frenchmen"; the British, to educate Africans who would remain rooted in their own culture. In practice, however, both colonial powers wavered between assimilationist and adjustive educational policies. Therefore, the educational consequences of British and French policy were often quite the same in spite of any disparities in official ideology. Nonetheless, two differences between British and French colonies are significant: First, the provision of educational opportunities started much earlier in British than in French territories, and their scope was much greater. This was the case at all levels. The very first lycée was not established in French West Africa until 1928, yet by that time, the British areas had developed a small but well-established secondary sector. Furthermore, the early access of West Africans to British universities and to Fourah Bay College had long preceded French adoption of such a policy. Second, the French language was always taught from the earliest years of schooling; whereas the British used local languages in the first years of primary school (Clignet and Foster 1964a).[3]

Throughout West Africa, Europe superimposed a new great tradition, as did Islam (although to a lesser extent). Its impact on the population at large varied considerably, and among the most educated there were early attempts to preserve the African heritage. In what was then the Gold Coast, the first African historian was the Reverend Reindorf, who in 1889 made an attempt to report oral tradition in his *History of the Gold Coast and Asante*. In the same year, the *Mfantsi Amanbuhu Fékuw* (Fanti National Political Society) was formed in Cape Coast for the purpose of reviving African culture. As a practical step, the founders planned to collect, discuss, and compile a record of Fanti sayings, customs, laws, and institutions. The Western suit, rather uncomfortable in the tropics anyhow, was rejected in favor of African dress. Intellectuals discarded their European names in favor of African ones and took an active interest in their mother tongue, a cause advocated, paradoxically, in the English-language journals they edited (Kimble 1963, pp. 150 and 518ff.).

With the call for political independence came renewed attempts to establish a distinct cultural identity. African personality, negritude, became a leitmotiv. The change in elite aspirations found its conspicuous expression in dress. During the colonial era, numerous observers had commented on the considerable spending on Western-type clothing; the African with a degree of formal education had thus underlined his claim to equal standing with Europeans. African dress has since become fashionable throughout West Africa, and West African styles have spread elsewhere in the world. In other spheres as well, traditional behavior was resuscitated, but with new meanings. Where such behavior is purely symbolic, the meaning is precisely the quest for a separate identity for Africa. When Kwame Nkrumah poured libation to the gods at the Independence celebrations of Ghana, he did not reaffirm religious beliefs in the ancestors but encouraged his people to take pride in their past.

Living in times of change

Achebe, in his first novel, *Things Fall Apart,* has set a monument to the victims of rapid change. For his hero, Okonkwo, the impact of change is overwhelming when he returns to his home village from exile. As one of the leading men in the village, he is unable to reconcile himself to the fact that the young follow the white man's god. He cannot endure the abuses of the foreign government that have been imposed on his people. Okonkwo comes to a tragic end.

Historical change has forced people reared in one tradition to adopt new behavior, to accept foreign beliefs, to embrace different norms, and ultimately, to change their values. But the changes West Africa has experienced have not simultaneously affected all the different subsystems of its societies to the same extent. Insofar as society itself constitutes a system, there is a degree of interdependence among its subsystems. Thus, the introduction of wage employment not only brings economic changes but also affects the relationship between old and young. However, a change in one subsystem usually does not affect all other subsystems; although all parts of a society are interrelated, there is a certain looseness in the whole structure.[4]

From a survey of adult-class students in Ghana during the middle fifties, Gustav Jahoda (1961, p. 53) concluded that Western values were preeminent in some subsystems, traditional ones in others. He emphasized the stresses inherent in this situation. First of all, although many spheres were dominated by either Western or traditional values, there was a wide and fluid no-man's-land in between where uncertainty reigned. Such indeterminateness creates a source of insecurity for the individual.

A second source of stress lies in the interdependence of the various subsystems. The polarity between Western and traditional values can lead to interpersonal and intrapersonal conflict. Workers may continue to feel that a younger man should show respect and deference to an older man, thus carrying a traditional expectation over into a formal organization that does not share it (Kapferer 1969, p. 238). If a man adopts social and economic advancement as his goal, that, in the new economic context, will have repercussions in several other spheres, such as his relationship with and attitudes toward his extended family and the demands it makes on him, the kind of woman he will consider for his wife, or the way he proposes to train his children (Jahoda 1961, p. 54).

A different kind of norm conflict is typically urban in that it derives from the heterogeneity of the urban populace. Given the recent arrival of most urban dwellers in West Africa, an enduring source of such conflict lies in the diversity of their traditional backgrounds. Balandier (1955, p. 261) proposed the notion of a jural void to characterize the clash of different traditional legal norms. With interethnic marriages, problems arise over the rights to children when parents separate and over inheritance.

City life is frequently assumed to be stressful. Migrants from rural areas are believed to find personal adjustment particularly difficult. However, there is little evidence to support such propositions.[5] The Harvard Project on the Social and Cultural Aspects of Development produced relevant data from six different countries (Inkeles and Smith 1970). It demonstrated that exposure to the reputed impersonality of urban life, to its plethora of stimuli, to its frenzied pace, and to its crowded conditions does not unmistakably induce psychosomatic symptoms. Nor was there evidence that migration itself brings about psychic distress.

One of the studies was carried out among Yoruba in Western Nigeria and

Lagos. It was limited to men aged eighteen to thirty-two who were asked about psychosomatic symptoms: difficulty in sleeping, trembling limbs, nervousness, a hard beating of the heart, shortness of breath, sweating palms, headaches, frightening dreams, being affected by witchcraft. Fewer such symptoms were reported by those who, in response to other questions, indicated job satisfaction and the desire to continue in their present employment, who reported that their parents and teachers were trustworthy and treated them decently, and who evaluated their treatment and the quality of their experience at work positively.

Farmers, whether compared with new factory workers or with longtime urban workers, were not significantly less prone to psychosomatic symptoms. Nor were there significant differences between workers born and raised in the countryside and their fellow workers who were born in town and came to the factory without intervening migration.[6] However, when cultivators were compared with a sample of urban nonindustrial workers that included craftsmen and artisans, workers in small retail shops, and domestic servants, the urban group showed a significantly higher incidence of psychosomatic symptoms. Similarly, those factory workers reporting lower earnings and possessing fewer consumer goods were significantly more prone to manifest psychic stress.

Arnold L. Epstein (1958, pp. 232ff.) has underscored the element of choice that the relative autonomy of subsystems offers the individual actor who is seen involved in "situational selection." A trade-union leader is concerned with the relations of white employer and black employees, but he can "seal off" his domestic sphere from the changes brought by urban living and Western culture. He can marry a woman from his home area, and in his family, he can continue to observe traditional custom. However, Epstein emphasizes the limits to such situational selection. Although the subsystems are not synchronized, they are interdependent.

Such a feedback is illustrated in those cases in which a man rising to elite status finds that the wife he married when in a more humble position is unable to adapt to some of the social requirements of his new station in life. In Ouagadougou, some educated men, including several Catholics, decided that the need for a "modern" wife was sufficiently pressing to justify polygamy or concubinage (Skinner 1974, pp. 138f.).

From another perspective, the individual actor can be seen as confronted with the conflicting demands made on him or her through simultaneous participation in different groups. The trade-union leader is faced with the expectations of his followers, the black employees; those of his people, both in the town and in the home area; and those, different again, of his peers in the urban setting, the new elite. The neighborhood constitutes a significant fourth reference group. Neighborhood composition will determine what demands are made on the resident. The neighborhood appears as an independent variable insofar as the choice of residence is restricted (e.g., where housing is allocated by public authorities or employers or where there are severe housing shortages). Neighborhood pressures are felt in particular by children who have not yet ventured beyond its confines and by women tied to the home because of child rearing and household chores. Roger Sanjek's (1972, pp. 286ff.) analysis of interactions in Accra, based on the accounts given by forty individuals of their encounters over a four-day period, demonstrates the greater social range of men. Women had many more interactions in their home and considerably less in the homes of others, in the street, and at their workplace. The neighborhood is thus a primary arena of socialization for women and children. Women who have no role outside the neighborhood, such as employment or trading, will tend to find themselves in close-knit networks within it. For men, however, the urban environment offers the option of keeping their network loose-knit, thus limiting the intensity of cross-pressures.

Situational change

How do we interpret change at the level of the individual actor? This has been the central theoretical issue in the discussion of urbanization in Subsaharan Africa. The "detribalization" model (gradual unidirectional change away from traditional culture as the immigrant adjusted to city life) was soon abandoned. A generation ago, Max Gluckman led the attack: "In a sense every African is detribalized as soon as he leaves his tribal area, even though he continues to be acted on by tribal influences: he lives in different kinds of groupings, earns his livelihood in a different way, comes under different authorities" (1945, p. 12). Later, Gluckman put it provocatively and succinctly in a statement that became a classic: "An African townsman is a townsman, an African miner is a miner" (1960, p. 57). Such an "alternation model" of change (Mayer 1962, p. 579) is particularly pertinent where men continue to move between urban employment and agriculture in their home area.

Short-term migrants from northern Ghana to the cities in the South offer an example of alternation. Grindal (1973, pp. 336ff.) describes how some persons, when in Accra, consult Moslem medicine practitioners in times of personal crisis. Even those who do not regard themselves as Moslems often take advantage of the protective qualities afforded by Islamic herbal remedies and amulets. Upon returning to their home area, this affiliation is usually discarded in the light of the renewed protection of one's ancestral and spiritual shrines.

Mitchell (1962, p. 128) referred to such shifts in behavior following participation in different social systems as "situational change." He criticized the tendency to confuse it with historical change, a hazard implicit in the view that sees urban patterns as rural changes to come: "Customs and values in tribal areas are part of a particular social context and cannot be compared with their counterparts in urban areas where they fall into another context" (1966, p. 45).

In spite of this emphasis on the distinctive character of the urban system, social scientists working in Subsaharan Africa have for the most part ignored the major theoretical strand in urban sociology that goes back to the writings of Georg Simmel [(1903) 1950] and Max Weber [(1921) 1958] and that found its most eloquent expression in Wirth's classic "Urbanism as a Way of Life," a school of thought that attempts to draw sociological inferences from the demographic attributes of the city: the size, density, and heterogeneity of its population.

However, two contributions derived from the observation of urban patterns of interaction in Subsaharan Africa do fit into this tradition. Mitchell's (1966, pp. 52ff.) concept of categorical relationships refers to situations in which, by the nature of things, contacts are superficial and perfunctory (e.g., in crowds, in markets, on buses). In such situations, people are stereotyped in such terms as race, ethnic group, or social class, and behavior is organized accordingly.[7] Categorization is based on easily perceived attributes but is subject to error. This type of relationship is characteristic of mass or collective behavior, especially mass violence. Communal rioters require easily discernible characteristics to recognize their victims; in warfare, the easy and fast categorization of "we" and "they" was perfected with the introduction of the flag and the uniform.

Aidan W. Southall has been concerned to operationalize the distinctiveness of urban life. Nearly twenty years ago, he suggested that

in general, town life is characterized by role relationships that are more narrowly defined, more specific, more unequally distributed between persons, more extensively developed in latent role structure, more numerous as a whole in relation to persons who are themselves living at a high spatial density, and more fleeting in their duration over time. (1959, p. 29)

Southall (1973) has elaborated this approach since. He focuses on the number of role relationships activated by an aggregate of persons within a particular space. He proposes a continuum from rural to urban social structure based on an increase in the number of role relationships. He suggests that such an increase is accompanied by qualitative changes in the majority of role relationships toward narrowness, specificity, latency, short duration, and unequal distribution and by changes in the frequency of predominant content or type of role relationships away from kinship to economic and occupational, political, and recreational, leisure time, or voluntary role relations, with the greatest eventual increase in voluntary leisure role relationships.[8]

Contributions to a critique of the "Urbanism as a Way of Life" tradition were made in two specific contexts. Students of Yoruba urbanization such as Bascom (1963), Krapf-Askari (1969), and Peter C. Lloyd (1973) pointed to the lack of fit between their observations and Wirth's analysis (see Chapter 1). On the other hand, research concerning plantations in southwest Cameroun encountered features usually thought of as urban. Not only did the planta-

tion constitute a dense settlement of considerable numbers, but the labor force
was heterogeneous in terms of origin, if not occupation, and interaction was
characterized by secondary contacts. Edwin W. Ardener (1961) further
pointed out how many characteristics of the plantation population resembled
those of rapidly growing towns: high turnover by immigration and emigration,
special age structures and sex ratios resulting from the selectivity of this migration, a high proportion of persons in wage- or salary-earning employment.
Plantations in Cameroun thus exhibited many problems typically associated
with urbanization. Overcrowding was common, and marriage instability, tran-
sitory unions, and venereal disease affected not only the plantation population
but also the long-established peasantry in the area (Ardener, Ardener, and
Warmington 1960, pp. 97ff. and 299ff.).

Urban research in Subsaharan Africa has been even more oblivious to Central American studies that have defined the ideal type of the folk society, char-
acterizing, by implication, its supposed opposite, urban society.[9] The one
application in West Africa is Horace Miner's study of Timbuktu in 1940. He
describes a mixture of traditional folkways with secular and impersonal behavior among what was then a stable population of over 6,000 people.

City–folk in Timbuktu*

Our problem does not imply that if urban traits are present in Timbuctoo,
they will exist to the exclusion of the contrasting traits of sacred and personal behavior and social organization. Our knowledge of the American
metropolis tells us that many aspects of urban life do show these latter
traits. We ask, rather, can we characterize any aspects of the community
life by non-folk traits and, if so, what sort of relationships do they typify?

Cultures in Contact

Reviewing what we have seen of life in Timbuctoo, it is apparent that the
family and ethnic group constitute social spheres of great importance. Leaving aside for the moment those recent innovations traceable to French influence, a person's occupation, status, marriage arrangements, and supernatural beliefs are patterned by his family and ethnic origins. While the customs differ among the ethnic groups, the traditions of each are in large part
sacred to its members. The extended kinship pattern is important in determining the nature of relations with local co-ethnics. Birth and marriage ceremonies, religious and magical beliefs and practices, circumcision and age-
set rituals and duties, even occupations and especially crafts are traditionally defined for the various culture groups of the city and even for status
groups within these ethnic units. Relations with kin are preponderantly personal in character, as are those with co-ethnics, the only marked exception
being the frequently impersonal nature of economic relations.

In spite of the exceptions, the Songhoi, Arabs, and Bela, taken as separate groups and considered only with regard to their internal relationships,

* Excerpt from the concluding chapter of Horace Miner, *The Primitive City of
Timbuctoo,* first published 1953, pp. 290–301 in revised edition 1965, by permission of
the author and the American Philosophical Society. Based on research in 1940. Footnote renumbered.

are strikingly folk in character. They are, however, a city folk. Their lives are not limited to contacts with their own kind. Commerce, age-sets, worship, government and law, marriage, and amusement – all draw together in interaction the peoples of different cultural backgrounds. It is in this interaction between the different population elements that behavior is the most secular and impersonal and the society shows the greatest disorganization.

The Songhoi called themselves "townsmen" and dislike the greedy "outsiders" who live in Badyinde. The rough play of *alkura* and subsequent fights reflect interethnic hostility. The Alkhali Sidali and Bela battle out their antagonisms. The Arab and Songhoi marabouts degrade and discriminate against one another. The age-set system is weakened by the introduction of *koterey* for each of the different ethnic stocks.** The children of mixed cultural marriages are made to feel they are social misfits.

Commerce, of course, was the activity which drew the heterogeneous population of Timbuctoo together and functioned to maintain the community for centuries. In the market relations between the culturally diverse people, profit motives appear to be paramount. They are not mitigated by the cultural patterns of prerogatives and obligations which typify economic relations within a homogeneous culture. Cultural values as to what is fair, honest, or humane are effective within a folk culture because faith in these values is supported by strong sanctions and each individual can see for himself that conformity is to his advantage as well as that of the whole "we-group" with which he identifies. Between people of a folk culture, economic relations are but one aspect, even a minor one, of a totality of social relations of all sorts. But when the ethnocentric individual relates himself commercially to an unknown person of another culture, he feels little unity with the stranger and the primary sanctions which operate are the economic sanctions of the market; the only motives are those of profit. We have seen the similarity between such market relations and the ethnocentric behavior of nomadic, bush folk who feel free to cheat or pillage outsiders. In market relations between two people of different cultures, the economic relation is often the only kind of interaction. The specificity of their relationship is reflected in their impersonal behavior. The anonymity of the market relationship is also important. When the other person is not known personally and his customs are strange, not understood, or even repellent, it is not difficult to treat him impersonally – to wring all the profit possible from the situation.

The market is an aspect of division of labor which relates diverse people to one another. Structurally, the peoples of Timbuctoo and its hinterland are as necessary to one another as are the people of a small, homogeneous folk society. There is a need for the heterogeneous market community to find or develop values consistent with their broad interrelations. Community-wide government and law are such developments. It is noteworthy, however, that such new social structures arise with difficulty. Community government did not develop independently in Timbuctoo. It was imposed from without by the power of a homogeneous society. As soon as that power was removed, the local organization began to fall apart. Even the universally accepted system of Koranic law was not generally operative except under outside control. The community failed to defend itself against outside aggression, when it could have done so. Some attempt was made to

** *Koterey* is the Songhoi term for an age-set.

extend the *koterey* system to include non-Songhoi, but all of the Bela and most Arabs are still excluded.

Not only was there resistance to the development of a body of community-wide culture, but the distinct culture units show internal disorganization traceable to life in the city. The secular, impersonal attitude of the market invaded intra-ethnic and intrafamilial relationships as the interdependence of individuals within each ethnic group became less necessary, less obvious to its members. The folk culture was no longer a closed system. Essential, everyday functions continually took one out of one's own group. While the necessity for interrelations with one's own kind diminished, the possibility of escaping its sanctions increased. In Timbuctoo it was possible to abandon one's family and still marry and make a living.

The city provides a social milieu in which economic success may be achieved with less regard for activities which are not primarily economic in nature. In the folk community, because of the close-knit functional organization of its culture, religious and family behavior have definite economic implications. In fact, it is exceedingly difficult, if not impossible, to say what is economic behavior and what is familial. In Timbuctoo it is often easy to make such a distinction. A market economy requires specialized and individualized activity. In these activities the market rewards secular and impersonal behavior. This fact, plus the inherent conflict between different traits of cultures in contact, results in interrelations of a non-folk type. The obvious need for community-wide organization is smothered in the lack of mutual understanding bred of heterogeneity and the obvious rewards attainable by disregard for tradition. Traditional behavior is operative when it is conceived as the only legitimate method of achieving success. Changes in economic structure and weakened sanctions may make it apparent that the traditional ways of life are not so successful as other forms of behavior and that the traditional ways may be successfully questioned. Then secular behavior challenges the sacred traditions.

The Gradient in Urban Behavior

Throughout our study of this primitive city, when we have found urban traits exemplified in relationships between kinsmen, the same sort of behavior has been found between unrelated co-ethnics and in interethnic relations as well. But urban traits evident in interethnic relations do not seem to show the same prevalence in intra-ethnic contacts and, in turn, the extended family is least marked by them. Conversely, folk behavior appears to be most typical of family relationships, next most common in intra-ethnic behavior and least evident in interethnic relations. It is true that these statements are based upon the comparison of data which are not expressed in metric terms. Yet it has seemed possible to discover certain basic relationships by simply examining extreme contrasts, which we shall now consider.

Islamic dogma provides the focus of much of the traditional belief in terms of which all residents of the city can relate themselves to one another in an organized and personal manner. The whole religious dogma is not thus shared, but everyone is a Moslem. The importance of this identification to group life is to be seen in the refusal of the community to admit non-Moslems before the French conquest. The Koran, the marabouts, the mosques, the obligations of prayer, alms, *Ramadān*, and the Pilgrimage are symbols which are common knowledge. Koranic laws find universal acceptance and the role of the cadi as arbiter and judge is recognized by all. The basic contract of marriage and the laws of divorce and inheritance are thus universal to the community.

Public participation in the work of repairing the mosques is markedly folk in character. People of different ethnic groups work shoulder to shoulder. Even the rich, who escape the labor through money donations, participate in the activities as honored spectators. The raids by small boys on the market are a special and authorized sanction against merchants who may try to compete with the communal mosque work.

At other times, the functioning of the market and of general commerce demonstrates additional factors of city-wide organization. Currency units were standardized long before the arrival of the French. Legitimate methods of price determination, payment, measurement, and transfer of goods are known to all.

The *alkura* games and victory feast are another organizing factor in the city. It is true that interethnic hostilities find expression in the games, which become extremely impersonal and rough. However, the fact that teammates come from the same city quarter contributes to quarter solidarity. The victory feast is a warmer, more personal occasion, financially supported by all of the players and attended by all but the losers. Thus *alkura* contributes to community solidarity by providing catharsis for tensions as well as being a focus for cooperative action.

Two types of what is essentially intra-ethnic organization were so generally recognized and respected that they should be considered factors of community-wide structure. One is the guild system. In pre-French days the monopolies of the guilds within particular ethnic groups were accepted by all groups. Likewise the internal status structure of the different ethnic groups is generally recognized, as are certain types of status equivalence. This equivalence finds common agreement only with regard to classes higher and lower than one's own. Freemen and slaves agree that slaves of any group are of lower status than freemen. Slaves of different groups, however, do not agree that they are of equal status. The same situation adheres between nobles and between serfs. Both class and guild traditionally pattern the legitimate expectations of personal relations.

In contrast to the city as a whole, each ethnic group possesses a much larger body of common customs. The life crisis rites of each are in many ways distinctive. These characteristics both separate the groups from one another and provide a basis of common understanding and cohesion within each. The factor of common language facilitates effective relations within the ethnic unit. Even strangers are housed with co-ethnics. Contacts with people of one's own group are naturally more frequent than with others. Such contacts result not only from the linguistic situation but also from group-limited institutions and rituals.

The Songhoi age-sets came to include the descendants of the Moroccan army through the acculturation process which drew both into a common ethnic unit. The Bela have their separate system and the Arabs possess mutual cooperation societies. Within each group, this sort of organization provides a strong basis for well-ordered relationships of a personal character.

Except for the Arabs, with whom circumcision is a family ritual, the circumcision ceremony is another focus of activity for the whole ethnic group.

The sociograms of birth and naming customs illustrate the manner in which the subgroups of each ethnic unit are also organized around the event of birth. The different ceremonies vary in such a fashion that their cohesive effects are most widespread among the Songhoi and the least extensive for the Arabs. We note also the special custom of New Year's gift giving, which further contributes to the unity of the Songhoi.

The members of each ethnic unit are in considerable agreement with regard to supernatural beliefs. This operates to obviate some types of friction within the group. Differences in belief become the point around which marabouts and their followers in one group are organized in power conflicts with those of other groups. From the point of view of intra-ethnic structure the effect is cohesive.

Most important to ethnic organization is the fact that marriages are preponderantly within the ethnic group. This functions to keep the totality of life crisis rituals and family connections as elements of structure which strengthen ethnic unity. By the same token, of course, these organizational factors tend to maintain the pattern of endogamy. Even some non-kin patterns of a folk sort are cast in kin terms, such as the relation of the circumcision "father" to the initiates, or the Arma to their Gabibi "cross-cousins."

This brings us to family organization itself. In the family, the patterns of ethnic solidarity are reinforced by kinship systems which define mutual rights and obligations in the greatest detail. The potentiality of withdrawal of the rights provides strong sanctions for the maintenance of the obligations. These obligations of kinship preclude impersonal behavior.

A folk aspect of family life which is most distinctive is the extent to which economic behavior is sacred and personal. In contrast to the profit motivated transactions of the market, the sharing of wealth within the elementary family of children and parents, and even their siblings, is striking. Traditional behavior associated with circumcision, courtship, engagement, marriage, and annual religious ceremonies is full of gift-giving patterns between relatives. The economic responsibility of children for parents continues after the offspring have families of their own. Even more distant relatives are assisted when in need. Adoption customs transfer potentially productive and desired offspring from one household to another purely on the claim of kinship. The patterns of expected behavior among kin clearly order their interrelations. Behavior oriented around these expectations is personal in nature. The legitimacy of the patterns seems rarely to be questioned.

The foregoing material seems to substantiate the observation that there is a gradient in the degree of "folkness," which increases from the community unit to the family. The polar concepts of "folk" and "urban" are drawn in such a way that a relative decrease in the characteristics of one is by definition an increase in the importance of the other. What evidence have we that the logically expectable reverse gradient in the occurrence of urban traits actually exists?

While kinship organization is strong, it is not free of disorganization, impersonal acts, and challenges to the sacred order of things. Most noteworthy is the conflict and deception which occurs over the question of polygyny. The marked difference of values between husbands and wives on this issue is a common source of strife. Men may take secret wives, but the deception is ultimately discovered and divorce ensues. Another device, employed by Arabs, uses the wife impersonally and uses the law secularly. An Arab can publicly take a second wife and divorce his first, with the intention of divorcing the second before the end of three months, and taking back the first wife who cannot legally remarry before that time.[1]

The impersonal economic behavior of the market even invades the family of extended kin. Arabs must be urged to aid starving, out-of-town relatives. Arab sons cheat their rich fathers. All groups demand interest on loans to their relations. A kinsman is not favored commercially unless he is in dire need.

Clearly the Arab family is less folk in character than the other family types. The African Arabs have experienced centuries of heterogeneous culture contact. Both on the basis of the hypothesis and on the evidence from the Sudan, it would therefore seem probable that this group was urbanized before its arrival in Timbuctoo. Yet the Arab family is much more urban in Timbuctoo than I found it to be in a homogeneous Arab oasis of comparable size in North Africa. The primitive city seems to have affected the Arab immigrants in ways comparable to the manner in which such a Western city as Algiers alters them.

Impersonal and secular market behavior, which is not generally typical of family economics in Timbuctoo, characterizes commercial relations with non-kin. In this regard, little distinction can be made between interethnic and intra-ethnic behavior. It may be easier to deceive a person of different background, but dishonesty and trickery are common practice. The stranger is housed with a co-ethnic. The latter may try to escape his obligations as host. Host and guest must both be alert for the other's chicanery.

Outright robbery is common and dealers in stolen goods prosper. The grain merchant who has cornered the market will let non-relatives starve if they cannot pay his inflated price. It is normal to take advantage of a man who is known to need money. The market vendor saves her goods for no one and extends no credit. Merchants capitalize on the local belief that the whims of a pregnant woman must be satisfied, to the consternation of the husbands who must buy the things their wives select from the merchant's wares.

Even the age-sets, which operate as cohesive factors in each group, are secularized. Their power to apply sanctions to their members for misbehavior is sometimes used only after outside pressures force such action. Thus a known thief may be retained in the group as long as he fulfills his obligations of cooperation. *Koterey* membership is open to other ethnics who participate economically but not personally.

Among the various ethnic units, sexual relations are primarily organized through prostitution – a strikingly impersonal occupation. Courting and marriage between members of different groups of equivalent status results in open conflict between the groups. Co-wives of different ethnic origin are in greater disaccord than are other co-wives. The children of such marriages are obviously marginal, torn between their two cultural heritages.

Ethnic differences in supernatural belief result in conflict between the Arab and the Songhoi marabouts and between the marabouts and sorcerers. The fear of the supernatural power of strangers and of the genii of strange

1 It should be emphasized that we are not citing the frequency of divorce as evidence of disorganization, as contended by Hansen (1954) and Sjoberg (1955). It is the nature of the conflicts leading to divorce which seems urban. A sex difference in the perception of the structure of the family can hardly be other than disorganizing. Similarly, it is the *abuse* of Islamic divorce law, not its *use*, which is urban in character.

ethnic quarters expresses the same inherent conflict. Even marabouts of the same belief compete for the trade in charms and for students in the manner of the market.

Within the framework of the sacred ideologies, the people's behavior is strikingly secular. The money evaluation and impersonal trading of the market permeate religion and magic. One bargains with God, the saints, and the marabouts. Supernatural services are either on a C.O.D. basis or the efficacy of charms is conceived as being proportionate to the amount paid for them. Some of the religious values are disregarded. Usury is common practice; the marabouts charge for their services; impostors use the sacred title of shereef; the rich fail to make their pilgrimage; non-public daily prayers are slighted; and false oaths are sworn on the Koran.

Post-Conquest Changes

Forty-five years of French occupation in Timbuctoo have brought about still further changes away from folk beliefs and practice. The coming of the French, of course, added to the cultural heterogeneity of the community. Yet the French have been present in small numbers and for a relatively short time. They have done little to alter native customs, aside from attempts to stop sorcery and the sale of slaves. New institutions of the French – the colonial administration and court, the French school and doctor, and the Army – have touched relatively few of the native citizens directly. French trading houses have had direct contact with a wider range of people and French currency has replaced cowries. These commercial innovations have resulted in little basic change for they fall almost completely within the old trading patterns of the people. As we have seen, the natives are sometimes more secular, impersonal, and shrewd than the French when it comes to dealing in credit and interest. Fixed price is the principal new commercial trait, but it has shown little tendency to spread beyond the trait complex of store trading. Commercial dealing with Christians, both French and the Syrian, is something which could never have occurred before the occupation. It is certainly evidence of secularization, considering the fact that no known Christian could have survived in Timbuctoo earlier.

Among other departures from traditional patterns, we have noted lower status people building themselves houses or dressing in clothes previously reserved for higher classes. We find Bela who cheat their fathers as they could not have done before. Marriages are concluded between low status men and higher status women. Even the crafts, hitherto limited to upper class people, are invaded by persons from lower classes, in utter disregard for tradition and the supernatural sanctions which protected the class-craft system. None of these changes is the direct result of French action and design. The fact that they have occurred following French conquest certainly indicates they are indirect effects of the contact.

We can attack the problem of these recent changes by posing the question, "What would have happened before the French conquest if the craft-guilds had been invaded; if a Bela had dressed as a noble; if a Bela son had stolen from his father; if a Gabibi man had tried to marry an Arma?" The answer is that the individual who behaved in this manner would have been severely beaten or killed outright by the individual or group whose rights and prerogatives had been infringed.

While the French have not tried to change native culture, they have assumed complete control of all major physical punishment. The French do not use such punishment to enforce all of the native culture patterns of Timbuctoo. It is used to protect the persons and property of the residents of the city and to enforce French administration and much of Islamic law. With the sanction of physical punishment no longer in native hands, social forces which have long been present can now make themselves felt. Other sanctions of the ethnic groups and families, such as ostracism, supernatural punishment, or disinheritance, cannot make an individual conform when he can gain a better livelihood by ignoring them and finding his social contacts with those who will judge him on the basis of his improved condition.

It is true that the cities of West Africa are distinct from rural communities in the size, density, and heterogeneity of their populations. Villagers know each other as individuals and are dependent on one another for social reputation; categorical relationships occur only with strangers. The urban immigrant who gets off the truck or bus or arrives at the railway station confronts a social structure that, in terms of role relationships, is quite different from what he or she is accustomed to. However, although more numerous role relationships that are more narrow, more specific, more frequently latent and of short duration are associated with urban life, they do not preclude complex primary ties; rather, they supplement them. As we have seen in the case of Timbuktu, obligations of kinship largely preclude impersonal behavior within the family (i.e., between children and parents, among siblings, and to a lesser extent, among extended kin). Furthermore, within each of the three ethnic groups, age-sets provide a strong basis for well-ordered relationships of a personal character. Very few people in any city live in isolation, with their social intercourse limited to impersonal transactions. The urban immigrant experiences situational change as he finds not only a new occupation but also different relationships at work; however, he is also likely to reestablish significant primary relationships. It is to this process of adaptation to a social environment that is both new and different in character that we now turn.

Biographic change

The reaction against the notion of detribalization and against the politics that went with it steered interest away from differential change between individual actors, away from the choices that the individual urban dweller can make. Southall's more balanced proposition went unheeded: "There are both gradual and sudden changes in the norms of migrant workers, while the set of norms operative in an urban situation changes gradually, picked up afresh by every migrant worker on arrival and reverting to latency for him each time he returns to the country" (1961, p. 19).

Here, then, we have both a recognition of situational change and a distinction between historical change at the system level and what we will call "biographic change" at the individual level. Subsequently, Epstein (1967, p. 276) has emphasized that the exclusive concern with situational change disregards the very process of becoming a townsman because it does not take sufficient account of the fact that urbanization of the immigrant, in at least one of its dimensions, involves a process of individual growth and change.

Perhaps because the discredited notion of "detribalization" was couched in cultural terms, or possibly because of the theoretical background of the social anthropologists who did most of the urban studies in Subsaharan Africa, there has been heavy emphasis on social relations as such, and interest in culture change all but disappeared. Philip Mayer [(1961) 1971, pp. 288ff.], however, combines a cultural and a structural approach. He emphasizes the interaction between cultural patterns and the structure of social relationships. A traditionalist outlook on the part of an immigrant encourages incapsulation in a close-knit network of like-minded associates who enforce conformity with the pattern of behavior prescribed by the group. A loose-knit network, on the other hand, indicates a more open outlook on the part of its members, who can take advantage of the choices that the urban setting offers and who decide for themselves whom to associate with and which cultural pattern to adopt. The moral pressures exerted by associates in the heterogeneous urban setting will not necessarily be consistent, and changing one's values, norms, beliefs, and behavior need not lead to general ostracism; it may only strain relations with some associates. Mayer's analysis represents cultural background as the only determinant of patterns of association in the urban setting, but Banton (1973) has focused attention on a second variable: opposition among social groupings in town. He suggests that the social density which characterizes the village is encouraged among urban groups both by the degree of discontinuity between the rural and the urban systems and by the extent and strength of structural opposition in the urban system.

Pons (1969, pp. 269f.) formulates a model of "cultural extension." In learning and acquiring new norms of behavior through urban socialization, some individuals "forget" or grow away from some of their rural ways, but most do not abandon the will or lose the ability to enter into social relations governed by less urban norms, whether in the town or in their home areas. In other words, becoming urban involves an extension of cultural equipment, but it does not necessarily imply a commensurate rejection or loss. Dorothy Dee Vellenga puts it this way:

In Ghana, people do not live in isolated sectors of the society – one traditional, another modern (if, indeed, they do anywhere) – but in increasingly interconnected spheres. One individual is confronted with a variety of behavioral patterns. An increase in one's resources does not necessarily mean a movement from one way of life to another but can often mean an attempt to expand one's choices to include all. (1971, pp. 136f.)

To this day, the urban–rural nexus is a major determinant of the biographic change experienced by most urban dwellers in West Africa. For those who anticipate ultimate return to rural areas, biographic change cannot be a one-way process. Prolonged urban residence may well be a cumulative experience, but the security ultimately to be found in the rural areas is not forgotten. A model of one-way change may apply better to urban dwellers permanently committed to the city. This is most obviously the case among those who have taken refuge in town from rural areas where their positions had become untenable. Others may become discredited in the eyes of their home people because of the particular role they play in the urban setting. Still others may make commitments unacceptable to their people (e.g., entering into an interethnic marriage).

The linkages between historical and biographic change can be easily seen but have been little commented upon. Epstein (1961, pp. 56ff.) has proposed a distinction between the effective and the extended network. Those people with whom an individual interacts most intensely and most regularly and who are therefore also likely to come to know one another (i.e., the part of the total network that shows a degree of connectedness) Epstein identifies as the "effective network." Those others with whom ties are more or less close but who are met less frequently and who are strangers or have only tenuous links among themselves constitute the "extended network." Epstein suggests that new norms and standards of behavior tend to arise more frequently within the effective network of those who rank high on the prestige continuum and that through the extended network they gradually filter down and percolate through the society.

How fast do the three types of change that we have distinguished proceed? Situational change is abrupt by definition. Historical and biographic change tend to occur more slowly. However, societies sometimes do experience abrupt change of great magnitude. The achievement of Independence by Guinea-Bissau in 1974 can be seen as such an event. Also, an individual may undergo profound changes within a short span of his or her lifetime. Joining a Fundamentalist church provides a good example of such change. So it is that the models of historical and biographic change generally denote gradual processes, although they can at times proceed very rapidly indeed.

Gradually or abruptly, historical change sets the context of biographic change and the conditions of situational change. The analysis of social change in West Africa profits from the distinction of these various types of change, and a full understanding of the unfolding historic process demands the capacity to recognize the interplay among them.

7 The family: continuity and change

A person who has worked must rest. My children pay for my food and light and washing. I've done as much for them: I brought them up since they were small, and married the senior ones to good wives. They can't leave me to suffer now.

Elderly widow in Lagos, quoted by Peter Marris (1961, pp. 38f.)

The family or, more precisely, the extended family has always been an important institution in West African societies; in some ways, it has been the core organizational unit. Currently the composition and function of the family are undergoing some modification as the process of urbanization and historically associated social changes strain its traditional structure of relationships. But in agreement with the point made recently by Peter C. W. Gutkind (1974, p. 103), we would argue that the changes the family has undergone do not mean it has come to play a role of lesser significance. In this chapter we emphasize the dynamic role of the family in changing society.[1]

The general discussion of the African family in labor migration, with complementary rural and urban components, has been complicated in West Africa by the lengthy urban history of the region. In addition to the pattern of urban workers separated physically but not economically from rural family members (see Chapter 4), various degrees of conjugal family nucleation and patterns of extended family adaptation may be found within the city;[2] therefore, generalization with regard to urban family form is hazardous. Generalization about rural family structures prior to widespread migration and urbanization is also inadvisable because of the range of variations and the tendency to compare current actual patterns with ideal types constructed to characterize the past. The consequence of such a perspective is a misplaced emphasis on the breakdown of the extended family, as opposed to its continuity, in the analysis and prognosis of the role of the extended family in the urbanization of West African societies.

The family appears to function in a number of ways as an active agent – rather than as a passive medium or impediment – in the process of urbanization. Able members are sponsored in migration in search of urban employment; members in need are supported by the kin network in crises; and through an internal division of labor, the family bridges the gap between the advantages offered by the urban and the rural sectors of the economy: cash income and security, respectively. Although other institutions, such as ethnic unions and more casual friendly associations with similar bases, have taken up some of the extended family's functions, it continues to provide certain unique securities to its members in the crowded cities where work and accommodations are in short supply.[3] Moving to the uncertainties of the city in search of the potential rewards of relatively good-paying work does not dissolve one's family ties. Uncertainty provides the condition for sustained family relations in the absence of alternate agencies of security. Among urban-based families, need and interdependency also arise. Marris writes of Lagos:

The family group, therefore, assumes responsibility for the welfare of its members: as yet, there are few public services in Nigeria to relieve it of any of these duties. A strong sense of mutual obligations sustains ties of kinship as the dominant concern of everyday life. Every member of the family group has a status, rights and obligations, and enjoys the sense of security which comes from these. He is protected against unemployment, old age, the cost of sickness, and can appeal to it in any difficulty. In return, he will be expected to support others, to contribute to family celebrations, to attend meetings, and reciprocate visits. (1961, p. 39)

The extended family in industrialization and urbanization

During the past two centuries or so, Western societies have experienced some rather profound structural changes generally associated with the process of industrialization. The transition has altered relationships not only among nations but among institutions and individuals. William J. Goode [(1963) 1970, pp. 169f.] has made the point that the core element of industrialization is a social factor; when we speak of industrialization we refer, not to the proliferation of factories, but to the growth of individualized wage labor, whether on plantations, in mines, or in cities. The division of labor, the increase in expertise, specialization, a market economy, and the development of individualized remuneration and liability signal the presence of industrialization; it is the redefinition of roles and relationships that indicate the condition.

However, in West Africa and much of the remainder of the Third World, this condition is better described by the term "urbanization" because of the absence (as we have seen) of large-scale industrialization. Here, service as a mode of employment surpasses the importance of manufacture. Urbanization, then, is a more suitable proxy for the individualization of contract. What does this individualization mean for traditional forms of family organization?

There is a substantial history to the development of thought on this matter for the Western industrialized countries. An early argument grew into a conventional wisdom and was widely accepted until recently. It had a number of proponents [Moore 1951; Parsons (1949) 1959; Nimkoff 1965; Blood 1972]. The following statements summarize the position, although perhaps too strongly for some members of this school of thought.

The trend in industrializing nations the world over is toward the independent family system. The line of influence here is from the economy to the family. Industrialization is the independent variable and the family the dependent variable. (Nimkoff 1965, pp. 61f.)

It is perhaps the kinship system in non-industrial societies that offers the most important single impediment to individual mobility, not only through the competing claims of kinsmen upon the potential industrial recruit but also through the security offered in established patterns of mutual responsibility. (Moore 1951, p. 24)

This line of reasoning gradually came under criticism. Goode noted that what had become a common hypothesis – that "the conjugal form of the family emerges when a culture is invaded by industrialization and urbanization – is an undeveloped assumption" [(1963) 1970, p. 10]. It remained unclear just how industrialization or urbanization affected the family system or how, in turn, the family facilitated or hindered these processes [Goode (1963) 1970, p. 2].[4]

The question regarding the actual nature of the relationship between the family and industrialization or urbanization arose as empirical evidence accumulated to demonstrate that extended families continued to function in important ways in Western society. Michael Young and Peter Willmott (1957), Eugene Litwak (1959; 1960a; 1960b), and M. B. Sussman and L. G. Burchinal (1962) were among those who found the image of the "isolated nuclear family" to be overdrawn. Research was beginning to show the advantage of extended family ties for facing the problems of urbanized and industrialized society, as well as the importance of extended family for those caught up in the transition (Anderson 1971). At the same time, the idea that a tradition of extended family cohabitation had been extinguished by the Industrial Revolution was being reexamined. It seems that nuclear families as residential units had been the typical pattern before the advent of widespread industrialization and urbanization (Greenfield 1961). It also appears that the English household may have increased in size as the Industrial Revolution gathered momentum, with the dwelling unit reaching its greatest complexity between 1850 and 1880 [Laslett (1970) 1973, p. 23].

One of the problems in determining what effect industrialization had on the family in the experience of the West has been that investigation is limited to a large extent to crude measures (such as household size) in dealing with the distant past. Studies of contemporary society have led to a call to abandon domicile (Adams 1968, pp. 48f.; Goody 1972, pp. 3f.; Winch 1972, pp. 10f.) and even general propinquity (Litwak 1960a; 1960b) as criteria for determining family size or cohesiveness. In today's rapidly urbanizing countries, we have a chance to witness firsthand and in greater detail the manner in which the family articulates with and is changed by the new definition of relationships that accompany the transition.

Institutional continuity in a changing environment

According to the pattern that is still most typical, migration is an individual affair in West Africa. Contact and visibility are reduced among family members as ties between migrants and home village become stretched out and communication becomes more difficult and far less frequent. Yet, the family has played a most important role in sponsoring the training of the migrant and in securing accommodation and work upon his or her arrival in the city.[5] It will continue to provide him with help in times of need. Thus, the migrant stands on the margin between the promise of a new freedom from family ties and the accumulated reciprocal obligations to those who have helped in the past and on whom he or she may have to depend in the future.

The strain on traditional family structure that is introduced by distance in cases of individual migration is compounded by two mutually reinforcing elements: the individualization of legal contract in the market economy and the increasing emphasis on romantic love as the basis for marriage. These forces create for individuals and couples a general tension in the direction of independence from larger family structures. The momentum of the Western ideology of the couple is carried out in the law and in court practice and is reflected in the nuclear family housing units provided for urban residents by employers and public authorities. Arrayed graphically (Figure 7.1), the trends that are straining the extended family would seem to pose an impressive threat to its continuity. Nevertheless, there are some potent factors contributing to its survival. And just as structure and ideology are mutually reinforcing in the direction of change and family breakdown, the ideology of mutual support combined with the individual experience of sponsorship, which is reinforced by the economic insecurity of the urban present and future, provide a strong complex of motives for sustained, active participation in the wider family group.

The divisive forces affecting the family are the ones most visible to the urban observer. They catch our attention and lead us to emphasize change. When Goode [(1963) 1970, pp. 175 and pp. 202ff.] surveyed evidence of family change in Africa a number of years ago, he saw migrant offspring becoming independent of their parents. He observed, too, a growing freedom of choice in town based on the new economic independence afforded by wage labor. Although he did note the persistence of some home ties, he predicted their continued decline in accordance with his general theoretical orientation. But as we saw in Chapter 2, the job boom in the cities that came with Independence was followed by an increase in migration that continued long after the demand for additional workers had subsided. The need for a flexible, multipurpose agent of support such as the extended family may be required by today's migrant more than it was by those of the earlier period. Migrants remain dependent on the goodwill of those at home (Chapter 4). Whoever wants to be able to fall back on the rural economy in case of a crisis or just in retirement is concerned about landrights there. If a man has left his wife and children behind, whether it is because he cannot support them in town or because they are the guardians of his home rights and can reap the current income from his interests there, he is dependent on kinsmen at home to assist them in crisis and controversy.

The extended family frequently plays a crucial role in the very process by

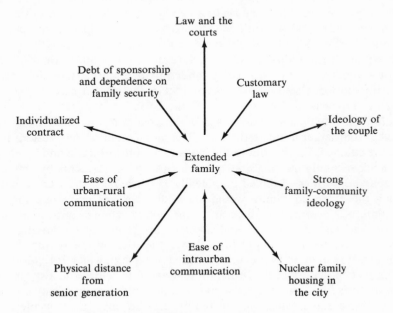

Figure 7.1. Forces supporting and straining the extended family

which individuals become established in the city. This role has recently been well documented in the case of Dar es Salaam, Tanzania (Flanagan 1977). There, the great majority of rural-urban migrants reported that they had been sponsored by members of their extended family who provided for their education, accommodated them in the city while they looked for work, and assisted them in periods of crisis. Aronson (1970, pp. 165f. and 270f.) has observed in the case of Ijebu Yoruba people in Nigeria, that a boy finishing primary school may decide for himself what kind of career he will enter, but his father, uncles, and older brothers and sisters can play a major role in the choice, especially if they do not like his original idea. In any event, his family, utilizing a chain of mutual kin obligations, will attempt to secure an apprenticeship or find a sponsor with whom he can stay in the city. The content of the binding relationships of family membership has shifted from matters of agricultural production and land allocation procedures to that of providing school fee payment, room, and sometimes board for recent migrants. Aronson emphasizes, in contrast to other authors, that people who have secured a foothold in the urban economy are happy to sponsor junior relatives and thus begin to repay their own obligations. Here is one of the accounts of Ijebu Yoruba families that Aronson presents. It illustrates our point that the physical nucleation of the domestic unit obscures important dynamics of membership in the extended family.

Struggling together: the Odusanya family*

Michael *Adétólá* Odusanya was born in Ilu-Ijebu on April 21, 1933. His father was a Christian born around 1901, who had gone to primary school and then migrated to Lagos, where he became a railway clerk, but also learned and practiced English tailoring in his off hours. Before Michael was born he had returned home to marry, and while keeping up his tailoring trade he also became the Anglican primary school headmaster. Michael's mother, from the same town, sold dried fish and *gàrí* (cassava meal), and did well enough at it to support herself and her only living child, Michael, when the senior Odusanya died three years after Michael's birth. Although there was some pressure put upon her to marry her deceased husband's younger brother,[1] neither she nor the brother's wife would hear of it. She has remained in her husband's family compound to this day.

Michael started school late, in 1944, and his mother managed to pay his school fees right through to Standard VI (sixth grade). He took entry examinations for secondary school, but his father's brother advised him instead to go and learn a trade. At first he did not want to do so, and he taught primary school for a term. But his uncle persisted, and arranged to have Michael go to Ibadan, where he stayed with an older cousin on his mother's side.

This cousin discussed careers with Michael, and they decided together that he should learn carpentry. A friend from home was apprenticed to a carpenter who was from a small town not far from Ilu-Ijebu, and Michael signed on as well. His mother paid the five guineas ($14.70) "tuition" fee for the three-year apprenticeship. He finally stayed four years instead of three, gaining his "freedom" in 1956, at the age of 23. He was in his own room by then (in the house where his future wife was also staying), though his mother sent him the rent and he continued to eat with his cousin.

His own master was head carpenter for a large-scale Ijebu building contractor, and hired Michael on at the end of his apprenticeship. The pay was low, though, only four or five pounds ($11.20 – $14.00) a month. So he wrote an application to an Italian contracting firm operating in Ibadan, and was hired at £15 ($42) a month. At the same time he did odd work on the side, as he had opened a shop jointly with a friend after he got his "freedom."

Work at Palladino and Sons was eased by the number of machines for cutting, planing, drilling and the like. But it was also exacting in a human

* Excerpts from Dan R. Aronson, *The City is Our Farm: Seven Migrant Ijebu Yoruba Families*, 1978, pp. 46–54, by permission of the author and Schenkman Publishing. Based on research in 1966–7. Subtitles and one footnote omitted, remaining footnote renumbered.

1 This is termed the "levirate" technically. It operated regularly in Yoruba culture but was rarely forced on unwilling parties.

sense, with strictly kept hours, only two short breaks during a workday that lasted from 7 a.m. to 4 p.m., and little feeling of or hope for self-advancement. As soon as he had enough work to keep him going on his own, he dropped the salaried job entirely. Now, four years later, he thinks he makes a net profit for himself of about £25 ($70) a month, though he does not have a bookkeeping system which allows him to tell very accurately. He is sure, though, that he spends more carefully than when he was on a salary, since he is never sure when his next few pounds will come in.

Florence *Ayòdélé* Odusanya is six years younger than her husband. Born in 1939 in a large village south of the Ijebu capital, she is also of a sturdily Anglican family. It was her grandfather who gave the land on which the village church was built. When Florence was a child her father had two wives, and he has added a third since she herself got married. In all there were nine children born to her mother, but only two remain alive. Her mother does some trading in rice and beans, buying in Ibadan (rice comes through a long-distance trade route from the north), and selling in small markets in the villages near her own. Florence's father farms, but also buys and sells a little cloth.

Florence finished the six grades of primary school when she was fifteen, and immediately went to Lagos, where she clerked in the shop of a male cousin of her mother's in return for room, board and £1. 5s. 0d. ($3.50) a month. She wanted to go on in school, but there was not enough money for her to do so.

At Christmas the following year she visited Ibadan and stayed with her father's brother. A friend of hers from home had a job at the Nigerian Tobacco Company, and was earning three times as much as she was. In those days the personnel man just walked along the lineup of applicants at the company gate and chose new employees by looking at them. Florence went one morning, and was selected. After ten years at the company she is earning £17 ($47.60) a month taking finished cigarettes off the machines for packaging. She is one of only a few hundred industrial workers in Ibadan, and considers herself lucky to have such a (relatively) large and steady income.

Michael was living in the same house as her uncle. He would come up to visit now and then, but was impressively reserved and soft-spoken. At the same time, she says, several much more active suitors were around, too. Thus, when Michael proposed to her, she was both surprised and overwhelmed. She didn't answer immediately, but communicated with her mother at home. In return her mother asked for the name of the boy, his parents' names and their home town. Next her mother came to Ibadan to meet Michael and, when they discovered that the two mothers often met at rural markets and liked one another, the young couple knew that family consent would be forthcoming. Many months, dowry payments, betrothal ceremonies, gifts, and promises later, they were married in a brief ceremony at Michael's paternal home and blessed at the church – three months after Deji's birth.

After Deji, who was born at home in Florence's village, all the children were born at the general hospital in Ibadan. All four have been quite healthy, except for a case of chicken pox each, and various sores and rashes like the one presently afflicting Wole. An only child himself, Michael is determined to have as many children as he can: he feels strongly the lack of immediate family. (In fact one reason for his family's rejection of a church marriage was the possibility that he might not have children who survived him unless he remained open to a second or third wife.) He does, however, claim to practice the Yoruba family planning technique of not resuming sexual relations with his wife until more than a year after each new baby. It is likely now that the Odusanyas will have six, seven, or more children before their family is completed.

By that time they will have even further outgrown their present lodgings. Right now they manage only barely. With seven-year-old Sola away, five members of the family are only the core of the household living in, or out of, their one large room. Bose, the maid, sleeps on the floor with the children. Three boys, all brothers and the sons of Florence's father's younger sister, sleep in the hallway or on the open porch outside the room. Except for an occasional meal, however, they otherwise are rarely at "home." One has a job as a carpenter, having learned the trade from Pa Deji. The other two are apprentices, one to a barber and one to a mechanic. And two other boys, Pa Deji's kinsmen and apprentices, also sleep in the hallway and store their few possessions in the room. They eat with another relative who lives not far away. . . .

The Odusanya family is enmeshed in at least four separate networks of social relations, respectively involving kinsmen, neighbors, friends and acquaintances, and workmates and customers. In their home towns, as indeed in most non-urban societies throughout the world, the separability of these networks would not now or in the past have been nearly so great. There, the extended family compound, where other individuals were simultaneously kinsmen, neighbors and workmates, was the basic building-block of both the physical and the social structure of the community. Of course the closure was not complete, especially in the centuries-old Yoruba urban tradition. Political associations, trade and marketing, and friendship as well as warfare drew people together who were not kin. But modern migrants approach the other extreme: although *some* workmates, for example, may also be neighbors or kin (Ma Akin, or Pa Deji's** apprentices for example), by and large the various networks consist of different sets of individuals. . . .

The Odusanyas are still very much kin-oriented. Their own nuclear family is, obviously, very much intact. They have five young relatives presently living with them, of whom Michael has provided occupational training for three, and yet other relatives have stayed with them in the past. Meanwhile they themselves have sent first Deji and now Sola to stay with Michael's mother in Ilu-Ijebu in order both to be of help around the house to her and to gain for the child small-town virtue and discipline. Ma Deji's father cultivates a piece of land he bought for her, though she has now directed the proceeds toward her younger half-brother's education; in a return gesture Ma Deji sends home the two free cartons of cigarettes she is given at the factory every month for her grandmother to sell for pure profit. Letters and verbal messages, containing much advice or request, pass frequently through travellers to and from the rural area. And one or both the adults travel home as often as once a month to see to some family business, spiritual, or personal affair, often giving several pounds in cash to each of several relatives when they go. The frequency, the complexity, and the will-

** Ma Akin is a neighbor as well as a co-worker of Mrs. Odusanya; Pa Deji is the father of Deji, that is, Mr. Odusanya.

ing undertaking of these activities attest to a continuing vitality of kinship bonds despite the departure from the intensity of traditional kin group interaction.

Perhaps the dominant theme of contemporary urban kinship behavior is the relative freedom of choice that now underlies it. People *can* choose these days to ignore their kinsmen, though neither the Odusanyas nor most other Ijebu migrants choose to do so. . . .

Neighborly interaction in the city evinces a strong sense of living under public scrutiny. This second theme of urban life . . . is a carry-over from the intense interaction of the kinsmen and co-wives of the traditional compound. The following description was given, by the late sociologist N. A. Fadipe, of extended family life in the rural compound fifty years ago, but it might apply almost equally to the Odusanyas and other Ijebu migrants today:

"A large part of the day is spent in the open . . . . everyone eats and drinks and talks in the full view of everybody else; and as the rooms are hot in the day-time . . . , most of the life of the compound has to be passed on the open verandah [now, in the yard]. . . . quarrels and rebukes take place within the full hearing of neighbors . . . each individual's weaknesses and vices are open to the observation of the other[s]. . . . People outside the immediate family are interested in its members and their welfare. . . . This makes exclusive family life in the Western sense impossible. Only a limited amount of privacy is possible . . . (1970:101-102)."

There has always been, of course, an etiquette governing life in the compound, and it continues with but minor adjustment. Husbands can discipline their wives, and mothers their children, without the intervention of neighbors – unless the punishment, in *their* eyes, exceeds the crime. A woman who is sensitive to criticism of her children by others will be left alone, though liked the less for her touchiness. A younger person of whatever age in the urban compound will obey any elder without bridling, will tolerate his idiosyncrasies, and may seek his advice, voicing disapproval only by seeking out another elder to mediate on his behalf. When Adunni [a neighbor] calls Pa Deji "our husband" during [an] exchange, . . . she brings into focus through her use of humor the tension between the shifting relationships of neighbors ("our husband" is the correct term of reference between traditional neighbors, who were co-wives as well), and the continuing inter-familial intimacy of the urban migrant compound.

Probably the major change in the interaction of neighbors parallels that among kinsmen. It consists of the *possibility* of privacy, which is available in the Odusanyas' house especially to those without families, and to other migrants in the city who want to keep to themselves and can afford either to rent an entire floor (four or more rooms) of a building, or to rent or build a small house on the sparsely settled fringe of the town. Few avail themselves of this potential secretiveness, in part because the personality characteristics that would lead to it are discouraged from the outset of one's life. But the choice is there.

Within these two networks, of kin and of neighbors, the urban household is a discrete entity, which has relatively more solidarity (and the stresses that go with solidarity) than it would have in the home town. Men's and women's roles and activities there are more distinct than they are in the city (but much less suffused by values of male superiority than in many other cultures in Africa, the Middle East, and elsewhere). For example, if Ma Deji needed to be away from home in a village situation as much as she does, other female compound-mates would see to the children. In Ibadan Pa Deji adjusts his schedule of eating and shop hours to the demands of his wife's factory job, and looks after the children more directly. As well, the couple shares financial responsibilities more cooperatively than in the traditional situation, where their purses would have remained separate, the husband providing shelter, tools, medicine, school fees and major items of clothing, and the wife the food and the minor utensils, school items, and everyday clothing. The monogamous family has probably always implied less segregation of roles and activities by sex than the polygynous one, but the migrants blur the differentiation even more. Finally, while Michael and Florence attend meetings, go visiting, and sometimes travel home independently, they and other migrant couples spend more time with one another and with their children than do their counterparts at home: their own room structures more nuclear family activity in this sense than do the small, dark, sometimes windowless sleeping rooms of the rural compound.

The Odusanyas, thus, have a joint domestic venture. Michael's income pays for the rent and electricity, his own clothing, Deji's tutoring, meals at the shop, association dues, gifts and remittances to kinsmen, and reinvestment in his small business. In addition, he gives his wife £8 ($22.40) each month as "chop money," that is, for basic food supplies. Florence's £17 ($47.60) per month income covers: additional food expenditures, especially on ready-cooked food sold by itinerant hawkers and some neighbors for meals when nothing has been prepared at home, and for lunches at the factory for herself; Bose's salary, £1. 5s. 0d., or $3.50 a month; clothing and school needs for the children; other household items like soap, firewood, and cosmetics; her own gifts and remittances to relatives at home; and £4 or £5 ($11.20 to $14.00) in savings for major clothing purchases, or a trip home. Florence and Michael each supply the money for their own relatives, but they discuss mutually all the major amounts that they are planning to send or take. . . .

Their gifts to relatives are not without relation to fairly basic needs of their own. Although they do not conceive it so in direct terms, their continuing contact and assistance provides them virtually the only potential social welfare insurance they can count upon, since they have no long-term savings. If anyone in the family, but especially Michael or Florence, had a serious illness, if Michael lost his business, if Florence were laid off, or if someone in the family were accidentally to die, the limited government medical service available for short-term care would be the only substantial assistance the Odusanyas would get from anyone besides their home-town relatives. Even in desperate circumstances they could find no relief from government or voluntary agencies, which simply do not exist except in rudimentary form. Seen in these terms, the network of kin ties is one that most urban families cannot easily afford to give up. Here, as in many situations in many cultures, people enjoy doing some things that they almost have to do in any case.

That social security is a concern for those who struggle together is evident. But what of the others who are better off, who are by virtue of their current position less concerned about what setbacks the future may hold for them?

Christine Oppong (1974, p. 63) found that 54 percent of a sample of Akan senior civil servants in Accra had provided for the education of the children of relatives. As these men understood very well from their current position, one of the strengths of the extended family is that it can pool incomes to secure training for individual members. The pay-off for the wider group comes later on. Typically, those who have attained higher qualifications and, therefore, positions of relative affluence, are the ones who have incurred the deeper obligations to a wider pool of kin. Many Akan youths who were educated in the 1940s and 1950s needed more than talent and hard work to get ahead: The majority had to rely on the support of parents, grandparents, brothers and sisters, and their parents' brothers and sisters. Oppong (1974, p. 62) reports that, virtually without exception, the senior civil servants she studied, whose parents and guardians were now elderly and, in some cases, in need, recognized their duty to reciprocate, and almost all gave money regularly or intermittently for support of kin.

Similar evidence abounds. Four-fifths of a sample of Ghanaian college graduates who had already found employment felt that they were obligated to provide at least a tenth of their income to relatives outside the nuclear family (Caldwell 1968a, p. 60). Peter C. Garlick (1971, pp. 97f.) observed that among successful traders in Accra and Kumasi, the demand to contribute to the education of relatives' children in addition to that of one's own children could require a sizable outlay. In Monrovia, in the late 1950s, sponsorship was found to extend beyond family to "adopted" wards. In addition to the loyalty and support of these younger persons, the prestige of the status of patron accrues to the benefactor (Fraenkel 1964, p. 119). As Diana Gladys Azu reports from two Ga neighborhoods on the outskirts of Accra:

One characteristic of the lineage which has persisted is the aid given to members. This is particularly so among members living in other towns. In the Ga town itself, there is reciprocal giving between children and relatives of the parents' and grandparents' generation, but the children tend to give more than they receive. What they give is usually money, mainly to the old men and women, and for bereaved members. As Marris (1961:137ff) also noticed among the Yoruba, it is the salaried workers who are mostly "taxed" in this sphere, and though most of them perform this duty, it is not done happily. (1974, p. 75)

Distance from home, the friction that impedes communication and contact, might be expected to reduce the flow of urban remittance. However, Caldwell (1969, pp. 153f.) found that the greatest proportion of households receiving remittances from town was in the most distant northern hinterlands of Ghana. He attributes this not to regional differences in strength of family ties but to the greater poverty of the northern regions and the lack of alternate sources of cash income, hence the greater demand for aid by relatives left behind.[6] And although time, like distance, might be expected to wear down ties, there seems to be a positive correlation between length of time in the city (away from home) and remittances. The long-term urban resident is generally in a better position to help kin than the newly arrived migrant who is struggling to establish himself in a job or trade.

Family, of course, is more than a refuge for those in need. The content of family ties and exchange cannot all be measured in terms of cash; support has meaning beyond the realm of economics. Marris (1961, p. 26) reported the distress, the longing for news, of migrants to Lagos who were physically separated from kin by the lack of means to visit home. That isolation must be appreciated relative to Yoruba habits of socializing. Here is the way a prosperous Lagos shoemaker describes things:

On Sunday the family will come, you know we Yoruba are not like white people, we do not wait to be invited. If I have a brother in Abeokuta, his son may come, let us say, or a cousin. So in the afternoon there is fried yam, beer for an aged person, Coca Cola for the children. It is because of our belief that in this way they will help us when we are old, and when you die, they will remember the uncle who did this or that for them. That is why we are careful never to offend them, and treat them like that so they will never forget it. (Marris 1961, p. 29)

For those with the means, visits among relatives living within easy reach, especially those in the same town, were frequent; visits with relatives in distant towns were often of long duration. In addition, there were the formal occasions when the family came together in an expression of unity, with family branches sometimes appearing in the uniform of matching cloth when the occasion was such that there was time for this kind of planning and preparation (Marris 1961, p. 31).

Reciprocity and enterprise

The heavy demands made on those successful in the urban arena have raised the question of what the potential effect of extended family demands on individual enterprise might be. That is, can it be that the net effect of the extended family is to impede or frustrate individual aspiration and ambition, whether in business or employment, because success only means increased demands from needy relatives? This is too simplistic a line of reasoning.

E. Wayne Nafziger (1969, pp. 25ff.) found in his Nigerian study that the extended family boosted entrepreneurial activity by financing training and furnishing initial capital outlay but that the expansion of these firms was hindered by the increase in the number of dependents asking for support when there was any increase in the size of business. Although Garlick (1971, pp. 99ff.) lays emphasis on the drain extended family demands constitute for businessmen in Ghana, he also notes that family helped in starting up businesses and in directing contracts or patronage to them. In Monrovia, family was an important source of funds for initial capitalization of enterprise, and friends tended to supply the necessary training in the skills of the trade (Handwerker 1973, p. 291).[7]

With regard to the danger of the extended family leading enterprise down the path to bankruptcy, W. Penn Handwerker (1973, pp. 293f.) suggests that African businessmen be credited with enough rationality not to ruin themselves by overextending aid to relatives or friends. Faced with unbearable demands, the economically successful man or woman may feel obliged to leave town in order to escape, but some have hit upon a more lasting solution: to reduce the costs of family support by setting up in business formerly dependent relatives or by educating them. The strategy fulfills obligations while creating them for others, who thus become better able to share family responsibility (Garlick 1971, p. 98).

In terms of motivation, the notion of family parasitism begs the question. The member who accepts the demands that the extended family makes on him as legitimate and who derives satisfaction from the contribution he can make to the extended family's well-being has every reason to make a maximum effort. Do men in Western society reduce their efforts when they get married and start raising children? Only when the extended family is put in question does the individual see the product of his work dissipated to others. It is precisely the ideology of the conjugal family that proposes such a perspective.

Variations in family form

Although we emphasize the continuity in patterns of extended family relationships in urbanization, it may be noted that the family has survived because it was flexible and able to change. Individualization and spatial disruptions have resulted in a number of residential arrangements. In addition to the rural–urban family with one or more representatives vying for a place in the urban sector, the long urban history of West Africa has provided for the development of the urban family network among towns or indeed with a single urban base.

The complementarity of roles in the rural–urban family type was noted earlier; yet, Skinner (1974, pp.103ff.) reports the beginning of the erosion of ties in Ouagadougou as established migrants came to feel that the utility of relationships with rural kin had lost most of its importance. However it was among the long established, urban-based coastal peoples in Monrovia that the social security function of kinship operated most effectively (Fraenkel 1961, p. 149). In both examples, the clue to understanding the processes observed lies beyond the pattern of family residence. Ouagadougou is unusual in that unoccupied or unused peri-urban land is available for farming. A large proportion of the households surveyed by Skinner were in fact those of farmers; the great majority of them were immigrants. They had not migrated to remain farmers, but at least, they had found a means of subsistence beyond the reach of immigrants in most major cities in West Africa. Also, politicans, civil servants, and even ordinary clerks had acquired farms near Ouagadougou and brought in rural relatives to settle on them or hired youths in Ouagadougou to work them (Skinner 1974, pp. 51 and 54ff.). Still, politicians, civil servants, and top-level clerks were beginning to build houses among those of their relatives in the rural areas (Skinner 1974, pp. 107f.). In Monrovia there was a pronounced inadequacy of public services, of alternate agencies of care to aid those in need. Kinfolk were forced to rely on each other, and the city administration depended on the general acceptance of the duties of kinship (Fraenkel 1961, p. 149). Complementarity in this situation rests on the alternation of periods of crisis and meager prosperity among the various city-based family members.

Among Yoruba, traditionally urban based and yet at the same time tied to the security of the land, the support structure of the most primary of all primary groups has been formalized. Family corporations have emerged whose job it is to orchestrate, arbitrate, and administer the lives of the members of the family collective. The Yoruba *ìdílé* is a named corporate body with membership based on descent; its duties include holding and managing property, seeing to the economic welfare of members in need, caring for the children of incapacitated parents, and arbitrating disputes among members.[8] Headship titles and chieftaincies are conferred upon the most active members (especially males), and all members are obligated to attend formal meetings and carry out duties associated with their allocated roles (Sandra T. Barnes 1974, pp. 87f.).

The peristence of the *ìdílé* is as remarkable as its formalized structure. Sandra T. Barnes concludes on the basis of her findings that

neither the passage of time and generations nor the lack of residential proximity has managed to diminish the persistence of descent group relationships among migrants. If anything there is a growing tendency toward strengthening these kinds of ties in Lagos. As more and more migrants commit themselves to living permanently in a new location, the number of active *ìdílé* in that place can be expected to increase. (1974, pp. 115f.)

One change she does expect to take place is a shift from the present dispersed urban corporation to a family type with a more focused urban base (Barnes 1974, p. 116). "Wing" family groups, urban-dwelling fragments of family not now large enough to constitute a family headquarters in themselves, currently pay dues and submit important disputes for arbitration to larger family units living in other towns (Barnes 1974, pp. 91f.). These will become family centers themselves over time as urban growth continues and the focus of local family authority and activities shifts inward. It seems, however, that continued development of Nigeria's many large urban centers would continue to lure increasingly mobile family members away from the home base. Hence, it may be too early to signal the close of the dispersed Yoruba family corporation as it appears today.

The functioning of the Yoruba family corporation recalls the fact that in addition to security, family business includes the holding of property. One of the most important processes with regard to family property is its transfer between generations. Changes that are occurring in this process may forecast changes in kinship configurations in some societies, but changes in the shape of the extended family do not necessarily portend a decline in its importance.

Corporately held properties such as land or housing lead individual Yoruba in Lagos to emphasize matrilineal, patrilineal, or bilateral affiliation, depending on where the family wealth lies (Barnes 1974, pp. 95ff.). The optional nature of figuring descent among Southern Yoruba, Barnes (1974, pp. 102f.) speculates, may increase the incidence of matrilineally traced descent lines because successful businesswomen tend to invest in housing and because women may be considered the founding ancestors of descent lines. On the other hand, in her history of the elite Brew family, Margaret Priestly (1969, pp. 183ff.) indicates a decline in the importance of customarily matrilineal channels of inheritance in Fanti society. The pattern in which "property was owned collectively by the clan and the concept of unrestricted, individual, private ownership was exceptional" was antithetical to a situation in which ambitious men accumulated and preserved considerable personal wealth. "Property acquired in this way took on the different connotation of association with a person rather than a group, and rights of disposal tended to be viewed accordingly. In such circumstances, it became not uncommon for a father to think of his own children as heirs" (Priestley 1969, p. 184). Yet, in the late 1960s, it was found that the wives of Akan senior civil servants maintained a segregation of their resources, fearing that if they pooled their money and holdings with those of their husbands, excessive demands by the husband's matrikin would deplete their assets, thus jeopardizing their own offspring's security (Oppong 1974, pp. 92f.).

New laws and the courts are playing an increasingly important role in decision making in these matters. As they do so, they contribute to the strain on the extended family and structurally advance the ideology of the nuclear family through legal patterns copied or adapted from those of Western countries. Attempts at change are most apparent in the areas of inheritance and the dissolution of marriage. Whereas the parent generation used to take a couple to task and apportion the blame and conditions of settlement according to custom in marital disruption, its role is more and more limited to advice giving. In divorce, the custody of children is increasingly awarded to the mother. Whereas bridewealth previously would have been refunded unless fault was found with the husband, urban courts may now require him to provide support for his divorced wife and their children. Upon the husband's death, the widow, who at one time would have been at the mercy of her in-laws, may now find support in the courts.

Thus, the point is reemphasized that the extended family has not remained unchanged in the urban transition. Physical fragmentation is another obvious symptom of this. Where multiple generation or laterally extended families are found in the city, the range of kin is modified, some members are absent, and the *domestic* unit constitutes a subset of the extended family network. Kin in the city are sought out by new arrivals, not according to the closeness of ties, but on the basis of which relative might fulfill the most pressing need (Sandra T. Barnes 1974, p. 49). Some number of urban households contain, in fact, nonkin who bear a variety of relationships to the core of residents, from boarder to "adopted" family members. Yet, for all the variety of family forms encountered, the nuclear conjugal family unit, isolated functionally from the extended body of kin, has yet to emerge as a widespread pattern in West African cities.[9] In the relatively rare case in which a couple might choose to isolate themselves from kin, perhaps because they feel their financial future is secure indefinitely, they would find it difficult to do so. Kinship is not something that is taken up or put down unilaterally, and the poor are reluctant to ignore a blood tie to a more comfortable present or to a secure future. As we pointed out earlier, those who have found security in the urban economy usually owe their success in no small measure to their family's support, and there are strong and lasting moral prescriptions to acknowledge these obligations.

Parental control and the lure of love

Change in traditional relationships started in the rural areas with the emancipation of those young adults who broke the monopoly on wisdom held by the old. A few years in school, a spell of employment or military service left them better equipped to deal with a new age than the knowledge transmitted by generations and a lifetime's experience in the village could have done. The young had some ability in the language used by the representatives of the new forces, whether they brought schools, churches, or dispensaries; whether they offered trade or employment in distant places; whether they demanded taxes or changes in agriculture. The young were more than interpreters of a foreign language; they also had some understanding of the new relationships entered into, an appreciation of the strength of the new powers, a vision of the future.[10]

The young men who went to work in the towns weakened the parent generation's exclusive control over economic resources.[11] In fact, the old frequently became dependent on the wage earnings of the young for the little luxuries of modern life that they had come to enjoy and sometimes became dependent even for their subsistence. In those cases where fathers had been expected to provide bridewealth for the marriage of their sons, it was now earned by the groom himself in labor migration.

It is not only the economic base of the parent generation's power that has been eroded; new values have been introduced simultaneously. Print, radio, and screen extol the overriding importance of love and challenge parental control over the selection of marriage partners. Janet E. Pool (1972, pp. 240f.) found a considerable difference in attitude between urban and rural women on this matter in Ghana and Upper Volta. A substantially higher percentage of urban respondents felt that both sons and daughters should be free to choose their own spouse. And, indeed, in an extensive survey among married women in two ethnic groups (one patrilineal, the other matrilineal) in the Ivory Coast in the early 1960s, those in Abidjan and two minor urban centers reported less frequently than those in rural areas that their husband had been selected by their parents (Clignet 1967, pp. 269f.).[12]

The emphasis on freedom in selecting a marriage partner increases the tension between generations. As one young man wrote to the advice column of a Ghana newspaper in the 1950s, "What can I tell my mother just to make her understand the word 'love and understanding in marriage'?" (Jahoda 1959, p. 181). In any case, free choice is increasingly important in partner selection; kin are excluded from the selection process or their numbers more restricted, and the significance of consultation reduced.

Love that promises emotional fulfillment within the conjugal family breaks husband and wife away from their respective kinship groups. As Goode puts it: "Strong love ties, like deep friendships, are often a nuisance and sometimes a disaster for others outside that dyad" (1973, p. 246). Gluckman (1955, pp. 57f.) also made specific note of the tension arising between husband and wife bound together in a relationship based on romantic love and the rest of the kin group, who stand outside this relationship. And Kenneth Little and Anne Price offer their insight into the process taking place:

Socialization in the traditional system has ingrained in each of its members a very deep sense of obligation and loyalty to kinsfolk in general. They have been brought up to give these attachments priority over all other interests . . . since deeply felt emotions persist, it is only by replacing familial feelings with an alternative and equally strong moral sentiment that many individuals who have been so reared can avoid an acute feeling of personal guilt.

This suggestion may explain why many of the younger men as well as the women find in the notion of love for a single partner a solution for their emotional dilemma. (1967, pp. 415f.)

The family in West Africa is adapting to the new physical and economic environment created by urbanization and also to a new environment of values involving the ideas of individual freedom and responsibility, a condition prescribed both by the relationship of individual contract in the market economy and by the modern idea of love. The realities of urban life, the probability of proximate personal crisis, and poverty in both city and country stand opposed to these notions of individuality. Security is a collective, not an individual, matter. Therefore, the extended family can be expected to continue to be an indispensable bridge between the individual's condition and his or her aspirations.

8 Changes in the position of women

It is traditional in Africa to regard marriage as an active association to which the woman has her daily contribution to make – an idea which is so recent in the West that it is still only accepted in some sections of society. Unaccustomed to relying on anyone but herself, the African woman will have no need to acquire a feeling of self-confidence, since she is already rarely without one.

Denise Paulme [(1960) 1963, p. 15]

Before a discussion of the position of women can be entered into, a question must be asked: Changes from what? What were the relative positions of the sexes in West Africa in the past? These positions may not have been subjected to evaluation in terms of "higher" and "lower" because frequently there was a strict division of labor between men and women. In the chapter epigraph, Denise Paulme emphasizes the self-assurance women used to enjoy in Africa. In some societies, role differentiation went so far as to create a considerable economic interdependence between the sexes. However, if we apply the criteria usually employed in stratification analysis, that is, power, wealth, and status, women can be seen in most societies to have enjoyed less of these than men.[1]

Forces for change

Western ideology, if not Western practice, has been a potent factor in changing the position of women in much of West Africa.[2] Most Christian missions propounded a doctrine of the equality of marriage partners, and schools taught both boys and girls. Print, radio. and screen extolled the overriding importance of love. When general suffrage was introduced toward the end of the colonial era, it was not "one man, one vote" but the vote for every adult.

Women thus found new aspirations, and men faced pressures to reform institutions, lest they be considered backward. These demands were articulated by the educated women.[3] The discussion on national legislation on marriage, maintenance of children, divorce, custody of children, and inheritance took account of world opinion. However, after lengthy debate, such legislation was not enacted in Ghana in the early 1960s (Vellenga 1971, pp. 141ff.); and the legislation that was passed in the Ivory Coast in 1964, although a radical departure from traditional norms in several respects, recognized the husband as the head of the household (Levasseur 1971, pp. 161f.).

Furthermore, there is the gap between law and practice. Alain A. Levasseur

135

(1971, p. 163) reports that family legislation decreed in 1939 and 1951 for what was then French West Africa and French Equatorial Africa failed completely in its purpose.[4] A survey conducted in 1967 by the Jeunesse Ouvrière Chrétienne among Ivory Coast youths aged thirteen to twenty-five revealed that many had never heard of the civil code passed three years earlier; among those who had, many indicated a continued preference for marriage according to customary law. Thus, even among the relatively educated young persons who had been reached by a Christian organization, the impact of the code was severely limited. In fact, Ivory Coast officials themselves expressed doubts concerning its actual effect (Levasseur 1971, p. 166).

The spread of modern methods of contraception is a major factor for change in the position of women. The very possibility of effective birth control gives women the prospect of greater power over their futures. Spouses are induced to agree on the number of children they desire. They may deliberate what method of contraception to adopt. Most important, to the extent that family size is effectively reduced, women are less bound by home and children and therefore in a better position to pursue career opportunities.

The position of women may well have improved, but as is generally true for the rest of the world, they certainly have not yet achieved equal status with men. Today, they are clearly lagging in the key areas of education and (as we will see) economic opportunity. In every West African country, women are underrepresented in the educational system (Table 8.1). In most countries, for every girl there are about two boys in primary school, though in five (Guinea-Bissau, Ghana, Nigeria, Sierra Leone, and Senegal) the proportion of girls enrolled at the first level is significantly higher. Although there is a tendency for the proportion of girls in primary schools to be higher in the countries with (relative to the total population) the larger student populations, several countries are at variance with this pattern, and a full explanation has to take into account the cultural, economic, and political contexts of education in individual countries.[5]

Along with dramatic increases in student enrollments the male–female ratio at the first level improved in most countries. The exceptions are The Gambia and Benin, where the ratios remained unchanged between 1965 and the early 1970s, and, most strikingly, Mauritania, where the proportion of girls in the first-level school population actually dropped three percentage points. Present underrepresentation at higher levels is a function of past underrepresentation at lower levels. However, this is only part of the explanation. In every country except Guinea-Bissau, the proportion of females at the second level is below that at the first level in 1965, the difference amounts to eight percentage points or more in the case of Mauritania, Senegal, Mali, Guinea, the Ivory Coast, and Ghana (UNESCO 1976, pp. 135ff. and 156ff.). Higher rates of attrition for female students thus emerge as the principal explanation for their low share in second-level enrollment in most countries.[6]

As the education stream contracts further from the second to the third level,

Table 8.1. *Student enrollments, totals and percent female, for West African countries, early 1970s*

Country (year)	First level[a] Total (thousands)	First level[a] Female	Second level[b] Total (thousands)	Second level[b] Female	Third level[c] Total (thousands)	Third level[c] Female	Students in total population
Mauritania (1971)	35	28%	4.4	12%[d]			3.3%
Senegal (1971)	270	39%	59.4[e]	28%[e]	6.7[f]	16%[f]	7.5%
The Gambia (1973)	21	29%	5.9	25%			5.4%
Mali (1974)	276	35%	11.3	18%[d]	0.7[e]	11%[e]	5.2%
Guinea-Bissau[g] (1971)	104[h]	44%[h]	8.1	41%			13.9%
Guinea (1971)	169	32%	68.4[d]	22%[d]	2.0[e]	8%[e]	4.8%
Sierra Leone (1971)	177	40%	37.6	29%	1.5[f]	15%[f]	7.9%
Liberia (1972)	139	34%	22.6	23%	1.4	24%	11.6%
Ivory Coast (1973)	606	37%[i]	94.3	24%	6.1	16%	11.5%
Upper Volta (1974)	134[i]	37%[i]	15.8[i]	30%[i]	0.4[f]	17%[f]	2.6%
Ghana (1973)	1,455[i]	43%[i]	94.8[j]	27%[j]	7.5	16%	16.6%
Togo (1974)	329	34%	48.4	23%	1.5[f]	13%[f]	17.4%
Benin (1973)	244	31%	40.8	28%	1.9	17%	9.7%
Niger (1973)	110	36%	11.1	26%	0.3	4%	2.8%
Nigeria (1973)	4,662	40%	516.7	33%	23.2	15%	7.3%

[a] Public and private schools.
[b] General, vocational, and teacher training in both public and private schools.
[c] Institutions of higher education such as universities, teacher-training colleges, and technical colleges, both public and private.
[d] General education only.
[e] Data for 1970.
[f] Data for 1973.
[g] Guinea-Bissau includes the Cape Verde Islands.
[h] Cape Verde Islands first-level enrollments data for 1972.
[i] Provisional data.
[j] Public education only.
Sources: First 6 columns from UNESCO (1976, pp. 135ff., 156ff., and 222ff.); the total population figures for the computation of column 7 were extrapolated from World Bank (1976a, p. 12).

women in every country but Liberia are even more severely underrepresented. Actually, the data on enrollments at the third level fail to fully reveal how inequal the share of women in higher education is. The third level comprises a wide range of institutions and women are likely to be disproportionately found at the lower-status programs. In addition, substantial numbers of West Africans continue to go overseas for higher education, and women have probably an even lower share of these opportunities. National comparisons are also distorted by the fact that the major West African universities are hosts to students from the entire region.

Western ideology, changes in the law, family planning, Western education – all make their strongest impact in the urban setting.[7] Not only are urban dwellers most exposed to these innovations, but an older generation that might oppose them is far away. Women have additional bargaining power in the towns because the sex imbalance allows them to be particular in selecting more or less permanent partners. Little (1965, pp. 133ff.) suggests that voluntary associations allow young women to get to know young men personally in a way that ordinarily might be very difficult; this facilitates an informed choice. Claude Meillassoux (1968, pp. 127ff.) reports that girls settled on permanent or semipermanent partners in neighborhood dancing associations in Bamako, even though marriage, for the girls, still depended largely on the parents' decision.

Women are probably better off in town than in rural areas in terms of relative female-to-male position. Still, the new economic opportunities in the urban areas are largely the preserve of men. Women hold only a small proportion of the positions in employment. In none of the three countries for which we have information does their share of employment reach even 15 percent (Table 8.2). Underrepresentation in employment in these countries is thus even more severe than underrepresentation at any level of the educational system. Only in sales and, most important, in professional and technical occupations are the participation rates of women similar to those in the secondary school system. It is ironic, then, when social scientists emphasize the attraction that life in town holds for rural women. The comment "It is hardly surprising that there should be a widespread desire among African women to exchange a village life of hard toil for an urban life of leisure" is surprising when it comes from so ardent a protagonist of the cause of women in developing countries as Ester Boserup (1970, p. 191). An emphasis on idleness appears misplaced when, in fact, many urban women are without gainful occupation, not out of choice, but because opportunities are woefully limited.

Urban opportunities for economic independence

Many women do eventually find a measure of economic independence in town. Some, especially those who have some formal education or training, obtain employment. Others resort to prostitution. However, the most widespread pat-

Table 8.2. *Economically active women, by occupational group, Sierra Leone, Liberia, Ghana, and Nigeria*

Occupational group	Sierra Leone, 1963		Liberia, 1962		Ghana, 1970		Nigeria, 1963	
	Total (thousands)	% of all such persons	Total (thousands)	% of all such persons	Total (thousands)	% of all such persons	Total (thousands)	% of all such persons
Employees	5	5%	4.3	7%	82	14%	n.a.	n.a.
Professional, technical, and related employees	2	29%	1.8	27%	24	23%	66[a]	15%[a]
Clerical employees	1	16%	0.6	13%	13	16%	22[b]	10%[b]
Sales employees	1	26%	0.3	13%	8	38%	n.a.	n.a.
Other employees	2	3%	1.7	4%	36	10%	n.a.	n.a.
Self-employed	22	23%	4.3	20%	537	73%	n.a.	n.a.
Self-employed traders	17	43%	3.0	37%	339	91%	1,692[c]	60%[c]
Other self-employed	5	10%	1.2	9%	199	55%	n.a.	n.a.
Family workers	6	42%	1.5	41%	24	81%	n.a.	n.a.
Family workers in trade	5	82%	0.6	62%	16	92%	n.a.	n.a.
Other family workers	2	18%	0.9	39%	8	66%	n.a.	n.a.
Unemployed	2[d]	8%[d]	n.a.	n.a.	57	29%	73	21%
Total outside farming, fishing, hunting, logging and related work	37	27%	10	11%	699	46%	3,440	42%
Total as proportion of women aged 15 and over		5.2%		3.1%		30.2%		21.6%

Notes: Some figures do not add because of rounding.
n.a. = not available.
[a] Includes professional, technical, and related self-employed and family workers.
[b] Includes self-employed and family clerical workers.
[c] Includes employees and family workers in sales.
[d] Persons not at work.
Source: International Labour Office (1973, pp. 11 and 150f.; 1975, pp. 10ff. and 162ff.).

tern is for women to secure some earnings from trade. Self-employed traders constitute close to a third of all women economically active outside agriculture in Liberia, close to half in Sierra Leone, Ghana, and Nigeria, the only countries for which data are available (Table 8.2).

The role of women in trade is particularly impressive in Ghana, where they hold more than nine-tenths of the positions, numbering over 300,000 in a predominantly rural population of less than 9 million in 1970. This is indeed the country of the "market mammies." As Miranda Greenstreet observes:

The market women have formed strong and effective associations for the protection of their commercial interests and the ventilation of their grievances. Some have become comparatively rich and have shown considerable business acumen. Many Ghanaian market women have gone on to assume more important business responsibilities, dealing in local produce or imports. Some run very prosperous concerns and have invested their profits in real estate. The influential position of market women was recognized by the government when they were given representation in the Constituent Assembly of 1968–69 which adopted the new Republican Constitution. (1971, p. 123)

In Ibadan, women trading in cloth have established associations for bulk buying to take advantage of quantity discounts or to combat the monopoly power of one or two expatriate firms selling to many small buyers. They also created exclusionary associations such as the Ibadan Women Block and Madras Association, which restricted the number of sellers of a particular type of cloth imported from India by charging a high initiation fee for membership (£5, or about $12) and by fining (same amount) those who attempted to sell without joining the association. A potential member had to have a sponsor and be approved by the group before she could join. Both economic and personal criteria entered the decision to accept a new member. Monthly dues amounted to 1s. (about $.12); additional money was collected for bulk buying of cloth and for assistance in court cases as necessary. Cloth traders were among the wealthiest traders and played an active role in Ibadan politics. Economic benefits for traders were exchanged for the market women's vote. However, when tensions in Western Nigeria increased over the 1963 census, the Federation of Ibadan Women Traders split from top to bottom, and united political action for the benefit of market women generally became impossible. Women with adjacent stalls no longer talked with one another (Remy 1968).

The successful woman trader, the merchant princess, is legendary throughout much of West Africa.[8] Her advance is facilitated by the absence of the kinds of restrictions on her control of land, houses, and goods that are found in many rural societies. But the very number of traders suggests both that competition is stiff and that the merchandise turnover of most is petty indeed.[9] A man interviewed in Enugu told Unokanma Okonjo that he gave his wife 1s. 8d., or (at that time) about $.25 to start trading. He explained:

When I give my wife one shilling and eight pence, she buys a basket of cassava [a staple food]. This she prepares and sells. At times she makes two pence, at times six pence [about seven cents]. It depends. From the cassava, she is able to reserve some: maybe we eat this, two times . . . three times . . . , then she makes another. You see? (1970, p. 125)

For married women, earnings have particular significance where there is a strict separation of resources between husband and wife. In central Lagos, Marris (1961, pp. 53f.) found most wives engaged in trade. Unless their parents had already provided them with the needed capital to set up stock, they expected it from their husbands. This money was often a wedding gift from the groom to the bride, one of the conditions of her consent. A wife's profit was her own, and she spent it mostly on personal needs, on their children, and in aiding her relatives. She might have helped her husband if he was in difficulty; in fact, the initial capitalization may be seen as his insurance or social security. But first and foremost, through her earnings, a wife secured economic independence that protected against the failure of her husband to support her. Here is Colette Le Cour Grandmaison's account from Dakar:

The economic position of Dakar women*

Let us rapidly recapitulate the historic evolution that led to the present-day economic independence of women within the household. In the rural context, the couple constituted a work unit, and the wife was responsible for the sale of produce. She obtained personal income, frequently minute, from the sale of the products of the small field she had cultivated or from the sale of fish her husband had presented her with, and she was completely free to use that small gain as she pleased. This custom is by no means peculiar to Dakar women but, on the contrary, is widely established in West African societies, as reported by numerous studies (Paulme 1952:116ff, Dupire and Boutillier 1958, Dupire 1960:50ff, Southall 1961:54, McCall 1961:287, Vincent 1966:168).

In the case of Lebou women, specific conditions – we retrace their historic evolution at length elsewhere [Grandmaison 1972: 158ff] – have unified the rule of devolution of assets that followed three different patterns in the old society. The maternal assets (land and cattle), left in trust with the maternal uncle or the oldest nephew, remained undivided. The paternal assets were shared; one-third was returned to the maternal line, and two-thirds were inherited by the children. The personal assets acquired by work or saving remained the property of each individual. In half a century, the total breakdown of the system of keeping the maternal assets intact was completed; cattle had disappeared among the Lebou, and land speculation, the appreciation of land values through market gardening, had led to the transformation of the rules governing the access to land.[1] A new law had confirmed individual property titles, provided that land and building lots were developed and that all assets, without exception, were inherited individually.

* Excerpt from Colette Le Cour Grandmaison, "Activités économiques des femmes Dakaroises," 1969, pp. 147–50, by permission of the author and the International African Institute. Based on research in 1964–5. Footnotes renumbered. Translation by Josef Gugler.

1 Colonial law specified for the agreement on the Tound area, the present city center, that "the attribution of the lots confers to the holders a personal right of occupation that can be transmitted only by inheritance. This right is transformed into a property title after a certain period of occupation and after development has been confirmed."

For all Dakar women, the Islamic rule that puts on the husband the entire responsibility for the support of the family and that makes the obligation unconditional has reinforced their independence in the utilization of their gains or of the assets acquired through their work. "We have to remember that the Koran imposes on the husband the charge to completely maintain his wife and his children, whatever his poverty, whatever the wealth of his wife; furthermore it gives the married woman the independent control over her personal assets" (Tillion 1966:169). In the contemporary context, there is thus no legal obligation whatsoever for a wife to contribute to household expenses; the income from her work is recognized as inalienably hers, to be used at her pleasure.

The women take advantage of their legal position to keep their gains separate from the family budget. This norm can certainly be transgressed for various reasons, but even in such an eventuality, the woman's assistance remains conditional – that is, it is given if the husband momentarily faces difficulty finding work and suspended as soon as he is again assured of regular income. This holds for all women, whatever the source of their income.

The share of receipts taken by women in the sale of the products of fishing and gardening varies according to the agreement reached by the couple. It can be a modest sum if the wife wishes to help her husband; it can be a very important part if a contract is established between husband and wife. There are thus different types of contracts concerning sales: Either the husband gives his wife his entire production and they share the income equally, or the wife evaluates the approximate income she can expect from the sale, pays her husband a fixed sum, and keeps the surplus.

Estimates of the income derived from sales allow an appreciation of their importance. The receipts calculated for vegetable sellers according to their daily turnover varies from 360,000 to 540,000 Fr CFA.** If taxes and delivery charges estimated at 60,000 Fr CFA are deducted, the lowest annual net income of a vegetable seller is about 360,000 Fr CFA.

Fishmongers, on average, have a higher daily turnover than vegetable sellers. The average gross annual income of fishmongers is about 450,000 Fr CFA, or a daily income between 1,000 and 2,000 Fr CFA, but it can reach 5,000 to 10,000 Fr CFA, which then carries the gross annual income of certain women beyond 1 million Fr CFA. If we retain the average figure of 450,000 Fr CFA, the annual net income of a fishmonger, after deduction of taxes and delivery charges, comes to about 400,000 Fr CFA.

A sales contract between a man and his wife thus assures her of gains that are certainly not negligible. Yet, it is not the most remarkable type of contract as far as the economic results and the implications for the couple are concerned. The contract established between the wife who owns a pirogue and her fisherman–husband is even more notable.

In fishing, certain women have been able to acquire the means of production because of the substantial income obtained from the sale of the catch and the role of intermediary that some play. The many women on the peninsula who own pirogues, occasionally entrust use of the vessels to their husbands.[2] They apply, then, without modification, the rules established in fishing for the division of the catch between employer and employee. These rules apply either to the catch, which is shared daily, or

** At that time, 1,000 Fr CFA were equivalent to U.S. $4.

2 "Occasionally" because certain women prefer to entrust this exploitation to a member of their lineage, most frequently their brothers.

to the receipts realized from the sale of the catch, which are accounted for at the end of the run.

We will present two of the instances of these types of contract that we encountered during our enquiries.

Magatte M., living in Grand Dakar, is the owner of a pirogue equipped with an engine; her husband uses it, and she sells the total catch at Sandaga every day, with the proceeds of the sale to be shared with her husband. She states: "If there is a big catch, I make from 10,000 to 15,000 Fr CFA a day. If it's smaller, I make 5,000 Fr CFA." We can estimate the couple's gross annual income to be 1,500,000 Fr CFA (200 catches, at 7,500 Fr CFA each), half of it her share; whereas the husband is responsible for the subsistence of the family, which numbers seven, including five children. The gains accruing to her allowed her to replace the old sailing pirogue, inherited from her father, with a new motor pirogue.

Awa G. is the owner of three motorized pirogues and their fishing nets. Her husband, to whom she has given the use of one of the pirogues, goes out to sea with a crew of three men. The shares are allocated as follows: one part for the owner of the pirogue, one part for the owner of the net, one part for the owner of the engine, and one part apiece for the four fishers. Thus, of these seven parts, Awa G., as the owner of the boat, the engine, and the nets, retains for herself three, whereas her husband gets only one. If the net annual income from a motorized pirogue is estimated at about 1,400,000 Fr CFA, Awa G. has a net income of 600,000 Fr CFA a year at her disposal, whereas her husband has only 200,000 Fr CFA. As the owner of three motor-pirogues, she has an income of more than 1.5 million Fr CFA, which has permitted her to acquire, among other investments, a minibus and a taxi that run for her account in Dakar.

Certainly, these are exceptional cases, that is women with very high incomes who, furthermore, strictly apply the separation of resources between husband and wife. They nevertheless give an indication of the economic independence of married women and explain the importance of the investments that certain women traders have made in motor transport, in house construction, or in the means of production. Such women are a minority, but they utilize their double affiliation with the old social organization and the modern economic sector in surprising ways. Depending on their goals, these women concurrently follow a policy of sociological and of economic investments (Balandier 1960:11) that makes them akin to entrepreneurs in many respects. They ensure their social integration by agreeing to prestige expenses and exploit, when it is within their reach, transformations of the organization of production to their advantage.

Magatte N., a market gardener in the peninsula, is an outstanding example. She personally supervises four Sérère laborers who work on her land throughout the year. She is in charge of selling the produce on the Dakar markets and has contracted with a school in M'Bour to supply fresh vegetables. Recently, she has granted herself the prestige of a pilgrimage to Mecca, from which she returned with jewelry that she sold at very good prices. She has acquired two taxis and a building lot on which rental construction is going up. . . .

Thus, these women, less absorbed than the men in the sumptuous expenses of social and ceremonial life,[3] patiently accumulate, under the cover of

3 An uninterrupted process of expenses is incurred by the men: payment of bridewealth, marriage, baptism, arrival of the wife in the conjugal home.

custom and of their legal right, a capital that allows them to acquire the means of production and eventually to transform a husband into a salaried employee – quite a paradox in this society, where the men hold authority in law and the women enjoy uncontested power in fact.

Claude Tardits (1963, pp. 274ff.) also emphasizes the independence illiterate women in Porto-Novo find in trade. He contrasts this with the dependency experienced by educated wives who stay at home. For Ghana, Dorothy Dee Vellenga (1971, pp. 148f.) reports that no legislator, man or woman, would be prepared to come out in favor of community property within marriage. Very few husbands let their wives know their total income. For her part, the wife is free to control and invest her capital as she wishes. Even some of the most militant women Vellenga interviewed were ambivalent concerning the idea of a common budget. Some attributed the continued viability of their marriages to the fact that the partners had not pooled their resources. With the wife's and the husband's relatives making different demands regarding school fees, funeral contributions, and the like, community property would create considerable difficulty. There were further problems in relation to inheritance, children outside the marriage, and other wives.[10]

In the Ivory Coast, the new civil code established a matrimonial regime in which the earnings and incomes of the spouses are community property. The survey by the Jeunesse Ouvrière Chrétienne that we referred to earlier in this chapter found this to be one of the most favored aspects (Levasseur 1971, pp. 162 and 166). In Upper Volta, most educated couples adopt community property at the time of marriage. However, few such ménages à deux survive the strains of competing demands from their respective families of orientation or of the husband getting involved in extramarital affairs or marrying a second wife. Most ménages à deux break up sooner or later, leaving in their wake an almost armed economic truce between husband and wife. Thereafter, the men provide the basic economic needs for their households; and the women, like their mothers in the rural areas, use their own resources to give extra help to their children. Women often become economically quite independent of their husbands; they start their own bank accounts, and some manage to build houses that they then rent (Skinner 1974, pp. 163f.).

The urban couple

Whatever his views, many a man who wants a woman to live permanently with him in town has to accept that she will gain a degree of economic independence because his earnings will be insufficient to support a family in urban conditions. However, conflict is rife. There is some evidence that women tend to be quicker than men to embrace innovations that promise to improve their position. In a sample of literate persons in Porto-Novo in the early 1950s, men overwhelmingly intended to keep their young children in case of marital breakup, which is in accordance with the patrilineal custom.[11] However, a sizable minority of women thought that their sons ought to stay with them, and a majority thought that their daughters should remain. Also, although the majority of men felt that girls should have a smaller part in succession than men, the majority of women pleaded for equal division (Tardits 1958, pp. 51, 68ff., 113, and 118). The stage is thus set for a radicalization of women. In a survey of the senior students in a sample of secondary and teacher-training institutions throughout Ghana in the late 1950s, women were found to be more radical than men on the subject of marriage and the family. They were more set against polygamy; they took a stronger view against inheritance from the maternal uncle; they were more determined to provide for their offspring themselves, rather than to rely on others; and they would rather be married in church than in any other way (Omari 1960, p. 207).[12]

Among the elite, with whom the ideology of the conjugal family based on the Euro-American ideal has taken root most strongly, the new expectations can lead to severe interpersonal tensions and frustrations between husband and wife. Of twelve families studied in depth by Oppong (1974, pp. 147f.), half were characterized as being "tense" relationships. In five of the six, the wife complained of deprivation or dissatisfaction, citing the "Euro-American ideal." Areas of disappointment that were commonly referred to involved the sharing of tasks, responsibilities, and leisure activities. Husbands who mentioned the model selected features such as loyalty and dependence in the role of the wife. Each partner's references were selective; they were not opting for the entire model. However, where the wife had educational or important economic assets of her own, her share in decisionmaking improved and husbands took a greater part in household chores and child care (Oppong 1974, pp. 121f.).

If demands for emancipation constitute one source of conflict, another source of stress arises out of the fact that many women remain more shielded from the rapid changes in urban Africa than their husbands are. First of all, discrimination in education means a considerable educational gap between most spouses. Second, women, tied as they are to the home because of child rearing and household chores, tend to be more restricted to their neighborhood than men. This is especially true if they have no occupational or other roles outside the neighborhood. Finally, the interchange between spouses that might compensate for unequal exposure to change tends to be limited. Peter C. Lloyd (1967, pp. 145ff.) reports that in Ibadan, husband and wife spend little leisure time together, even in elite families. Women share few close friendships with their husbands, and each spouse spends much of the nonworking day visiting or entertaining his or her own friends in exclusively male or female gatherings. We should not be surprised, then, if there are sharp differences in attitudes toward modern changes and, consequently, severe stresses within the marital relationship.

Some women in Muslim areas live literally secluded lives. In Hausa cities, the wives of the traditional ruling class experience the most restrictive form of marriage, *auren kulle,* in which a woman may never go outside the confines of her husband's compound. In such a household, many of the normal household duties are carried on by servants, and social contacts and common interests between husband and wife are at a minimum. During the colonial period, the educated personnel in clerical and technical capacities formed a new elite group. Rachel Yeld (1964) reports that they firmly adopted the status symbols of the aristocracy, particularly in their emphasis on Moslem rather than Western culture, including a strict conformity to Islamic custom on the seclusion of wives and general attitudes toward the position of women. Dorothy Remy (1975b, p. 363) found that the wives of unskilled workers at a factory in Zaria were in *auren tsare,* a form of marriage involving partial seclusion which allows the wife to visit her relatives and to attend the health clinc when it becomes necessary. However, in the households of the two men Remy knew who had been promoted to skilled jobs, the conditions of total seclusion had been imposed on the youngest wife because now these men could afford it.[13]

It has been suggested that the urban couple are more dependent on each other for carrying out familial tasks and for emotional support and that this mutual dependence will encourage a greater degree of equality (Plotnicov 1962, p. 101). However, such an assumption – that more joint relationships imply more equal relationships – requires scrutiny. The overall inequality between the sexes would seem to stand in the way of conjugal equality. First, the statuses assigned to men and women in the society at large presumably have a bearing on their relative position within the family. Second, educated men usually marry women with less or no formal education. Third, the general theme of male dominance is reinforced by the fact that most women get married quite young to men who are several years their elders. Typically, though, women in town wield increased control over the day-to-day affairs of the household. With the separation of workplace and home, most husbands are away for much of the day, leaving to their wives the running of the home and the education of the children.[14]

Two policy issues

For the governments of the new nations of West Africa, two policy matters concerning women stand out. One revolves around the position of women in the family. It remains to be seen how effectively lawmakers can legislate in the sphere of personal status. As Aristide R. Zolberg observes:

Such activities as the registration of births and deaths, the enforcement of rules concerning marriage and divorce, the definition of personal rights, the inheritance of property, the regulation of work, are clearly important areas of policy-making . . . It is therefore highly significant to note that the activities of the West African party–state in this entire sphere are extremely limited. The regime is concerned with extending its authority in this direction by making laws that will affect these activities, but of course, there is a vast difference between the staking of a claim to do so and the genuine operation of allocative authority. Yet . . . we know that rules exist, that they are enforced, that they undergo change, that conflicts occur, and that they are settled, hence that the political system allocates values authoritatively in this sphere. (1966, p. 133)

The other issue concerns the access women have to education and career opportunities. Frequently, a lack of political initiative thinly veils a policy of discrimination.[15] Continued discrimination is an insult to aspirations for sexual equality, to which much lip service is paid. Furthermore, unequal access to economic opportunities in the urban setting imposes heavy costs on societies that seem so contented with the status quo. Families are separated, and/or a large segment of the population is dependent on urban services but constrained from realizing its potential contribution to the urban economy.

Many urban workers have left their wives and children in their rural home areas. The costs of such separation are difficult to assess. One indication is the high rates of labor turnover that were common until quite recently. With unemployment widespread, those fortunate enough to secure a job cling to it. What used to be an economic cost to employers has become a social cost to employees; high labor turnover has been replaced by an additional strain put on the relationship between the worker and his family. Another cost of separation is increasingly in evidence; venereal disease is one of the major medical problems in urban areas. Unbalanced sex ratios constitute a principal cause inasmuch as they encourage short-lived unions and prostitution.

We have discussed the constraints that motivate rural–urban migrants to maintain strong ties with their areas of origin and frequently to leave their wives and children there (see Chapter 4). Clearly, more women would join their husbands if the urban economy offered women earning opportunities that compensated for rural income.

Where men do bring their families to town, the women have only limited or no opportunity to contribute to the urban economy. Most women become economically inactive or join the already overcrowded ranks of petty traders. There is not only a loss of rural income forgone by such families, or, to the extent that they are compensated by profits from trading, a reduction in the business of other traders, but also a considerable cost to the national economy. If women were fully integrated into the urban economy, a smaller population would have to be accommodated in urban centers to perform the same economic tasks. Accordingly a lower investment would be required in infrastructure, major elements of which are notably more expensive than their rural equivalents (especially housing and sewerage).[16] As Boserup points out:

Villagers in developing countries usually build their own homes of local materials, supply themselves with water, light and fuel, arrange their own local transport . . .

In towns, by contrast, public investment budgets are burdened by investment costs to provide migrant families with dwellings, light, water, sanitation, schools, hospitals, etc. . . . If employment is provided for both men and women from immigrant families, this investment for infrastructure will be lower per person employed, and if employment is given only to hitherto idle wives and daughters of families already living in the towns, little additional infrastructure will be needed. (1970, pp. 206ff.)

In short, sex discrimination in the urban setting carries high costs. Urban dwellers bear the cost in terms of the separation of their families, and nations pay for the additional urban infrastructure required for the underemployed wives of the predominantly male work force.

9 Stratification and social mobility

Class contradictions in independent Africa are less dramatic than in Southern Africa and many areas of the underdeveloped world. Moreover, they are blurred by racial, ethnic, and nationalist dimensions which hamper the development of subjective conditions favorable to radical change. The development of a rural proletariat and of an urban lumpenproletariat will steadily restructure this situation, but for some time to come class antagonisms are unlikely to contribute in a determinant way to the internal dynamics of independent Africa.

Giovanni Arrighi and John S. Saul [(1969) 1973, p. 84]

The degree of stratification varied greatly among the precolonial societies of West Africa. Many societies knew little occupational differentiation and minimal concentration of political power. This was frequently the case in stateless societies such as those of most Ibo peoples. Elsewhere, the political hierarchies of centralized states displayed marked inequalities. Their rulers were held in high esteem, controlled considerable resources, and at times, had arbitrary power over life and death. Such states were particularly important in the Sudanic belt.[1]

Political organization was the nearly exclusive determinant of stratification. Craft specialists were important in West Africa, and its traders are justly famous. However, they did not establish a power base in juxtaposition to that of the political authorities. We may speculate about the difficulties of storing wealth and the technological limitations on converting wealth into productive capital, but the general pattern is clear: "The predominant tendency has been for political structures to dominate and enclose economic ones and hence for authority to be the principal basis for stratification" (Fallers 1964, p. 120).

Political power meant control over people. A surplus could be extracted from them for the court; they could be made to man the military expeditions. However, land was not scarce on the whole, and disaffected subjects could simply pick up and move away. The support of the lieutenants, in turn, was based on little else but personal loyalty. Wealth had to be redistributed in a bid for support. In these circumstances, stratification, where it was pronounced, was usually accompanied by a high degree of mobility.

Transmission of power and wealth to descendants was particularly difficult. In some societies, political office could not be inherited.[2] Invariably, persons of high status had many wives and numerous offspring, with the result that in each generation, there were many more elite children than could possibly inherit their parents' status. Rival claims to succession and the dispersal of wealth in the effort to rally personal followings were typical.

149

Thus, turnover in elite membership was usually substantial. Slaves moving into high office provide the most striking instance; slaves were appointed as generals to command standing armies by the Fulani rulers of Zaria between 1870 and 1880 (Smith 1959, p. 242). Different status groups were further bound together by a network of intermarriage. Ruling groups in the major states were rarely, if ever, endogamous. In the kingdom of Gonja, in northern Ghana, there was so little objection to low marriage that a Gonja prince remarked to a social anthropologist that "all our mothers were slaves" (Goody 1971, pp. 588ff.).

Mobility and intermarriage were facilitated by the fact that cultural differentiation between social strata was limited. Elite subcultures lacked the technology of writing that would underpin a "great tradition." In Bornu, language, dress, and house style were visible symbols of status. However, these qualities were imitable. Commoners could buy the voluminous robes worn by the elite. An upwardly mobile person could, with some effort, pronounce words as the elite did and drop from his conversation the ribaldry and slightly profane exclamations that colored and punctuated the speech of peasants and low-status people in general. If he acquired the means, the mobile person could live in a larger, better-built house with more dependents and more clients (Ronald Cohen 1970).

Integration with the population at large and dependency on personal followings impeded tendencies for the elite to form a distinct class. For example, even within the Yoruba town, the elite did not form a social group. They stood individually at the apexes of groups consisting of kin and followers, and most of their interaction was within these groups. Common interests did not bind the prestigious in distinction from, or opposition to, the masses (Peter C. Lloyd 1966b, pp. 331ff.).

International stratification

The problems facing mankind today call for a world society, but we are still living in a world of nation-states. This world system is characterized by severe inequalities among nations in terms of economic resources, political power, and cultural influence. The General Assembly of the United Nations is based on one country, one vote; but the permanent members of the Security Council, with their veto power, are recognized as major powers. The present designation of permanent members is an anachronism dating back to the end of World War II, but it is significant that neither Latin America nor Africa has been in a position to challenge effectively a situation that relegates all their countries to small-power status.

The nations of West Africa are among the poorest of the world. In addition, they have experienced balkanization twice. First, the region was carved up among European powers toward the end of the nineteenth century. The

Gambia would emerge with a population base that has grown to less than 600,000 people today; Guinea-Bissau finds itself with less than 1 million, Liberia with less than 1.8 million. Then, with Independence, the disintegration of French West Africa left behind nine sovereign countries, their populations ranging from 1.4 to 7.5 million today (Table 2.2). The countries of West Africa thus carry very little weight when bargaining with industrialized countries. The boost their position received from the East–West rivalry was limited, although it played some role in the support that the Federal Government was able to mobilize in the Nigerian Civil War.

The prestige of West African countries is narrowly circumscribed by their poverty and lack of power. Concern with prestige would seem to be reflected in the considerable resources sunk into industrial showpieces and the good looks of capital cities, enterprises that are best described as "conspicuous investment." In cultural terms, however, the position of West Africa has improved, with a fresh appreciation of its rich heritage; more recently, West African writers and artists have gained international recognition.

In the 1950s, Ghana attracted attention with Kwame Nkrumah's call for African unity. However, the Guinea–Ghana–Mali union initiated in 1959 never made much progress, and this chapter of Pan-Africanism came to a close when Nkrumah was deposed by the military in February 1966. In recent years, Guinea-Bissau, Liberia, the Ivory Coast, and Ghana have stood out among the West African countries by virtue of per capita incomes roughly five times those of several of their poorer neighbors (see the map preceding p. 1). Most recently, Nigeria is the state that has gained prominence. The sheer weight of its numbers, close to 80 million according to the latest estimate, easily outnumbering the combined populations of the other fourteen countries of West Africa, seems to predestine it for a major role in the region and, in fact, the entire continent. Added to the potential of this population base is the promise of Nigeria's petroleum resources. The remarkable success of the Organization of Petroleum Exporting Countries has further strengthened Nigeria in terms of both economic resources becoming available for industrialization and an enhanced stature at the negotiating table.

National stratification systems

The economic condition of African peasants and workers is largely determined by their position in the world economy. However, their political activity is confined within the states of which they are members, and understandably, the current popular perception of stratification tends to be limited to the national scene (Wallerstein 1973). Here, the masses experience income inequalities more glaring than those that characterize rich countries. The distribution of incomes recorded for taxpayers in Western Nigeria, although subject to serious qualifications with regard to its accuracy, provides some illustration (Table

9.1).[3] This highly unequal income distribution remains virtually unaffected by taxation. Although the nominal income tax rate structure in Western Nigeria is progressive, relief is granted to those earning more than £300, and the progressiveness of the tax is thus much diminished (Teriba and Philips 1971, pp. 91ff.).[4]

Stratification in the countries of West Africa can be seen as a three-tier structure. The urban elite enjoys a living standard similar to that of the middle class in rich countries. This elite is very small; in Western Nigeria, in 1966–7, it was made up of those 0.7 percent of income-tax payers who had incomes of over £700 and enjoyed 12 percent of the total income recorded.[5] Although few in numbers, the elite is highly visible. Along with foreign experts and tourists, its members shape the aspirations of the urban masses, aspirations these low-income earners are unable to fulfill. However, a major sector of the urban masses, those above the level of unskilled labor who are steadily employed in the regulated sector, appear privileged when compared with the majority of peasants. Rural incomes are difficult to estimate, but continued rural–urban migration in spite of the threat of urban unemployment bears living evidence to the attraction that urban employment holds for the rural masses.

This three-tier model of elite, urban employed, and rural masses represents a rather high level of generalization. The fit between rural–urban residence and income is not so neat. In Chapter 3, we looked at the growing urban *lumpenproletariat*. In some rural areas, on the other hand, farmers are long established in cash cropping and enjoy a standard of living that compares well with that of urban workers. In other places, a landed bourgeoisie has emerged. We will return to it when we explore the composition of national elites in the next section.

The three-tier structure is not just an economic one. It corresponds to the reality of political power. In most countries, political power lies with the elite or a section of it. As elections become meaningless or are no longer held, the peasants are without a voice. The urban workers, however, present an incipient threat to those in power.

Trade-union demands usually have political implications because government is the most important employer and the allocation of public resources is at stake. However, the power of trade unions is rather limited in every West African country. Trade unions are integrated into the party, as in Guinea and in Nkrumah's Ghana; their functions are narrowly circumscribed and their demands subject to compulsory arbitration and conciliation procedures, as in the Ivory Coast; or they are so weak that their autonomy does not constitute a threat to the government, as in Nigeria. Only in Sierra Leone did unions closely cooperate with an opposition party that subsequently gained power (Robin Cohen 1974, pp. 252ff.).[6]

On the other hand, the basis of support for political leaders is invariably so

Table 9.1. *Recorded income distribution of taxpayers in Western Nigeria, 1966–7*

Income range[a]	Persons		Gross income		Disposable income	
	number	percent	£ (thousands)[a]	percent	£ (thousands)[a]	percent
£1–50	541,853	62.76%	26,517	39.7%	24,920	39.7%
£51–100	226,313	26.21%	13,654	20.4%	12,801	20.4%
£101–200	50,277	5.82%	6,550	9.8%	6,116	9.8%
£201–300	23,398	2.71%	5,520	8.3%	5,115	8.2%
£301–500	11,768	1.36%	4,369	6.5%	4,149	6.6%
£501–700	3,510	0.41%	2,026	3.0%	1,943	3.1%
£701–900	2,106	0.24%	1,664	2.5%	1,602	2.6%
£901–1,100	1,227	0.14%	1,214	1.8%	1,163	1.9%
£1,101–1,500	1,333	0.15%	1,725	2.6%	1,636	2.6%
£1,501–2,000	737	0.09%	1,224	1.8%	1,131	1.8%
£2,001–2,300	266	0.03%	557	0.9%	522	0.8%
£2,301–3,300	458	0.05%	1,231	1.8%	1,090	1.7%
£3,301–4,300	81	0.01%	308	0.5%	264	0.4%
Above 4,300	51	0.01%	289	0.4%	224	0.4%
Total[b]	863,378	100.00%	66,868	100.0%	62,716	100.0%

Note: Two major limitations of these data are that they do not cover the whole range of assumed income earners in Western Nigeria and that by all accounts the incidence of tax evasion and avoidance is high.
[a] The official exchange rate was 1N £ = US $2.80 in 1966–7.
[b] Because of rounding percent do not necessarily add up to 100.
Source: Statistical Abstract of Western Nigeria 1968 (Ministry of Economic Planning and Reconstruction, Ibadan), reproduced by Teriba and Philips (1971, p. 92).

limited that they cannot survive the chaos that concerted strike action creates in the major cities, especially in the capital. Strike funds are virtually nonexistent, but as we noted in Chapter 4, in most countries, the bulk of the urban workers can fall back on rural subsistence. A strike by dock or railroad workers paralyzes economies that are heavily dependent on imports and on the receipts from exports. Miners occupy a similarly critical position in countries such as Mauritania and Liberia. Once strikers take to the streets, they are joined by petty self-employed and unemployed, and the stage for rioting is set. A minor incident can trigger violence and looting. The armed forces have to be called in to control the crowds, and they are likely to decide to control government as well. Given this precarious position of party governments as distinct from military governments, their efforts have to focus on co-opting the leadership of urban workers and on reducing the income disparity between themselves and urban labor.[7] The economic gap between the urban and the rural sector is thus further exacerbated.

In terms of prestige, the system of national stratification is less clear-cut. The political elites of West Africa reside in the major urban centers. Peasants flock to the cities in the search for employment. Therefore, the assumption that urban residence generally carries higher prestige than rural residence comes easily. This is not borne out by the few inquiries into the prestige of occupations that covered both rural and urban occupations (Foster 1965, pp. 268ff.; Clignet and Foster 1966, pp. 146ff.; Ronald Cohen 1970, pp. 247ff.; and Peil 1973, p. 207).[8]

The elite

The privileged position of the elite stands out starkly against the background of the standard of living of the population at large. The private car has become the symbol of elite status in societies in which most people can barely afford a bicycle. If wealth were distributed with perfect equity, there would be no passenger cars whatsoever; all motor transport would be by bus or truck. And, indeed, very few passenger cars are found in West Africa, only about 2 for every 1,000 people in 1969 (Table 9.2). However, passenger cars were much more widespread in Senegal, The Gambia, Sierra Leone, and the Ivory Coast, with rates ranging from 6 to 9 per 1,000. Road mileage built and its condition through the seasons differ greatly among West African countries, and so does the availability of railroads. The ratio of passenger cars to commercial vehicles eliminates some of these differences to the extent that both types of transport are dependent on roads. This ratio is relatively high in Senegal, Ghana, Benin, and Nigeria, where it reaches about 1.7, and especially high in Sierra Leone, where it reaches 2.8. Since the middle 1950s, just prior to Independence, the stock of passenger cars has expanded dramatically in most West African countries, with only Nigeria the conspicuous exception, and

Table 9.2. *Passenger cars and commercial vehicles in West African countries, 1956 and 1969*

Country	Passenger cars[a] 1956 (thousands)	1969	percent increase 1956–69	Commercial vehicles[b] 1956 (thousands)	1969	percent increase 1956–69	Ratio of passenger cars to commercial vehicles, 1969
Mauritania	0.1	4.2	4,100%	0.8	5.2	550%	0.8
Senegal	12.8	36.0	181%	11.3	21.4	89%	1.7
The Gambia	0.5	2.5	400%	0.9	2.0	122%	1.3
Mali	1.8	4.5	150%	3.7	5.7	54%	0.8
Guinea	3.0	8.0	167%	4.8	12.0	150%	0.7
Sierra Leone	3.0	21.2	607%	1.8	7.7	328%	2.8
Ivory Coast	7.5	47.0	527%	12.7	33.0	160%	1.4
Upper Volta	0.8	5.8	625%	2.2	6.3	186%	0.9
Ghana	13.4[c]	34.2	155%[c]	14.9[c]	19.2	29%[c]	1.8
Togo	0.9[c]	5.9	556%[c]	1.7[c]	4.5	165%[c]	1.3
Benin	1.6	11.2	600%	2.8	6.7	139%	1.7
Niger	0.6	3.8	533%	2.0	5.0	150%	0.8
Nigeria	23.5	42.8	82%	17.4	25.6	47%	1.7

Note: Military vehicles and vehicles operated by police or other government security organizations are excluded unless otherwise indicated.
[a] Passenger cars include taxis, jeeps, and station wagons.
[b] Commercial vehicles include vans, trucks, buses, tractors, and semi-trailer combinations.
[c] Vehicles operated by police or other government security organizations are included in 1956 figures, and 1956–69 increases are understated to that extent.
Sources: United Nations (1966, pp. 428ff.; 1976b, pp. 411ff.).

much more rapidly than the stock of commercial vehicles in all countries but Guinea.[9]

A decade ago, the term "elite" referred primarily to two somewhat distinct groups: senior civil servants and politicians. But in December 1965, the army took over in Benin, an experience that was repeated in six other West African countries within three years: in Upper Volta (1966), Nigeria (1966), Ghana (1966), Togo (1967), Sierra Leone (1967), and Mali (1968). The officer corps of the army, and to a lesser extent the police, came to be recognized as a third elite group. Finally, two other groups share the affluence, if not the power, of the elite: the businessmen and the emerging landed interests.

Concern about elite privileges used to center on the senior civil service. Here, privilege came to West Africans when they started assuming senior positions previously held by colonial officers. They obtained the same salaries and most of the perquisites that had been given to nationals of rich countries to induce them to work in the tropics. Any attempt to reduce such privileges spawned charges of racial discrimination. In Nigeria, the faculty at Ibadan University College provided the example for the country at large. An "expatriation allowance" that gave non-Nigerians a total salary approximately one-third higher than that of Nigerians drew such criticism that it was abolished in 1950, along with other differences in travel, leave, and fringe benefits. Nigerian staff were granted annual "home leave" to Britain on the same terms as the British, and the expatriation allowance was consolidated into a new, higher "basic salary" that was given to all staff, regardless of nationality (van den Berghe 1973, p. 20). The result is that a full professor earns almost thirty times as much as an unskilled worker. So does the permanent secretary (Teriba and Philips 1971, p. 97). The pattern is well illustrated by the salary scales in the Nigerian civil service, which are closely related to formal educational qualifications (Table 9.3).

The position in the former French colonies is somewhat different in that the lower grades of the civil service are better paid. In consequence, salary differentials within the civil service are more limited, and employment here is strongly preferred to the private sector. The clerk in commerce is a civil servant manqué (Skinner 1974, p. 50). Formal educational qualifications put an even stricter ceiling on opportunities for advancement than in the former British colonies, as is illustrated by the salary scales for the Upper Volta civil service (Table 9.4).

The bureaucratic elite can be described as a mandarinate. Claim to office is based overwhelmingly on having passed certain examinations in a highly formalized system of education. As in the classical case of the Chinese mandarin

Table 9.3. *Salary scales for civil service in Nigeria, 1966*

Educational standard	Minimum years required to obtain qualification	Entry point[a]	Ceiling[a]
University honors degree	16	£720	£1,584
University pass degree	16	648	1,584
Higher School Certificate (or GCE A level)	13	336	1,584
West African School Certificate (or GCE O level)	11	198	828
Secondary IV	10	156	397
Primary School Leaving Certificate	6	129	246

[a] The official exchange rate was 1 N£ = U.S. $2.80 in 1966.
Source: Report of grading team on the grading of posts in the Public Services of the Federation of Nigeria (Ministry of Information, Lagos 1966); reproduced by Teriba and Philips (1971, p. 99).

Table 9.4. *Salary scales for civil service in Upper Volta, 1967*

Educational standard	Minimum years required to obtain qualification	Entry point[a]	Ceiling[a]
Doctorate, graduate diploma, or professional school		CFA 727,500	CFA 1,940,000
Master's degree		582,000	1,155,000
Baccalauréat	13	426,800	1,008,800
Brevet d'études du premier cycle	10	291,000	582,000
Certificat d'études primaires élémentaires	6	194,000	407,400

[a] In 1967, 1,000 Fr CFA were equivalent to U.S. $4.
Source: Projet de classement indiciaire et échelle des traitements (Ministère du Travail et de la Fonction Publique, Républic de Haute-Volta, 1967); reproduced by Skinner (1974, p. 49).

trained in the Confucian tradition, the Western system of formal education to which West Africans have been exposed bears little relationship to the tasks of governance. New recruits are highly selected in terms of intellectual ability, but their energies have been directed to studies in an esoteric and recondite intellectual tradition that bears very little relationship to the realities of their society. In a sense, the problem of relevance is further aggravated in West Africa because that intellectual tradition is not only esoteric but entirely alien (van den Berghe 1973, pp. 59f. and 112).

In recent years there have been reductions in the salaries and fringe benefits of senior civil servants in several countries; their real incomes have been eroded by rising prices everywhere, especially by heavy import duties imposed on most of the imported goods they consume. But policies designed to curtail the incomes of civil servants face the opposition of a powerful interest group. Civil servants threatened with salary cuts and increased taxes played a major part in bringing down governments in Benin and Upper Volta (Skinner 1974, pp. 431ff.). Clement Cottingham (1974) emphasizes as a key variable in these coups the institutionalized autonomy bestowed on civil servants in countries with a French civil service tradition as against the situation in the English-speaking countries where political rights of their associations are not recognized. However, we also note that Benin and Upper Volta are among the poorest countries in the region and that the conflict over the allocation of scarce resources between administrative apparatus and development projects must be particularly severe.

An incomes policy for senior civil servants also has to cope with the contingency that the best-qualified may be tempted away to more affluent labor markets. The brain drain, a problem of long standing in many parts of Asia, is coming to be of major concern in West Africa, too. To prohibit the emigration of professionals, quite apart from the political undesirability and problems of enforcement, would discourage the return of those studying abroad. The only alternative appears to be to restructure professional training. Judicious cuts in the imported systems of training and a stronger emphasis on local conditions would produce a greater number of professionals whose skills would be more immediately relevant to West African conditions. Demand from rich countries for these skills would be quite limited. Guinea and Mali have gone some way in this direction. Already in the late 1960s Guinea allowed only students in advanced technical subjects such as engineering to study abroad, and even they had to work for one year in a factory as part of their course (Johnson 1970, p. 363, fn. 28). In Mali, sixty percent of students at higher educational levels were trained in the country itself in recent years, and they followed curricula and received degrees incompatible with those of other countries (Vera L. Zolberg 1974, pp. 13 and 16).

Colonial officers wielded considerable power. The legendary District Officer and his French counterpart, the *commandant de cercle*, ruled like little kings. The politicians who took over, first in local government, then in national self-government, and ultimately in an independent state, took a close interest in the workings of the bureaucratic apparatus. This interference was resented by the civil service, which had little respect for the politicians whose formal education was, by and large, much more limited. The legitimacy of political control was not helped by the fact that most politics were geared to parochial interests, if not to the filling of the pockets of individual politicians.

The nationalist movements in West Africa had their martyrs. Prominent among them were the workers on the Dakar–Niger railroad whose five-month strike has been immortalized by a distinguished Senegalese writer, Sembene Ousmane (1960). But, eventually, the colonial powers yielded political control without armed struggle, except for Guinea-Bissau. When the new political leadership emerged, it followed the example of the senior civil service in granting itself similar, if not higher, salaries and perquisites. In addition to such legal incomes, all too many politicians succumbed to the lure of corruption. In Nigeria, Ekotie Eboh, federal minister of finance from 1957 until he was killed in the January 1966 coup, was to become the sad symbol of widespread corruption. Foreign contractors eagerly joined in the game and deducted bribes on their tax returns in their home countries. Commissions of inquiry appointed after the military coups were to hear all too many sorry tales.

Civilian rule was to last less than a decade in seven of the fifteen countries of West Africa. Discontent with the displaced civilian regimes had been widespread. However, it soon became obvious that the military rulers brought little change. In Nigeria, the coup of the young majors was bungled, and the top brass who took over proved unable to effect fundamental changes (First 1970, pp. 278ff.). Anton Bebler summarizes the experience in Mali, Sierra Leone, Ghana, and Benin:

The impact of military rule [on the civilian administration and bureaucracy] was not appreciable or lasting. During the first several months it improved discipline (mainly reporting to the job, reducing absenteeism during the day, and so forth), but often without commensurate gains in efficiency. The change of masters produced some confusion and uncertainty, and temporarily even had a paralyzing effect. Regardless of the formal organization of power the real impact of military rule on state administration seems to have been an increase in its autonomy. The military removed or minimized party and "political" pressures on the bureaucrats, without bringing in their own system of effective control. Even if the juntas were to employ all the military officers and NCOs in the country on a full-time basis, they could not really supervise the civilian administration. Besides, the juntas espoused Western notions of the administration's corporate autonomy and apolitical nature . . . In the long run no junta changed anything of substance in the organization and functioning of the civil administration. Some, but very few, corrupt civil servants were sacked, and if anything the experience taught civilian bureaucrats about the dangers and unpredictability of associating themselves with political parties. It is doubtful that the efficiency and responsiveness of the civil bureaucracy improved, while corruption only took different and less conspicuous forms. (1973, pp. 203f.)

In fact, the organization of the army parallels that of the civil service, and the formation of its personnel follows similar patterns. Like their bureaucratic counterparts, the army officers have been recruited through channels of formalized training into clearly established careers endowed with similar salary scales, although the coups brought rapid promotion to quite a few. The military initiated little change, precisely because they represented so little difference. The need for sacrifice and austerity was proclaimed, but it was not meant to apply to the ranks of the military. The extravagances of the Nkrumah regime were widely decried after the 1966 coup, and the budgets of the National Liberation Council brought severe cutbacks in many sectors over the next three years. However, the allocation to the defense sector increased and by 1968–9 was 41 percent higher than under the last pre-coup budget (Table 9.5).[10] Although they failed to generate a new approach to development, the armed forces increased their claim on national resources. And as individual military and police got access to the levers of power, the myth of their incorruptibility was soon shattered.

Once the first euphoria had worn off, the basis of support of the military rulers turned out to be just as limited as that of the civilian governments they had toppled. However, they, in their exercise of power, can take advantage of the fact that they have unfettered control over the means of violence, the ultimate sanction; their preparedness to use it has been demonstrated in the very coups that brought them to power. Predictions about the staying power of the military thus turn on the cohesiveness of the armed forces. Divisions arise internally over the distribution of power and wealth, and they are also intro-

Table 9.5. *Comparison of National Liberation Council budgets with last pre-coup budget, Ghana*

Sector	Change in allocation from 1966 level			Average
	1966–7	1967–8	1968–9	
Defense	+ 4.0%	+20.0%	+41.4%	+22.0%
Agriculture	−16.5%	−36.7%	−28.3%	−27.2%
Industries	−56.2%	−77.4%	−78.2%	−70.6%
Transport and communications	− 9.8%	−54.1%	−47.5%	−37.1%
Trade	− 3.6%	−65.2%	−62.3%	−43.7%
Foreign relations	−25.0%	+27.7%	+22.4%	+ 8.4%

Sources: Ghana, *The Budget, 1966–67* (Accra); Ghana, *The Financial Statement, 1967–68* (Accra); Ghana, *The Financial Statement, 1968–69* (Accra); compiled by Price (1971, p. 425).

duced from the outside as the military rulers have to confront political issues. The allocation of resources among regions usually constitutes just such a major task.

We need to look briefly at two other privileged groups: the commercial and the emerging landed interests. Their members are as wealthy as those of the three elites we have discussed, perhaps more so. However, they do not have their hands directly on the levers of power. It is through corruption that they steer the execution of policy into directions that suit their interests. However, their influence on policy making is usually subsidiary to that of foreign governments and multinational corporations.

The traders of West Africa have been famous for centuries. In the colonial situation they constituted an indigenous middle sector, a sharp contrast with other parts of Subsaharan Africa, where most commerce was preempted by foreigners. Three important consequences may be suggested: Race relations were, and continue to be, more relaxed because the majority of the population had little close contact with Europeans; the nationalist movement was not diverted into struggles against resident buffer groups, but directly confronted the colonial power; and the successful trader bore living testimony to the capability of Africans.

A remarkable increase in manufacturing accompanied the advent of Independence. In 1957, industrial output (exclusive of craft production) was less than 2 percent of national income in Nigeria, Ghana, and the Ivory Coast. Then, starting about 1958, a rapid spurt of industrialization that carried into the mid-1960s raised the share of manufacturing to from 6 to 8 percent (Kilby 1975, p. 490). Still, manufacturing remains a rather small sector. Further-

more, it continues to be dominated by foreign firms. Studies of ,
preneurs suggest no lack of enterprise, but very serious problem.
ment (Kilby 1969).

Little systematic information is available on the commercial bourgeo.
West Africa. A survey of Senegalese businessmen stresses several weaknesses
of this sector today. The performance and even the mere existence of their
enterprise is dependent on the individual owner; when an owner dies suddenly,
his enterprise nearly always disappears with him. Additionally, the financial
base of Senegalese business is severely restricted. Finally, indigenous business
enjoys little independence. It is, by and large, dependent on foreign import
wholesalers, foreign-owned local industry, and foreign-controlled banks. It is
even more dependent on government both as the major client and the prime
force shaping the economic environment in which business operates (Amin
1969, pp. 180ff.).

Holders of political power, whether civil politicians or military officers, and
senior civil servants have established considerable interests in the commercial
sector. Michael A. Cohen (1974a) demonstrates for the Ivory Coast how
Nkrumah's adage, "Seek ye first the political kingdom, and all things will be
added unto you," came true for those at the top of the political-administrative
structure. Political power was used to establish urban economic interests. In
1969, out of 287 positions occupied by Ivoiriens on the *conseils d'administration* of 88 enterprises and economic associations, 179 were held by 23 members of the National Assembly, 15 members of the Economic and Social
Council, 14 ministers, 16 government employees, and 3 members of the first
political generation (Michael A. Cohen 1974a, pp. 62ff.). The political-administrative elite is particularly advantaged where it is directly involved in the
allocation of valuable resources such as state-owned land in urban areas.
From 1960 to 1965, 5 to 13 percent of all land grants were made to ministers,
deputies, and other national figures. The share of administrative personnel
increased steadily; by 1970, they received about 44 percent of all allocations
(Michael A. Cohen 1974a, pp. 42ff.). Michael Cohen concludes:

Political power is the key not only to public authority but also to the many goods
and services which public institutions produce and distribute. In a developmental
sense, political power precedes the public authority which is the means of access to
wealth and status. As such, it is the dynamic principle of social stratification in
African states. (1974a, p. 6)

A potentially very important development in West Africa has been the concentration of land in private hands. In the Sudanic belt, estates controlling
both land and people have been widespread for many centuries. However, in
the last few decades, wealthy landowners have emerged in southern Ghana,
southern Togo, southwestern Nigeria, southern Liberia, and the southeast of
the Ivory Coast. In the Ivory Coast, only a couple of hundred families could

be so described in 1950; but by 1965, about 20,000 landowners were estimated to control nearly a quarter of the land in the plantation zones, to employ two-thirds of the labor, and to enjoy incomes ranging from $1,400 to $4,000 a year (Amin 1967, pp. 91 and 277).[11]

Four elements were involved in making the establishment of such a rural bourgeoisie possible in the Ivory Coast. First, the traditional society in the region concerned was sufficiently hierarchical so that certain hereditary chiefs possessed enough social power to appropriate important parcels of land for themselves. Second, the area was characterized by medium population density. A low density would have made the private appropriation of lands ineffective because the potential supply of labor would have been insufficient; high densities would have made it difficult for the chiefs to seize control of sufficient land. Third, rich products (coffee and cocoa) made it possible to produce a surplus from farming that remained largely extensive. Fourth, the political atmosphere was not detrimental to this kind of spontaneous development. Specifically, the relative ease of private appropriation of land, the freedom of work, and the credit awarded individual farmers played important roles in establishing this rural bourgeoisie (Amin 1971b, pp. 320f.).

The heyday of this particular conjunction favoring the emergence of wealthy landowners is probably past. However, by rural standards, members of the urban elite have tremendous purchasing power. Especially in areas of high population density, individual ownership of land is increasingly affirmed, and transfer to nonmembers of the community is no longer unthinkable. At this time there is little indication that the political atmosphere is detrimental to such a development. The urban elite may thus gain greater security of status for their descendants, but it will be at the expense of a new group of rural landless. Such a development would have fundamental consequences in terms both of adding to the rural–urban flow and of weakening urban–rural ties and the security such ties promise.

In Liberia such a pattern is well established. J. Gus Liebenow (1969, pp. 209f.) reports that the "honorables" and others who have the ear of the president have engaged in one of the most extensive programs of private land acquisition outside of South Africa, Zimbabwe, Angola, and Mozambique. The actual extent of the transfer of title from customarily held land to freehold land is not a matter of public record because only the less consequential registrations of title are published in the press. However, the covert acquisition of land has been so outrageous that the late President William Tubman himself commented on the situation in his inaugural address in 1964. He noted that several citizens, including the chiefs allied with the Americo-Liberian ruling class, had acquired estates of up to 20,000 acres for as little as fifty cents an acre. Incidentally, it is the president's office that authorizes the transfer of titles, and President Tubman's own holdings were substantial.

Social mobility

Until now, formal education was the rapid transitway of social mobility in West Africa. The range of earned income is much wider than in rich countries, and remuneration is largely based on level of formal education. Government is both the most important employer and a major direct influence in regulating wages in the private sector. Government salary scales are tied closely to education qualifications, as we have seen. In fact, a distribution of the labor force according to education, read in conjunction with government salary scales, will give a good approximation of the income distribution. However, there are exceptions to the general pattern, such as members of the older generation who made their way in employment before more recent rises in the general level of education, politicians in office, and the more successful self-employed.

A sizeable part of the population never enters the educational system, and very few reach its apex. In Western Nigeria, universal free primary education was instituted in 1955. Although tuition was free, parents were expected to pay about £5 (or $14) for books and uniforms. Since 1955, almost all boys but only about 80 percent of girls started primary education. However, dropout rates are extremely high both in primary school and at higher levels. Peter C. Lloyd (1974, pp. 91ff.) estimates that only about 2 percent of those entering primary school reach university (Figure 9.1).

Although the educational system could be seen to be open to all members of society irrespective of their origin, the children of the educated do enjoy better educational opportunities.[12] In 1961 Philip Foster (1965, pp. 220ff. and 242ff.) administered questionnaires to fifth form students in a random sample of public secondary schools in Ghana. He found the children of fathers with university or equivalent education overrepresented by a factor of 18; whereas children of fathers without formal education were underrepresented by 60 percent.[13] It has been estimated that roughly half of the students at the University of Ibadan, Nigeria, were the children of illiterate or barely literate parents with a social background of small-scale farming, petty trade, or manual work. Economically, these families were probably above the mass of subsistence peasants, but they were not elite, nor did they even belong to the salaried, urban, petty middle-class of secretaries, clerks, and sales personnel.[14] The other half of the students came from literate, urban families with postprimary education and with salaried fathers who were most often artisans, teachers, clerks, civil servants, or independent professionals. University-educated professional parents accounted for only 11 percent of the students entering the university between 1948 and 1966; however that was twenty or thirty times their representation in the population at large (van den Berghe 1973, p. 153).

As the ranks of the elite swell and the drastic expansion of the educational system is slowed down, the children of the elite can be expected to preempt a

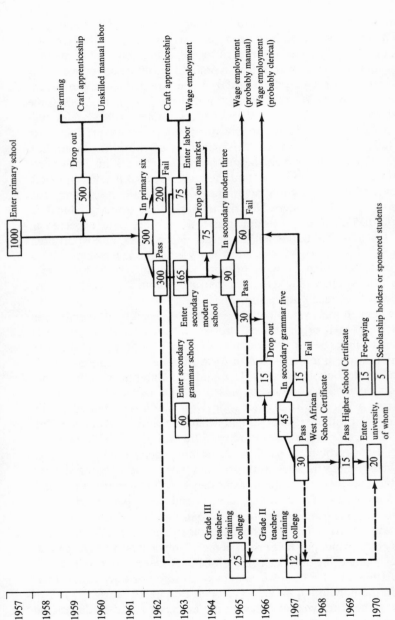

Figure 9.1. The education route in Western Nigeria, 1957–70. *Sources:* Western Region or State education reports and digests or abstracts of education statistics, presented by Peter C. Lloyd (1974, pp. 98f.). Reproduced by permission of the author and Routledge & Kegan Paul. *Note:* The figures are approximate only, allowing for distortions caused by regional boundary changes and marked annual variations in some data. The diagram ignores the intervals of work which sometimes separate primary and secondary schooling and usually divide secondary and university education. The dotted lines indicate the teacher-training route; the numbers cited are of students in colleges at the stated periods; these are not included within the thousand entering primary school in 1957 for they will be much older men, their training being interspersed with periods of teaching. "Drop-outs" refer to the entire periods of primary or secondary schooling, not to a single given year.

greater proportion of the places in higher education. The strain is compounded by the fact that the elite continue to rear a large number of children.[15] A time may well come when the absolute number of nonelite children in higher education starts declining.

Elite children have been, and can be expected to continue to be, inordinately overrepresented for two reasons: Only their parents can finance an extended education for all their children, and they are much better prepared for the severe competition in the educational system.

Sending their children to school represents a heavy economic burden for the majority of West African parents. School fees, uniforms, and books constitute a great expense even for an urban worker. The fact that many secondary schools are boarding schools adds to the cost. Where parents reach their ideal of numerous offspring, the problem is exacerbated. When parents have to choose which of their children are to continue their education, they tend to favor their sons. At Ibadan University, women made up only 11 percent of students registered between 1948 and 1966, and 58 percent of them were the daughters of professionals and semiprofessionals; whereas 32 percent of the men had fathers in these categories (van den Berghe 1973, pp. 152ff.).

In addition, the children of well-educated parents enjoy considerable advantages in entering the more promising channels of the educational system and competing for the higher rungs of the educational ladder. A longitudinal growth study in Ibadan demonstrates the slower physical growth of poor as against elite children from the age of four weeks (Figure 9.2).[16] Barbara B. Lloyd reports from a related study of differences in home environment.

Children of the Yoruba elite*

Class consciousness as known in Europe and America is not an outstanding feature of contemporary life in Western Nigeria. A cultivated feeling of classlessness may indeed be necessary to ensure government stability in the present situation of marked contrasts in wealth and privilege [see Peter C. Lloyd 1966b, pp. 328ff.]. Despite apparent adult disregard of class differences, a study of the child-rearing methods employed by well-educated Yoruba mothers indicates the emergence in the next generation of a fairly homogeneous group more distinct from their countrymen than their own educated parents, who had themselves been recruited rather widely from the population. The home and family life, the schools and educational opportunities, as well as the attitudes and values which the elite parent offers his offspring to assure him a bright future, will most probably produce adults quite different in experience, training, and motivation from the majority of their contemporaries. The contrast is heightened here by emphasis on the

* Excerpt from Barbara Lloyd, "Education and Family Life in the Development of Class Identification among the Yoruba" in the collection *The New Elites of Tropical Africa*, 1966, pp. 163–73, by permission of the author and the International African Institute. Based on research in 1961–3. Acknowledgments have been dropped, and footnotes renumbered.

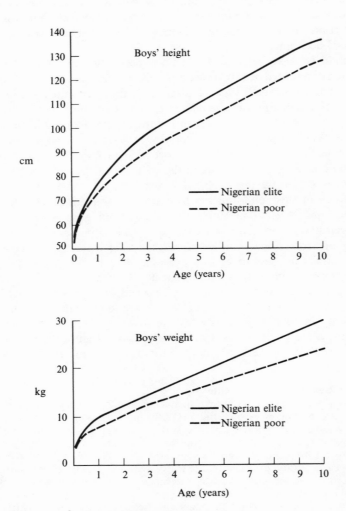

Figure 9.2. Growth of elite and poor boys in Ibadan

Note: The elite group was composed of children from well-to-do, mostly professional families; the mothers of these children had had a minimum of four years
secondary education. The poor group included children from one of the poorest
areas in Ibadan where polygamy, poor environmental sanitation and nutrition, and
a high level of illiteracy are common.

Source: Curves designed from data collected (between 1962 and 1974) and made
available by Margaret Janes (cf Janes 1975).

comparison of Yoruba home life in a traditional quarter of Ibadan with that of the well-educated professional group.[1] The sizeable middle category of petty officialdom and small businessmen is largely ignored.

Family and home life

Children of the educated elite are taller, heavier, healthier,[2] and begin schooling earlier and with more skills then the products of illiterate or traditional Yoruba homes. These are the most obvious results of superior housing, diet, medical care – in fact, of privilege. Of interest in this analysis are the social and psychological aspects of home and family life which set these children apart from their peers and which make the Nigerian situation unusual.

More so, perhaps, than in industrial nations, the educated Nigerian seeks his career in the professions or in the governmental bureaucracy. Unlike western middle-class suburban-dwelling children, however, these youngsters are not ignorant of their fathers' occupations. Due in part to the residential patterns set down during the colonial era, officers are housed near their work. Thus, today's Nigerian university staff live on the university grounds, senior government officials in residence areas near their offices, graduate teachers on their school compounds, and even among private lawyers it is common for the family to live on the first floor of a two-story building which houses the father's chambers on the ground floor. The children may go to school by car, together with their parents, who leave home for work at the same time in the morning, and in the early afternoon return together for dinner. On Sundays a busy father sometimes takes the children with him when he goes to work in his office for a few hours in the afternoon. Thus, elite children become familiar with the work of government officials, lawyers, professors, and teachers, and through observation learn the requirements of the roles they may expect one day to perform.

The pressure to provide funds to educate her siblings and later her own children sends educated Yoruba mothers to work in great numbers. Only a very few wives of top-level civil servants and politicians can afford the luxury of staying at home.[3] The majority, who have been trained as nurses and teachers, carry on their professional activities, despite the demanding hours required. Unlike the illiterate or semi-educated women who trade and can set their own hours and locations, often taking the baby along with

1 Most of the data presented in the paper are drawn from structured interviews concerning maternal attitudes towards family, marriage, and the raising of children carried out among sixty Yoruba mothers of five-year-olds. The thirty educated mothers were selected from a large number replying to a questionnaire designed to recruit educated women, those of secondary schooling or its equivalent, with children aged zero to three years for a study of physical growth. A traditional quarter of Ibadan had been surveyed before the medical study began, and it was thus possible to select children for the growth study and mothers of five-year-olds from our own census data. It was not possible to select at random mothers of five-year-olds from the larger samples, as it was scarcely possible to fill the quotas of each group. Throughout the educated mothers are referred to as either the elite or educated group, while those from the traditional quarter are referred to as uneducated, illiterate, or traditional.

2 The medical data is supplied by Dr. M. D. Janes of the Institute of Child Health, University of Ibadan, and is based upon the larger samples of elite and traditional children described in footnote 1.

3 Twenty-four of the thirty educated mothers were in full-time employment at the time of the interview.

them, the educated woman is a slave to hours, which, as one nurse assured me, must have been devised for unmarried nursing sisters resident at the hospital. Yet, difficulties notwithstanding, 88 per cent of the Nigerian, Western Region, government nursing staff is married.

The employment of teenage, primary-school educated, nurse-girls, and the profusion and popularity of nursery schools are the immediate consequences of mothers working away from home at least six hours of the day. Unlike the traditional Yoruba family, which lives in a lineage-based compound housing fathers, sons, wives, and children, the elite nuclear family lives in employer-provided quarters isolated from relatives, or in modern houses in the newer residential parts of Ibadan. When relatives live with the elite family they are often children pursuing an education.[4] In the majority of homes adult kinsmen, particularly grandparents, are frequent visitors, but are not often permanent guests. This is marked in Ibadan, which recruits professional people throughout the region. In the absence of relatives to mind their small children, working mothers employ young unmarried girls, who come to Ibadan from the provinces after primary schooling. Mothers who feel uneasy about leaving their children of three years or more with these semi-educated girls, or who wish to provide a more stimulating environment, send their offspring to nursery schools.

A surprising feature of educated families is their large size. While educated women in other parts of the world have tended to limit the number of children they bear, elite families of four are modal in this sample, and completed families of six children are common in Ibadan.[5] Thus, without further recruitment from outside its own ranks, the educated elite may well, if children reach the educational standard of their parents, double in a generation.

The large family with an ample supply of brothers and sisters is a boon to the elite child, who must often find his playmates among his siblings. Not only is the elite nuclear family isolated in a social sense from relatives, but it is also physically isolated. Typical of this isolation are the government housing areas, where homes are surrounded by large gardens. Children walking just a few houses from home along the tarred roads which cut through these areas risk the hazards of fast cars, as there are no pavements. In their concern for safety, parents may restrict children to their own gardens or those of the adjoining houses.

Children who live in the more densely settled parts of Ibadan, rather than in the spaciously laid out reservations, face another kind of isolation. In town, parents take pains to see that their children play only with other children from 'good homes', and they point out that children learn bad habits easily by imitation. Thus, naughty, stubborn, rude, obscene, and dirty children must be avoided. Rules are strictly enforced, and some children are

4 Twenty-seven permanent visitors were reported by elite mothers. Two-thirds of these were children and adolescent relatives, as well as three young adults and six adults of the grandparental generation, one a grandfather staying with the family until father returned from overseas duty.
5 Though families reported here are not complete, one can compare the mean of 4.7 children reported by educated mothers and 3.2 reported by traditional women. Though educated women tend to marry later it is difficult to determine whether the difference in numbers of children is a reflection of differential survival or of the six-year mean difference in age of mothers. Considerations are further complicated by the generally unreliable nature of illiterate women's memory of dates.

even restricted to their family apartments and veranda on the first floor, if the children on the ground floor of the building in which they live are not thought suitable companions. Though it is often maintained by the educated Yoruba that social class is a Western concept with limited applicability in Africa, it does appear that elite children are made aware of social differences which some might describe as class distinctive.

Life is not dreary for the elite child, despite parental rules for choosing playmates. Though neighbours may be unavailable, there are siblings and the children of family friends. Children often attend and play host at elaborate birthday parties. They are taken along to play with the children when parents visit their friends. Parents take care to see that their children learn manners appropriate for these occasions, i.e. to say thank you, sit quietly when necessary, and not to ask for too many things.

A child reared in a traditional family compound would find such social life strange and unfamiliar. All the compound children play together and are expected to get along well with one another. A mother who tried to choose her child's companions would be considered unsociable and rude. The compound child is seldom alone and is thought to be odd or preoccupied with spirit friends when seeking solitude; the elite child, however, is actively encouraged by his parents to learn to play by himself. Elite mothers believe solitary play gives a child time to think, to learn skills such as drawing or painting, and perhaps, most importantly, from a mother's point of view, it teaches him not to fret when there is no one about who can play with him.

The family car offers ease of movement and tempers the isolation of the nuclear family. Parents frequently visit friends in Ibadan, go to Lagos to shop or see people, and usually maintain active ties with their home towns. Residential mobility is also a feature of elite family life. Since occupation and dwelling are linked, and it is common for children to be born in the years when a father is becoming established, children move about frequently in their early years. One-fifth of the elite five-year-olds were born in England while both parents were studying. Frequently the child born abroad is boarded in a foster home until studies are completed. Children of civil servants often live with their parents outside Ibadan before starting school, but once their education has begun parents try to ensure continuity. This may necessitate children living with relatives in Ibadan, staying at boarding schools, or for mother and children, occasionally even father and children, to remain in Ibadan while the other parent is on transfer in another part of the country. Naturally permanent posts in Ibadan are sought. Though a traditional father might be employed outside Ibadan, his wives and their children would usually remain in his compound. Thus, compound children of five may have travelled no more than a mile or two from home.

Changes in home life and ways of raising children are apparent to most Nigerians. Uneducated mothers reported these changes mainly in terms of child health, and some spoke of the modern world as that of the hospital. Among educated mothers, the most frequently noted change is that in the atmosphere of the home. Of course, some educated women are themselves from educated homes, and these people are less often struck with modern innovations. Even when the overall change is only slight, from the stiffness of a Victorian, mission-patterned home, to current relaxed family life, educated mothers believe that today's children are more at ease with their fathers than they had been.[6] The transition from the traditional home in the parental generation to that of the current elite group is more sharply marked, and mothers mention the greater physical amenities now available to them. The modern educated father is reported to actively seek a warm, friendly relationship with his children; he plays ball with them, reads to them, and if need be, while living abroad, will help to feed and look after them. Generally, this attitude is not achieved by completely giving in to children's whims. Educated parents still expect children to be obedient, e.g. to fetch something when sent, but consideration is given to what the children are doing at the time they are summoned, and if the parent's request can be delayed children may be allowed to complete their activity.

Elite children still receive spankings and even beatings, though discipline is less harsh than in the traditional family. A few educated mothers have even mentioned that, contrary to traditional practice, their husbands refuse to spank the children, and thus they must be the strict parent in the family. Mothers take care to see that their servants never use physical punishments in their absence, but wait instead until the parents return to report any misdeeds of the children. Visiting grandparents would be allowed to discipline children, but it seems an almost universal complaint that they only spoil their grandchildren.

Schools and educational opportunity
Membership in the elite is currently determined primarily by education. Entry into the governmental and educational bureaucracies, in which the majority of educated people find employment, is relatively open to those with the essential academic qualifications. As rank is largely determined by education at the time of entry, promotion is mainly by seniority. Though private business and the independent professions of law and medicine offer greater opportunity for nonacademic abilities and the manipulation of influence, fewer positions are as yet established in these spheres. Generally the elite are not extensive land or factory owners, though they may have some rent-producing residential property. Thus, an elite child's principal inheritance is the education which his parents can provide.

Familiar with Nigerian educational institutions, elite mothers see their task as taking an interest in their children's schooling, giving help when necessary, and continuously offering support and encouragement. To improve their children's creative and intellectual capacities, parents are prepared to spend as much as their financial means permit in order to provide teachers, books, toys, and recreation. Mothers take special care to answer children's questions, since the belief is widespread that ignoring questions from children stifles their curiosity. Though academic achievement is the chief concern of an elite family, a majority of children will be taught additional skills. Some mothers mentioned plans for music lessons, others reported that older children were involved in the Scouting movement, while a number of mothers hoped their children could have swimming lessons.

To the young child in an elite home, going to school is often seen as a privilege to be won, especially where both parents and older siblings leave home together each morning. Though 4.2 years is the mean entrance age, one mother reported that a daughter began nursery school eight months after her second birthday. It is not unusual for children over three years to

6 Nineteen out of thirty reports of elite women include mention of changes of patterns [of] discipline or the approachability of fathers, factors described by the phrase 'atmosphere in the home'.

attend regularly. The nurseries may be attached to a private, fee-paying primary school, be part of a demonstration school attached to a Teacher Training College, or informally organized in the home of a trained Nigerian teacher or expatriate wife. A majority of the children attending nursery schools come from the homes of the elite, but a number of expatriate children are also enrolled, often affording Nigerian children additional opportunity to learn English – beyond that acquired listening to parents who converse with ease in both English and Yoruba.

Parents often teach their children numbers and the alphabet, even though they attend nursery school. A large number of elite children are registered in private, fee-paying schools, often with mixed classes of expatriate and Nigerian children. The Western Region provides free primary schools, and children from educated homes do attend them, either of necessity (with four to six children, a number of whom may be enrolled in secondary schools, fees mount up) or from genuinely democratic sentiment; but parents strive to provide additional training. Classes in state primary schools are larger, the teachers less thoroughly trained, and the curriculum narrow, as supplementary educational materials are expensive, and in short supply. In educated homes tutors are frequently employed to give two-hour lessons in the house each weekday afternoon, or parents themselves may regularly coach their offspring. With few exceptions, one parent, usually the mother, checks each child's homework daily. Though many parents believe they should not make corrections, they will give additional work in areas in which the child is weak, thus helping him to correct his own mistakes.

By contrast, traditional families send their children to school only when they are six or seven years old, and then with little preparation. They attend nearby state schools, to which they walk each morning. Even in the absence of fees, it may be difficult for parents to provide the requisite books and uniforms. Almost all boys attend school, though in a poor Moslem home there are still doubts about sending girls to school. Parents can offer little assistance with school work; sometimes they do manage to provide money for lessons, but most often tutoring, if any, would come from older children living in the compound.

In all homes primary school performance is a major concern. The competitive process of secondary school entrance selection sharpens this interest. No secondary education is free, though the older schools offer scholarships which are awarded on the basis of test performance, apparently without consideration of family means. Despite the formidable barrier of nearly one hundred pounds a year expenses for fees, board, books, and uniforms, there are more applicants than places in better boarding grammar schools. The well-established schools, the state-managed colleges, and older mission or church grammar schools recruit the brightest students, or rather those with the best performance on the common entrance examinations tests, largely based on primary school subject achievement. Though fees vary little, the quality of education is not constant, in part reflecting the finances available to a school. While Government Colleges may receive several hundred pounds a year to spend on school libraries, independent schools often have less than fifty pounds. Educated parents are acutely aware of these differences and do everything possible to ensure their children places in the best schools. Children are sometimes specifically coached for the common entrance examinations.

For many years a very small group of Yoruba children have been sent to Public Schools in England. Whether the opening of the International School at the University of Ibadan (with its close ties to Prince Charles's school, Gordonstoun in Scotland) will reduce the flow remains to be seen. From the press announcements that the son of the Western Region's Premier will be the first Nigerian to attend Eton, one may judge that the famous English Public Schools are still attractive to the elite.

University education for their offspring is the goal of most elite parents, and two-thirds of the mothers interviewed stated it explicitly, while the others mentioned professions requiring extensive study. Though such aspirations at first seem high, they become readily understandable in the light of the salary scale automatically offered to the graduate and the rapid increase in secondary education throughout the Western Region. Unemployment, already common among persons of primary and secondary modern education, is beginning to affect grammar school products as well. A university degree thus becomes necessary to assure occupational success.

Sentiment is strong for allowing children to follow their own inclinations and abilities in the particular career they choose. There appears to be little occupational prejudice, though great emphasis is given to the level of education sought for one's children. Medicine, the most popular choice, was mentioned by eight mothers, three of whom were reporting their children's own preference. Mothers' ambitions for their daughters seem as high as for sons. One mother expressed, with feministic fervour, the wish for her daughter to qualify as a physician, while another hoped a daughter might follow her father's medical career, as their son had already indicated that his interests lay elsewhere.

Uneducated mothers have difficulty verbalizing their educational and occupational aspirations for their children. They appear quite unaware of the expanding educational opportunities available in Nigeria. Most mothers say only that they want their children to be good people and to get an unspecified 'higher qualification'. When pressed, they would often reply that they wanted their children to attend a secondary school or go overseas to England for further study. These are unrealistic aims in terms of family resources, though for an exceptional child an entire compound might manage to provide financial support. Only two traditional mothers were explicit in mentioning a university education. On the vocational side, nursing or office work are seen along with medicine and law as occupations which would afford their children, and themselves, indirectly, a good life.

Unclear in their view of the educational system, illiterate mothers are at a loss to know how to help their offspring succeed academically. When questioned, about half say that they would pray to God and make certain to get the medicine necessary to ensure success, though a number do mention verbally encouraging their children, buying them books, but also praying for success. Prayer may seem an odd approach to education, but in fact, traditional parents have little else to give their children. Lacking capital for extensive trading or the educational qualifications to obtain well-paid employment, they are unable to finance costly education. They must be satisfied if their children can attend primary school and may hope to be able to finance an apprenticeship or secondary modern school. In addition, some Moslem parents provide lessons in the Koran, while others hope to arrange lessons in useful crafts, such as sewing and raffia weaving. Unfortunately, the careful primary school training provided by elite parents ensures that the Government's limited financial assistance for secondary education in the form of subsidies and scholarships goes primarily to the elite child rather than to the most needy, those from uneducated homes.

With the advent of Independence, preferential treatment for nationals became government policy. Implementation was most extensive in public administration, but new opportunities for nationals also opened up in private employment and commerce. The result was high mobility in employment for the educated. In commerce, those benefited who had already a foothold or who enjoyed privileged access to credit. Political influence might help to get a promotion, but it paid the biggest dividends in opening up credit and guaranteeing profitable sales.

The accelerated recruitment of nationals into jobs and their establishment in new entrepreneurial roles, were usually referred to as "Africanization." This was accurate enough in that most of the positions taken over by nationals had been held by Europeans. However, substantial numbers of West Africans were adversely affected. Such was the case of the Dahomeans (people originally from Dahomey, now called the People's Republic of Benin), who had occupied a disproportionately large number of the administrative positions throughout what used to be French West Africa; they were forced to return to Benin and reportedly were a major factor contributing to continued political instability in that country. Ghana added to the unemployment problem in neighboring countries when more than 100,000 non-Ghanaian Africans were deported in 1969 (Peil 1971, pp. 225f.).

With the increased output of certified manpower from the educational system, expatriates were replaced, and high-level employment approached the limits dictated by the poverty of these countries. Education ceased to be an automatic guarantee of high income. In this changed context, the social position of parents, relatives, and coethnics increasingly affects the real worth of educational qualifications.

As the process of replacing foreigners in employment and commerce is completed and the post-Independence expansion of high-level public employment is halted, an alternative avenue of social mobility may become prominent. We have already noted the limited role of manufacture in the economies of West Africa and the subordinate position occupied by African enterprise. The success stories of the next decade will probably be written in industry. Given the manifold impact of government policies in manufacture, parents and relatives strategically placed in government or administration may be expected to be again a major factor in success.

Class formation

An increasing share of higher education preempted by elite children seems a likely prospect. Furthermore, elite connections will probably become more important in securing high income, whether it be in employment or in commerce or manufacture. These tendencies point toward an entrenchment of the elite. Does the elite – do the several elite groups – constitute a class?

In terms of income, wealth, power, and prestige, the elite are conspicuously set off from the masses. Almost without exception, the elite in Ibadan name as their close friends persons of similar age, occupation, education, and income (Peter C. Lloyd 1967, p. 146). The language situation contributes to the increasing estrangement between elite and masses (van den Berghe 1968). A European language is the official language in every country (in Mauritania it competes with Arabic); usually, it is understood only by a minority. This foreign language is the medium of instruction, except in the first years of primary school in several countries, and elite parents frequently use it with their children in order to further their educational opportunities.

The elite are referred to as *"Jeleconnais"* ("Iknowhim") in French-speaking countries. This expression aptly summarizes both points: The elite member speaks a European language, and whenever he is introduced to another elite member, it turns out that he knows him already because they all belong to one small, close-knit network.

Social distance finds its spatial expression in residence patterns. Throughout West Africa, residential areas that were racially segregated de jure or de facto in colonial days have provided a ready-made location for the elite. And the hallmark of elite status, possession of a motorcar, has allowed surburban developments such as the exclusive Cocody quarter in Abidjan.

Members of the elite tend to emphasize that they continue to be in close contact with poor kin and to redistribute part of their income to them. Such redistribution doubtless is important (e.g., village improvements financed mainly by urban dwellers, particularly the elite, in Eastern Nigeria via their improvement unions). The extent of such redistribution is difficult to assess; at a guess, transfers beyond the nuclear family rarely reach one-fifth of earnings. Such transfers, furthermore, go only to a very limited section of the total population who happen to have links, typically of kinship, with members of the elite. As the consolidation of the elite proceeds, such links with other sectors of the population will shrivel. Even at present, given the minute size of the elite, redistributing part of their income can make only a negligible impact on the incomes of the masses.

The elite can be seen to pursue class interest. An observer of politics in Ibadan, Oyo, Ilesha, and Benin City describes rising-class interest groups (Sklar 1963, pp. 253ff. and 289ff.). An account of national politics in Sierra Leone from 1951 to 1967 notes that leaders of the governing party and of successive opposition parties were linked both by family, educational, and occupational ties and by personal friendship. The conflict over values was not a profound one; there was enough similarity of outlook that the government would be unlikely to treat opposition views as dangerous heresies that had to be destroyed, although this homogeneity of outlook diminished in the 1960s. In fact, at the national level, leaders of the government party shared personal patronage freely with opposition leaders (Cartwright 1970, pp. 266 and 275f.). As Michael A. Cohen puts it: "Classes are categories of people sharing common political and economic interests arising from their access to public

authorities and the public resources and opportunities which they control"
(1974a, p. 194).

There is little to suggest that a worker and/or peasant class is emerging in
opposition to such an upper class. In Ibadan, Oyo, Ilesha, and Benin City, the
rising class clashed, not with an urban proletariat, but rather with the indigenous community. And it could be said for Sierra Leone that every party of any
significance during the years 1947–67 except one that lasted less than four
years had its roots in a "tribal" cleavage (Cartwright 1970, p. 263).

Where the population at large has an opportunity to participate in the political process, alignments do not follow class lines. Popular support continues to
go to the champions of local interests. Such politics may be referred to as
"ethnic" if it is understood that they are based on loyalties to groups of origin
and descent and that these groups may vary from a section in the village to a
region in the nation, depending on the political arena involved. Thus, Yoruba
continue to see differences among themselves primarily in ethnic terms (i.e., in
terms of regions the inhabitants of which are said to have peculiar cultural
traits) and to divide the population of their own town into indigenes and
strangers (Peter C. Lloyd 1974, pp. 169f.).

Achebe, in his brilliant novel *A Man of the People,* portrayed the Nigerian
deputy as an intermediary between the government and the people of his constituency. He was elected on the promise of pursuing the immediate interests
of his constituency: to get the road paved, a new bridge built, piped water
supply or electricity, a new school or a maternity clinic established. Listen to
Achebe's account of an election meeting, the leader of a new party addressing
the crowd in the narrator's home village.

Grass roots politics*

Max began by accusing the outgoing Government of all kinds of swindling
and corruption. As he gave instance after instance of how some of our leaders who were ash-mouthed paupers five years ago had become near-million-
aires under our very eyes, many in the audience laughed. But it was the
laughter of resignation to misfortune. No one among them swore ven-
geance; no one shook with rage or showed any sign of fight. They understood
what was being said, they had seen it with their own eyes. But what did
anyone expect them to do?

The ex-policeman put it very well. "We know they are eating," he said,
"but we are eating too. They are bringing us water and they promise to
bring us electricity. We did not have those things before; that is why I say
we are eating too."

"Defend them, Couple," cried someone in the audience to him. "Are you
not one of them when it comes to eating aged guinea-fowls?"

This brought a good deal of laughter but again it was a slack, resigned
laughter. No one seemed ready to follow up the reprimand or join issue
with Couple for defending his fellow racketeers.

* Excerpt from Chinua Achebe, *A Man of the People,* 1966, pp. 117–19, by permission of the author.

Up to this point Max had spoken slowly and deliberately, with very little heat. But now, as he accused the present regime of trying to establish itself as a privileged class sitting on the back of the rest of us, his hands and his voice began to shake.

"Whether it is P.O.P. or P.A.P. they are the same," he cried.

"The same ten and ten pence," agreed someone in English.

"They want to share out the wealth of the country between them. That is why you must reject both; that is why we have now formed the C.P.C. as a party of the ordinary people like yourselves. . . . Once upon a time a hunter killed some big-game at night. He searched for it in vain and at last he decided to go home and await daylight. At the first light of morning he returned to the forest full of expectation. And what do you think he found? He saw two vultures fighting over what still remained of the carcass. In great anger he loaded his gun and shot the two dirty uneatable birds. You may say that he was foolish to waste his bullet on them but I say no. He was angry and he wanted to wipe out the dirty thieves fighting over another man's inheritance. That hunter is yourselves. Yes, you and you and you. And the two vultures – P.O.P. and P.A.P. . . ." There was loud applause. Jolly good, I thought.

"There were three vultures," said the ex-policeman after the applause had subsided. "The third and youngest was called C.P.C."

"Why don't you leave the young man alone to tell us his story?" asked one elderly woman smoking a short clay pipe. But many people obviously thought the ex-policeman very witty and I saw one or two shaking his hand.

Towards the end of his speech Max made one point which frankly I thought unworthy of him or of C.P.C. but I suppose I am too finicky. "We all know," he said, "what one dog said to another. He said: 'If I fall for you this time and you fall for me next time then I know it is play not fight.' Last time you elected a Member of Parliament from Anata. Now it is your turn here in Urua. A goat does not eat into a hen's stomach no matter how friendly the two may be. Ours is ours but mine is mine. I present as my party's candidate your own son, Odili Samalu . . ." He walked over to me and held my hand up and the crowd cheered and cheered.

An elderly man who I believe was also a local councillor now stood up. He had sat on the edge of his seat directly opposite the microphone, his two hands like a climber's grasping his iron staff. His attitude and posture had shown total absorption in what was being said:

"I want to thank the young man for his beautiful words," he said. "Every one of them has entered my ear. I always say that what is important nowadays is no longer age or title but knowledge. The young man clearly has it and I salute him. There is one word he said which entered my ear more than everything else – not only entered but built a house there. I don't know whether you others heard it in the same way as I did. That word was that our own son should go and bring our share." There was great applause from the crowd. "That word entered my ear. The village of Anata has already eaten, now they must make way for us to reach the plate. No man in Urua will give his paper to a stranger when his own son needs it; if the very herb we go to seek in the forest now grows at our very back yard are we not saved the journey? We are ignorant people and we are like children. But I want to tell our son one thing: He already knows where to go and what to say when he gets there; he should tell them that we are waiting here like a babe cutting its first tooth: anyone who wants to look at our new tooth should know that his bag should be heavy. Have I spoken well?"

"Yes," answered the crowd as they began to disperse.

Urban workers would appear to present a more promising ground for class formation. And while they constitute only a very small proportion of the total population, the close connection most of them have with rural areas provides a possible channel for the mobilization of more massive support there. Trade unions would offer a ready organizational framework for organizing the urban workers. In fact, any bargaining over wages and benefits relates directly to national politics because national governments are the major employer of labor and tend to set wages. It has been estimated that in the West African states half or more of the wage earners are employed in the public sector and that a far higher proportion of the well-educated are so employed. In such a situation the grievances of the wage earners are directed toward the government and its leaders; they become expressed in a political form; the politicians are not able to assume the role of arbitrators between wage earners and employers (Peter C. Lloyd 1971, p. 55).

The nationwide general strike of June 1964 gained Nigerian workers unprecedented political prominence and for a time united disparate elements of opposition in a challenge to the political elite controlling the federation. The Nigerian Labor Party was founded. But when the federal elections were held in December of the same year, they were dominated again by the established, regionally based parties. A few months later, when Lagos railway workers were asked what parties trade unionists should support, 43 percent said that workers should form a labor party; only 10 percent thought workers should support one of the existing political parties. However, when asked what parties they found most helpful, the proportions were reversed, with 49 percent indicating one of the existing ethnic parties and only 9 percent referring to a labor party. Over one-third felt that workers should not mix in politics, and a similar proportion reported that they found no party of help (Melson 1971, pp. 591ff.).

In 1971, violence erupted on the Ikeja Industrial Estate near Lagos when employers and government proposed to exempt certain companies in the private sector from the cost-of-living allowance (*cola*) recommended by the Adebo Commission. Managers were beaten up; their cars were stoned. In one company, workers threatened to burn down the administration building with managers inside unless they signed a document to the effect that *cola* would be paid. There was fighting with the police. The workers were successful in that they obtained *cola*, but no further political action ensued. Adrian Peace (1974) suggests that most workers interpreted their action as a variant on the normal processes of accommodation to the social order that, during periods of social calm, took the form of peaceful bargaining between unions and managements around the negotiating table. Violence was viewed as a complement to the established procedure rather than a rejection of it, induced by the military decree that forbade strike action or incitement to strike. When the Adebo Commission presented its final award seven months later, adding little to the interim award for the lowest-paid workers but giving sizable increments to senior civil servants, workers suspected that the government had exerted pressure on the commission or tampered with its report, but they continued to work peacefully.[17]

So, the urban worker seeks the support of patrons who might help him get promoted, secure a better job, or start a promising business of his own. He knows that he is better off than the urban underemployed and unemployed and the rural masses. He pins unrealistically high hopes on the future of his children while accepting for himself more limited contexts of prestige and status. In his home village, he is respected as a son who established a foothold in the urban economy. In his urban neighborhood, he may join a group that appreciates him in spite of his limited economic resources. He may excel in a sport or beat his friends at checkers; he may derive prestige from his speech or his experience; office in an ethnic association or an independent church may give him status. It is his children who will climb the broader and steeper steps of society.

Peter C. Lloyd (1974, pp. 180 and 190) relates how many Yoruba accept great differences in wealth and income as legitimate so long as they or, more realistically, their children can achieve high positions. However, they are becoming increasingly unsure of their chances of success. The rich are seen to be able to educate not only their bright children but also the dull ones; their wives receive lucrative contracts and quasi-monopolistic trading opportunities. The Yoruba norm of assistance to a wide circle of kin is often honored in the breach. The dichotomy and opposition between government and ordinary folk becomes more commonly asserted. But the alternative structure that is postulated is a traditional one in which the benefits of power and wealth fall more widely upon the entire community, less exclusively upon the children of those in eminent positions.

In four countries, Ghana, Mali, Guinea, and Guinea-Bissau, attempts have been made to introduce socialist policies. In every case, these policies were initiated by a party whose primary appeal was based on the quest for Independence. In Ghana and Mali, investments were directed to the public rather than the private sector; but when Kwame Nkrumah and Modibo Keita were toppled by military coups, it appeared that nearly a decade of Independence had wrought very little social transformation in either country. In Guinea, according to Samir Amin (1971a, pp. 115f.) rural–urban inequality remained virtually unchanged between 1960 and 1970, with the urban average income about ten times as high as the rural; the rapid growth of Conakry attests to that inequality (Table 2.3).[18]

The Partido Africano da Independencia da Guiné e Cabo Verde has made a firm commitment to socialism. It holds out the promise that a people who have gone through a prolonged violent struggle to win Independence will continue to put national unity over regional interests and remain committed to the equality they knew in the baptism of fire. As Amilcar Cabral described this experience in a lecture in 1970, three years before he fell in the struggle:

The leaders of the liberation movement, drawn from the "petty bourgeoisie" (intellectuals, clerks) or the urban working population (workers, chauffeurs, wage-earners in general) have to live day by day with the various peasant groups, in the midst of the rural populations, and they come to know the people better. They discover at the grass-roots the richness of peasant cultural values (philosophical, political, artistic, social and moral). They acquire a closer understanding of the economic realities of the country, of the problems, sufferings and hopes of the popular masses. The leaders realize, not without a certain astonishment, the richness of spirit, the capacity for reasoned discussion and clear exposition of ideas, the facility for understanding and assimilating concepts, of people who only yesterday were forgotten, if not despised, and who were considered incompetent by the colonizers and even by some nationals. The leaders thus enrich their culture. They develop personally and free themselves from complexes. They reinforce their capacity to serve the movement in the service of the people.

On their side, the working masses and in particular the peasants, who are usually illiterate and have never moved beyond the boundaries of their village or their region, come into contact with other groups and lose those complexes of their own that constrained them in their relationships with other ethnic and social groups. They realize their crucial role in the struggle. They break the bonds of the village universe to integrate progressively into their country and the world. They acquire an infinite amount of new knowledge that is useful for their immediate and future activity within the framework of the struggle. They strengthen their political consciousness by assimilating the principles of the national and social revolution postulated by the struggle. They thereby increase their capability to play the decisive role of providing the principal force in the liberation movement. (1975, p. 332)

Guinea-Bissau has set out to prove to West Africa what another very poor country, Tanzania, demonstrates on the other side of the continent: A road to socialism can be found in Africa today.

Conclusion: The incorporation of the West African peasantry

The Wolof peasants are not only the victims of vast impersonal forces, they are also subordinate elements in a local structure (social, economic, and political) in which they are both disadvantaged and resentful.

Donal B. Cruise O'Brien (1975, pp. 115f.)

A study of urbanization and social change that failed to pay attention to the rural masses would obscure the processes at hand; the economic, political, and cultural changes experienced by the cities of West Africa have also been felt in the rural areas. Historical changes may be first perceived in the urban setting, but they affect the society at large. They may progress further in the town, as we have seen in the case of changes in the family and in the position of women, but they are also at work in the vast expanses where the great majority of the people of West Africa live. There was a time when one could talk of rural societies, peoples whose economy, polity, and culture were relatively self-contained, whose contacts were restricted to neighboring groups. But already several centuries ago, the tremors of the international slave trade were felt in many parts of the region. Today, people everywhere have in varying degrees been drawn into the national and international context.[1]

The rural masses of West Africa have been incorporated into the national and international economy as they went to work in the urban areas and as they grew crops for export or food for the expanding urban populations. The migrant workers brought manufactured goods back; cheap and efficient products displaced many of the old crafts. Traders came to buy produce and to sell the new merchandise. The camel, the steamship, the locomotive, and the truck, each, in turn, spread the tentacles of the national and international system even farther until the remotest corners of West Africa were reached. Thus, the agriculturalists of West Africa became peasants as defined by John S. Saul and Roger Woods: "Peasants are those whose ultimate security and subsistence lies in their having certain rights in land and in the labour of family members on the land, but who are involved, through rights and obligations, in a wider economic system which includes the participation of non-peasants" (1971, p. 105).

Political incorporation of the rural areas was at a minimal level in the early empires; in fact, it has remained rather limited to the present. Colonial administrations, whether enunciating principles of direct or of indirect rule, were content to establish a secure environment for commercial activity and to extract a modicum of taxes from agriculture. The Independence movement brought out the rural vote, but party organization failed to reach the rural masses, except in Guinea and Guinea-Bissau.

Missionaries were effective agents in the cultural incorporation of the rural masses. The Koran class and the mosque came to parts of West Africa over 1,000 years ago, reaching the Bight of Benin in the nineteenth century. The schools and churches of Christ remained restricted to coastal areas for several centuries, but in the nineteenth century, they started spreading out fast, with Islam their only major obstacle. Western education became the stepping-stone to success in an urban economy largely dominated by Europeans. A further important channel of communication was established by migrant workers who returned with new messages such as the call to rally to the cause of the Independence movement. Today, the voices of the city are heard on the transistor radio in nearly every village.

It has been said, with reference to industrial societies, that one can no longer speak of rural-oriented regions, only of urban ones (Sjoberg 1964, 149). With technological breakthroughs in communication and transportation, distance has lost much of its import. Newspapers, books, radio, television, and film reach the most outlying regions of the rich countries. Rapid means of transportation have become accessible to much of their populations. Although the technological know-how is available to poor countries such as those of West Africa, the resources are not. Most of these countries have started television in recent years, but it is frequently available only in and near the capital city. Furthermore, only a minority of their populations can afford receiving sets for radio, let alone television. The printed word eludes not only the illiterate but many more whose level of literacy is low. Economic constraints operate also on the availability of transport for people and goods. In this respect, changes in rural settlement patterns are of considerable importance. The concentration of rural settlements, as well as relocation of settlements next to lines of communication, frequently spontaneous developments, increase the accessibility of the rural population. Major decisions face policy makers concerning the countrywide integration of the legal system and the propagation of a national lingua franca.

Distance from urban centers, then, does affect access to educational and cultural facilities in West Africa. But ideas travel fast, and as long as strong urban–rural ties are maintained there is no lack of intermediaries. Most important, these middlemen are known to the villagers, are considered *of* the village.[2] Migration may take the most promising sons away, but their counsel is heard. In Chapter 4, we emphasized the role that urban-based associations play in rural development in many parts of West Africa.

At the urban end, there is a "continual ruralization of the cities," to use Janet Abu-Lughod's (1961, p. 23) classic phrase. Most towns in West Africa are of recent origin; nearly all have grown very rapidly over the last three decades. Rates of urban growth remain high, and rural immigrants continue to make their contribution to the urban configuration. Many maintain, as we have seen, strong ties with their rural homeplaces. The estrangement of the urban sector from the rural is thus delayed.[3]

The issue presented by the rural masses, then, is not that there is a lack of communication or a low incorporation into the national system; rather, it turns on the conditions of incorporation. Decisions are made for the peasants by elites in regional centers, capital cities, and overseas centers of politics and finance. The Independence movement brought a vote to every man and every woman, but the leverage thus promised to the rural majority soon vanished because elections rarely offered a choice – if they were not abolished altogether. In most West African countries the peasantry has been disenfranchised. The rural areas are taxed, most importantly through government marketing boards that buy crops for export at prices well below the world market price.[4] Resources are disproportionately allocated to the urban sector, especially to the capital cities (as we have seen in Chapter 2). Cities are centers of power and privilege; such a summary statement holds true for West Africa today. The visitor is appalled at the urban poverty of West Africa, but the most severe poverty is experienced in rural areas.

The peasants of West Africa, frustrated in their aspirations, retain three options: to vote with their feet and move to the city, to withdraw into subsistence agriculture, or to rebel.[5] The 1960–1 population survey in Upper Volta found one-third of the men away from their homes (Songre, Sawadogo, and Sanogoh 1974, p. 392). Many were involved in agriculture elsewhere in Upper Volta and in neighboring countries, especially the Ivory Coast. But others, here, as throughout West Africa, had opted for rural–urban migration (a phenomenon we explored in detail in Chapter 3). As these migrants swell the masses of urban unemployed and underemployed, they are increasingly seen as a threat to those in power.

Senegalese peasants, threatened in their subsistence and disaffected from the cooperative marketing system, shifted from the cultivation of peanuts to growing millet for their own consumption, withdrew from rural development services, and intensified noncompliance with administrative regulations and laws. The amount of peanuts (the country's main export) marketed dropped from 1 million tons in 1967 to 550,000 tons in 1970. Part of the explanation is that the weather was drier and that soils were becoming exhausted. But there is also the fact that sales of peanut fertilizer, the linchpin of the government's rural productivity campaign, had fallen from 53,000 tons in 1967 to less than 5,500 tons in 1970 in spite of a 25 percent reduction in price (Dumont 1972, pp. 197ff.; Schumacher 1975, pp. 183ff.).

The *Agbekoya* ("farmers shall not suffer") rebellion in Western Nigeria was sparked in 1968, when the arrest of tax defaulters led to attacks on the authorities. It was rekindled in 1969; when the government renewed its tax raids, the police were ambushed. In September 1969, after reports of the deaths of prisoners in jail, farmers invaded Ibadan and released 464 prisoners. The police and army pursued the farmers, and six days of fighting ensued. Ambushes were carried out largely by hunters equipped with dane guns; they were supported by farmers armed with matchets. Fighting units were organized separately in each area; linked by messengers, they were deployed with apparent sophistication. The government compromised before the farmers implemented what was rumored to be their final plan: putting Ibadan ablaze by setting the gas pumps on fire. The rebels obtained a substantial reduction in tax, the suspension of other rates and fees, an end to tax raids and to army and police patrols, the withdrawal of local government staff from the villages, and an amnesty for most of the arrested farmers (Williams 1974, pp. 126ff.).[6]

Throughout our presentation, and especially in this conclusion, we have groped for a perspective that includes the contributions made by the rural masses, and the exactions imposed on them. We will make ours a statement René Dumont made about an angry book, his *False Start in Africa*:

I preferred to run the risk of annoying some of my African friends rather than show my disrespect by flattering them or withholding my essential ideas. That would have been a hypocritical form of neo-colonialist segregation. Confronted by the "childhood diseases of independence," I thought it was important to try to diagnose their cure. The tone I adopted was sometimes clumsy, but I was trying to defend the tropical peasantry (the true proletarians of modern times, even though, ironically, they own their tools of production). (1969, p. 21)

Notes

Introduction: Exploding cities in poverty-stricken countries

1 West Africa stretches from the Cape Verde Islands to the Cameroun Mountains, from the Sahara to the Gulf of Guinea. It includes fifteen countries, several of which reach well into the Sahara. (The Partido Africano de Independencia da Guiné e Cabo Verde, which forms the governments of both Guinea-Bissau and the Cape Verde Islands, is committed to the unification of the two countries and has begun preparatory work. We anticipate here, and throughout this study, that this aspiration will be realized in the not-too-distant future.) In 1978, West Africa's 6.1 million square kilometers (2.4 million square miles) hold a population of more than 140 million, over half of it living in one country, Nigeria. West Africa is about four times the size of the nine countries combined in the European Economic Community; it is nearly two-thirds the size of the United States. Its people number more than half of those in the European Community and close to two-thirds of those in the United States.

2 Most West African countries lag even further behind, according to more direct indicators of living conditions such as life expectancy, literacy, and energy consumption per capita (United Nations 1975c, pp. 14ff.).

3 "Urbanization" is one of those terms in the social sciences that has taken on many meanings. In this case, they range from the demographic (increases in the number of people or in the proportion of a population living in urban areas) to the characterization of individuals (the extent to which they are economically, socially, and culturally anchored in urban rather than rural areas) to social organizational changes that can be argued to be related to the transition from rural to urban society (e.g., the growth of bureaucracy). A narrow definition of urbanization will not do for the purpose of this volume; instead, where we do use the term, we have made every effort to clarify its meaning through the particular context in which it is being used.

4 The company town, with its paternalistic regime, is also virtually unknown in West Africa; compare Epstein's (1964) account of the situation in the mining townships on the Zambian Copperbelt.

5 For a discussion of the contrast between Kano and Lagos, on the one hand, and Ibadan and Zaria, on the other, in terms of the size and concentration of the industrial labor force, residential patterns, and the relative importance of economic activities in the informal sector, see Remy (1975a), who explores the implications of this contrast for collective industrial action.

6 This is in sharp contrast with Belgian colonial policy, which in the 1930s had already initiated steps to establish Africans permanently in town in what is now Zaïre.

7 These factors of attraction and rejection by the urban economy operated differentially according to the type and size of city and the conditions in the immigrants' area of origin. Hence, their impact on the three characteristics of the new urbanization varied. Ethnic diversity is less marked in some of the

smaller towns, and age structures and sex ratios vary greatly among different occupational strata and various ethnic groups.

1. Empires and trade

1 However, as we will see, Islam was at times the inspiration for crusades of purification and conversion that tumbled prevailing orders and left chaos in their wake.
2 The following account is heavily indebted to Levtzion's (1973) study, which combines an evaluation of Arabic and Portuguese sources with an appreciation of oral traditions and archaeological evidence.
3 A number of authors record old sayings that the first kings of Ghana were white. However, none of the Arabic sources before the twelfth century imply that the rulers of Ghana were, or had been in the past, other than black. Reports to the contrary date after the Almoravids' conquest of Ghana and the Islamization of that kingdom. Levtzion (1973, pp. 4ff.) argues further that the polity was Sudanic in form and character.
4 People living in hot climates, such as the Sudan, require a considerable amount of salt to compensate for the body's loss of it through perspiration.
5 The gold was most likely found in the Bambuk area, between the Senegal and Falémé rivers.
6 In 1066, at the Battle of Hastings, William of Normandy may have mustered about 30,000 men, although estimates vary greatly. In 1346, the English fought the Battle of Crécy with about 20,000 men, successfully opposing the French force of about 60,000.
7 For dissenting views on the location of the capital of Mali, see Meillassoux (1972) and Hunwick (1973).
8 Although Mali lost control over the Sahel, it maintained itself on the Gambia River and expanded southward. In the fifteenth and sixteenth centuries, the Portuguese found that the kingdoms along the Gambia acknowledged the ruler of Mali as their sovereign. Caravans that reached the Gambia traveled under his orders and were accompanied by Malinke warriors. And far away in Elmina the Portuguese experienced competition from Malinke traders for the gold from the Akan forest. About 1493–5, an ambassador of the Portuguese king visited Niani Mansā Mamudu.
9 Islam, in addition to being a system of beliefs, is a code of laws. Because the Koran is open to interpretation in some number of passages, schools have evolved around various themes through which the true meanings of the writings are sought. The Maliki school of northern Africa seeks understanding of the law through examining the traditions of the city where the Prophet lived, Medina, in the time that he was there.
10 For this attribution of the Ta'rīkh al-Fattāsh, see Levtzion (1971).
11 Some estimates run as high as 20 million or more (Curtin 1969, pp. 3ff.).
12 As Davidson has put it: "Men became mere trade goods. Not only that; with the expansion of the Great Circuit enterprise in the seventeenth century, men became the *only* trade goods that really mattered. African chiefs found that the sale of their fellow men was indispensable to any contact or commerce with Europe. Unless they were willing – and not only willing, but active in delivery – the ships went elsewhere. That is how the system was installed" (1961, p. 85).
13 Levtzion (1971, pp. 174f.) suggests that in the Western Sudan, where gold dominated the trade, it was vital that peace and security should prevail over

all the country between the gold sources and the market towns of the Sahel. The gold trade thus encouraged the formation of states, their integration into large-scale empires, and the spread of Islam. Intensive slave trade, on the other hand, was based on continuous raids that bred terror and hostile relations between the raiding kingdoms and the neighbors they invaded.

14 Benin was connected to the Yoruba towns and probably followed a similar pattern. When the Portuguese first visited Benin in 1485, it was already a well-established state, with a large army conducting long compaigns far afield (Bradbury 1967, p. 5).

15 Most of the generalizations commonly made about Yoruba urbanization apply only to the northern Yoruba. Peter C. Lloyd (1962, pp. 54ff.) describes the different Ijebu settlement pattern. The farmland belonging to descent groups resident within Ijebu-Ode extends only a short distance from the town wall. Beyond that lie numerous villages, each of which is a distinct social and political unit with its own chief, who is, however, ultimately responsible to the ruler of Ijebu-Ode. The difference is highlighted in the occupational pattern. According to the 1952 census, the typical northern Yoruba town had more than half its adult males engaged in agriculture. In Ijebu-Ode, by contrast, only one-fifth of the men were farmers; the remainder were in "urban occupations."

Aronson (1970, pp. 44ff.) relates the Ijebu-Ode pattern to the fact that the Ijebu have been long established in trade and therefore had an attractive alternative to farming. Peter C. Lloyd (1962, pp. 56ff.) notes the difference between patrilinear succession in the agnatic lineage among northern Yoruba and cognatic descent in Ijebu-Ode and argues the significance of rule of descent. The difficulty with both interpretations is that they fail to deal with the other Yoruba group, Ondo, which was never prominent in trade, is characterized by cognatic descent groups, and constitutes an intermediary case; it has both socially autonomous villages of the Ijebu type and a large number of socially allegiant hamlets of the northern type (Peter C. Lloyd 1962, pp. 34 and 110ff.). Following Mabogunje's conjecture, the most plausible explanation of these variations would appear to be that the autonomous villages represent pre-Yoruba settlement that was not fully absorbed.

16 At the same time, farmers were being driven to reside behind town walls for safety.

2. Urbanization and economic development

1 For a detailed account of how both exports and imports have been diverted from three formerly important Senegalese ports (Saint-Louis, Kaolack, and Ziguinchor) to Dakar, see Seck (1970, pp. 351ff.).
Surviving secondary ports that continue to grow do so at a drastically slower pace than what is in nearly all countries the one primary port. For instance, the population of Saint-Louis rose only from 30,000 to 50,000 between 1937 and 1966, that of Grand Bassam only from 4,500 to 12,000 between 1937 and 1968 (White and Gleave 1971, pp. 263ff.). Port Harcourt may be seen as a primary port in its own right, located as it is at one end of the extensive Nigerian railroad system.

2 Information for 1970 provided by Peter K. Mitchell, director of the Demographic Documentation Project, Centre of West African Studies, University of Birmingham.

3 Saint-Louis, the colonial headquarters for both Senegal and Mauritania, was

the only one to be abandoned. Dakar became the capital of Senegal as it relinquished its role as colonial headquarters for French West Africa. Nouakchott was founded to provide Mauritania with a capital on its own soil.

4   The urban-system perspective employed by geographers takes the city's function as the focal point of social and economic organization and maps the interrelationships among the various cities within national boundaries. A "mature" urban system is one that reflects the focusing of specialized cities and towns within national boundaries, a situation yet to be achieved in outward-looking West African countries. Although there is not a great deal of research available on the topic of the development or underdevelopment of West African urban systems, Ghana has been a favorite target for researchers. The lack of system development in this relatively advanced nation is instructive (see Berry 1962 and McNulty 1969).

5   The new Tanzanian capital is not just another example of the transfer of the capital to a small town in a central location. Dodoma also promises to demonstrate that there are low-cost solutions to the multiple requirements of constructing a new capital city. Progress to date suggests that it will provide a contrast to the experience of Brasília, which stands as a monument to the heavy burden the grandiose conception of a new capital city can impose on a nation.

6   Since this was written, the Federal Government has announced plans to move the capital to a federal territory to be established south of Abuja, in the center of Nigeria.

7   Table 2.2 shows considerable continuity in the urban growth rates in the 1950s and the 1960s for West Africa, a continuity that holds even within individual countries. This lack of variation between the two decades is to some extent a function of the estimates, interpolations, and projections employed in arriving at the figures for 1970.

8   This point is strikingly demonstrated by the fact that 53 percent of the population of Dakar cannot afford the cost of an empty lot and minimal services offered under the site and services scheme (see infra.).

9   A dynamic analysis would also have to take into account the impact of rural–urban migration on rural development. Not only does the rural sector usually lose the best-educated young men, but it is also presumably the more enterprising individuals who make the decision to migrate. In areas where rural development opportunities and/or decreasing land–labor ratios (migrations drain off only part of the natural population increase in the rural areas) require technological changes, many potential innovators have already left to seek the established opportunities available in town.

10   Quantitative data on open urban unemployment are scanty at best; their reliability, very doubtful. A survey of published data yielded information only for Sierra Leone (1967), the Ivory Coast (1963), Ghana (1960 and 1970), Dahomey (1968), and Nigeria (1963 and 1966–7), with the proportion reported unemployed ranging from 8 to 15 percent (Gugler 1976).

11   In Lagos, underemployment appears severe even among skilled craftsmen such as printers, radio repairmen, goldsmiths, and auto mechanics (Peil n.d., p. 14).

12   In Table 2.2, we have used gross domestic product (GDP), which measures the output from factors of production located within the country. This measure would seem most appropriate for comparisons between levels of production and urbanization. Gross national product (GNP) subtracts from GDP the net flow of payments to foreign recipients. GNP thus values the output

produced by factors of production owned by residents of a particular country. This measure is the most appropriate for comparison of income levels among countries and has been used in the map preceding p. 1.

13 Whereas in 1953, people dodged the Nigerian census, many reasoning that it was associated in some way with taxation, the 1962 census followed a campaign of official exhortation to be counted. The politics of the matter were that representation in the federal parliament was according to population. The results were canceled when it appeared that certain states had inflated their rolls. The 1963 retake (with elections scheduled for the following year) was denounced as "less than useless," and the 55.7 million figure for the total population of Nigeria at that date remains suspect (Udo 1968, 1970). Late in 1973, 120,000 enumerators again took to the field. This time, each was accompanied by a soldier. Provisional figures were released, after two delays, by General Yakubu Gowon, the head of state, in May 1974. Total population was said to have increased to 79.8 million. Even more extraordinary, the populations of three states, Kano, Kwara, and North Eastern, were reported to be 89 to 97 percent higher than they had been a decade earlier. General Gowon emphasized that the figures were subject to modifications and not to be used for planning in the meantime; at the same time, he announced that a postenumeration survey was to be carried out (Enahoro 1974). In July 1975, when Brigadier Murtala Mohammed took over, he announced that the results of the 1973 census were canceled.

14 The relatively high level of urbanization in Nigeria is partly accounted for by the special pattern of Yoruba urbanization.

15 The comparability of Tables 2.3 and 2.2 is limited because our sources use different estimates.

16 In Nigeria the Federal Government decreed a new structure of twelve states in 1967. One consequence was that seven new state capitals, Calabar, Ilorin, Jos, Kano, Maiduguri, Port Harcourt, and Sokoto, could now compete more effectively for resources with Benin City, Enugu, Ibadan, and Kaduna, the former regional capitals, now the capitals of smaller states, and Lagos, capital of both a state and the Federation. The process was carried further in 1976, when Nigeria was reorganized into nineteen states and Abeokuta, Akure, Bauchi, Ikeja, Makurdi, Minna, Owerri, and Yola joined the ranks of state capitals.

17 In Senegal nearly 80 percent of industrial enterprises, 66 percent of all salaried employees, and 50 percent of civil servants are similarly concentrated in the Dakar area (Bachmann 1974, p. 51).
    Even Lagos, not a primate city, boasts a major share of industry, the pattern becoming more pronounced in recent years. In 1964, 35 percent of employees in Nigeria's manufacturing industry were working within the boundaries of what has since become Lagos State; by 1972 the proportion had increased to 44 percent, and their share in the wages and salaries paid in manufacturing had risen from 41 to 53 percent. In terms of gross output (56 percent) and value added (55 percent), more than half of Nigeria's manufacturing industry was located in Lagos in 1972 (Berger 1975, pp. 205ff.).

18 Dakar, in the mid-1960s, received three-fifths of the national health budget and had four-fifths of the medical doctors and two-thirds of the midwives in all Senegal (Sankalé et al. 1968, pp. 279f.).

19 The term "metropolis" is used here to denote cities with a population over 1 million.

20 For a summary of recent research on spontaneous housing on the periphery of Dakar, Abidjan, and Cotonou, see Vernière (1973).

21   Most of them are not squatters; rather they have negotiated access to land
      with landowners, typically with representatives of local communities control-
      ling land use.
22   If the cost has been heavy for many of the more than 11,000 people evicted
      from central Lagos, the implementation of redevelopment has been character-
      ized by corruption and inefficiency. Eviction began in 1956, but more than a
      decade later, only 25 of the 70 acres of land designated had been actually
      acquired by the Lagos Executive Development Board; of these 25 acres, only
      3.6 had been redeveloped. The rest of the land was used as improvised play-
      grounds, parking lots, garbage dumps, or markets for itinerant traders (Baker
      1974, pp. 94ff.).
23   This has caused the World Bank to turn to the strategy of upgrading existing
      slums and unauthorized settlements. Costs for residents are thus further
      reduced. Such an approach is clearly preferable to the indiscriminate eradica-
      tion of substandard housing. But the strategy in itself fails to provide a means
      of planning the location of new low-standard housing developments. West
      African governments will have to face the fact that a substantial proportion of
      their urban population cannot afford to pay for house lots. Rather than react-
      ing to unauthorized settlement, it would seem desirable to anticipate it by the
      establishment of site and services projects that offer free land while charging
      for the minimal services provided.
24   The distinction among these three levels of analysis is derived from Safier
      (1970).

3. Rural–urban migration

1   The 1970 Ghana census found 22 percent of the population living outside
      their region of birth (de Graft-Johnson 1974, 474f.).
2   For an attempt to explain the high degree of receptivity to change of one
      people, the Ibo, see Simon Ottenberg (1959).
3   The reasons for rural–rural migration are strikingly similar to those for
      rural–urban migration, both in the case of employment being taken in planta-
      tions, see, for example, Ardener, Ardener, and Warmington (1960, pp. 248ff.)
      on Cameroun, and in the case of work for small-scale farmers in com-
      paratively wealthy areas, see, for example, A. D. Goddard (1974) on the
      Sokoto zone in Northern Nigeria.
4   Such a formulation would seem preferable to an analysis in terms of push or
      pull, which obscures the fact that a comparison between the points of depar-
      ture and destination is involved and which encourages undue emphasis on
      a single factor.
5   The only pertinent reference we can find is in a footnote on page 324 in
      which Parsons explains the distinction between rate and incidence and gives
      unemployment as an example. Personal inefficiency may well explain why
      one person rather than another is unemployed at a given time. But it is
      extremely unlikely that a sudden change in the efficiency of the working
      population of the United States occurred that could account for the enormous
      increase in unemployment between 1929 and 1932. The latter is a problem of
      rate, not of incidence.
6   The proposition that potential migrants take into account not only rural–
      urban real-income differentials but also the probability of securing urban
      employment has been incorporated into an econometric model (Harris and

Todaro 1968; Todaro 1969; Harris and Todaro 1970). The probability of obtaining urban employment is defined as the proportion of the urban labor force actually employed. For a critique, see Gugler (1976).

7 Skinner (1974, pp. 54ff.) reports that in Ouagadougou many immigrants who declare themselves unemployed in fact farm peri-urban land obtained for the planting season from local chiefs.

4. Townsman and absentee villager

1 Simon Ottenberg (1955) describes the beginnings of such involvement in home affairs in the Afikpo area in what was then Eastern Nigeria.

2 For accounts of associations that were particularly successful in this respect, see Smock (1971, pp. 27ff.) and Gugler (1969a, pp. 98ff.).

3 The conspicuous character of contributions made by or extorted from members is striking to a Western observer. The economically successful, in particular, are under constant pressure to contribute to village developments. Most continue to be committed to the village and to their standing in the eyes of people from the village (whether resident in the village or in town) and pay up. These patterns reaffirm community control over "our son," no matter how high he has risen in the outside world. They stand in contrast with the inequality inherent in patron–client relationships.

4 From rudimentary beginnings in colonial days, the scope of social security legislation expanded in all West African countries (except Senegal and Sierra Leone) to cover a wider range of contingencies, but only Ghana has a system of unemployment insurance, instituted in 1972. Benefits are limited to a first payment equal to 50 percent of the insured person's monthly wage after two months of unemployment and a second payment equal to 20 percent of that wage or 15 cedis (whichever is greater) at the end of the third month of unemployment. In Nigeria, the unemployed can withdraw their contributions (and if they have reached age fifty-five, their employers' contributions) with accrued interest from a provident fund (Mouton 1975, pp. 3ff., pp. 38f.).

5 Those who can anticipate a small pension know that its purchasing power will go farther in the village.

6 The precarious position of the urban worker contrasts with that of the rural–rural migrant, whose wife and children can contribute to production and who frequently is able to acquire land. Nevertheless, cocoa farmers in southeastern Ghana who bought land away from home two or three generations ago and who are fully resident in the cocoa area, together with their wives and children, still regard themselves as "camping" there, are involved in a constant to-and-fro movement with their hometowns, and put part of their profits into house building there (Hill 1963, pp. 1 and 17).

7 These expectations were shattered for some as the Civil War forced them to fall back on the support the village had to offer.

8 Udo (1972, pp. 4f.) reports successful moves by urban-based elites to forbid the lease of land in their home areas to migrant farmers and to eject already established migrant farmers.

9 To the extent that politicians rely on an ethnically circumscribed base and distribute patronage on the same lines, other elite members are dependent on them. This can apply to civil servants who are seeking to further their careers and therefore may be induced to emphasize their ethnic affiliation (Peter C. Lloyd 1966b, pp. 333f.).

10   The disgrace in death of not having a proper house at home for sympathizers to admire and to shelter mourners is also brought out in Agunwa's novel *More than Once.*

11   Pons (1969, pp. 75ff. and 99) strikingly shows how rural involvement varied within one town (Kisangani, Zaïre) among ethnic groups. The high levels of urban and rural involvements of the Lokele tended to reinforce each other. For the Babua, high urban involvement went hand in hand with low rural involvement. Conversely, the Topoke had limited urban involvement but a high degree of continuing rural involvement. Underlying factors included the accessibility of home areas, the degree of success in the urban economy, and for the Lokele, the opportunity to supply Kisangani with products from their home area and eventually to control the markets in fish, vegetables, and fruits.

5. Social relationships in the urban setting

1   Banton (1973, pp. 57ff.) emphasizes that the degree of discontinuity migrants experience between rural and urban social systems varies considerably. He suggests that continuity is greater in West Africa than in Zambia because the countryside has been permeated by urban values to a greater extent and the nature of the urban system with respect to employment and housing is less discouraging to the perpetuation of rural social patterns. Banton summarizes a number of factors affecting the degree of rural–urban continuity.

2   A great deal of education in West Africa has been provided by missions, which tended to operate within linguistically homogeneous areas. Religious differences thus became part of ethnic differences. Sometimes, this pattern is perpetuated in the urban setting. Plotnicov (1967, pp. 78f. and 293f.) reported from Jos that the urban elite sent its children to the schools of the missions with which its ethnic groups were historically associated.

3   There is very little information about stages of migration in West Africa. But this pattern of joining kin or covillagers suggests that migrants move directly to where they can expect a familiar welcome rather than following a pattern of stepwise migration by way of intermediate centers to the major cities. Where this entails long-distance travel, it is facilitated by the availability of fast and cheap transport.

4   For data from Lagos, Abeokuta, Aba, and Kaduna on the extent of ethnic homogeneity among cotenants see Peil (1975a, pp. 114ff.).

5   For more recent data on the ethnic identity of close friends in working-class suburbs of Lagos and Kaduna, see Peil (1975a, pp. 116ff.).

6   In a country with a long urban history, such as Mali, people are more frequently classed according to the town or area in which they and their immediate ascendants have lived than according to their often ambiguous "tribal" origin (Nicholas S. Hopkins 1972, pp. 45ff.).

7   For the social control exerted by the neighborhood, especially on women, children, and young adolescents, see Chapter 6.

8   Europeans and West Africans associated more closely up to about the turn of the century. At that time, the death rate among Europeans dropped drastically as the causes of malaria were understood. The number of Europeans increased, they now brought their wives out to West Africa, their young children lived with them, and a separate European community was firmly established.

9   This conceptual methodology was first developed by John A. Barnes (1954) in his study of a Norwegian fishing and farming island parish. Bott's (1957)

study of conjugal roles in Britain has been the classic application and point of reference. Both Mitchell (1969) and John A. Barnes (1969; 1972) have offered detailed discussions of social network characteristics that can be analytically important. A taxonomy may also be found in Wolfe (1970); he further proposes a matrix of frequencies of scores on twelve variables and a three-dimensional model for multiple comparisons. Recently, the clarification of concepts has been carried forward in work by Laumann (1973), Mitchell (1973, 1974), Niemeijer (1973), Thoden van Velzen (1973), White, Boorman and Breiger (1976), and Boorman and White (1976).

10   The discussion of ethnic unions and ethnic organizations draws heavily on our research among Eastern Nigerians in 1961–2, see Gugler (1971).

11   For an account of the activities of a clan association in Sapele and extracts from its constitution, see Imoagene (1967, pp. 58ff.).

12   For recent data from Tema, Lagos, Abeokuta, Aba, and Kaduna on affiliation with and participation in Pentecostal and Apostolic groups, Jehovah's Witnesses, and the Salvation Army, and on membership in church associations, see Peil (1975b).

13   Ifeka-Moller (1974, p. 68) suggests that both the ethnic union and the independent church are rooted in the collectivist norms of the village community. They carry the "kinship ideology" and the "ritual ideology," respectively, that Abner Cohen (1969, pp. 208f.) sees as the two major forms of ideologies to be found in "simple societies" and that he relates to the distinction between segmentary and centralized systems.

14   For a description of ethnic specialization in the markets of Niamey, see Bernus (1969, pp. 59ff.).

15   In Jos, we attended the practice dance of an organization representing the immigrants from an administrative district in Eastern Nigeria. People from neighboring villages that had been feuding over land for many years were dancing together. A few months later, in their home area, men were killed in renewed violence between the two villages.

16   Wolpe (1974, p. 6) uses "communalism" as a more comprehensive concept than "ethnic conflict." In particular it includes intergroup conflicts involving religion. In the context of Port Harcourt, "communal" is identical to "ethnic" in the extended sense in which we have used it. Wolpe's mention of "townspeople" refers to people from the same home area.

17   Formal ethnic associations are widespread but far from universal. Among many immigrants, a good deal of authority is wielded by more or less formally recognized leaders who settle disputes and organize the ethnic group in emergency situations.

18   In Mali, a long urban history is reflected in ethnic organizations that are based not on "tribal" origin but on town or area of birth. Such organizations did become politically involved during the nationalist movement and encountered the hostility of both colonial authorities and the independent government. Accordingly, they came to take on a very informal character (Meillassoux 1968, pp. 61, 69f., and 77ff.).
      In Niger, ethnic organizations were similarly discouraged in both the colonial and the postcolonial settings (Bernus 1969, pp. 166f.). In Upper Volta, many organizations were banned at the time of Independence (Skinner 1974, pp. 211ff.).

19   Ethnic associations and ethnic organizations alike are frequently referred to as "tribal unions." As can be seen from the discussion, this term is inaccurate because most represent groups of origin much smaller than could be called

"tribes" in any accepted sense of the term. The term current in Francophone countries, *"associations d'originaires,"* is more felicitous.

20 Most social scientists appear strangely insensitive to the importance of language in the everyday life of the masses, for the education and occupational career of the elite, and as the medium of ideology. Note, however, that intelligibility between languages is itself a function of interethnic trends and relationships, a point strikingly demonstrated by Wolff (1959) with examples from Nigeria.

21 At times, customs are revived in order to cater to modern needs. Thus, in a village where age-grade celebrations had been abolished, age-groups were brought to the fore of community life anew, and the competition among them, a traditional feature, was directed toward village development (Gugler 1969a, p. 103).

22 Cohen's description of this process as "retribalization" is less than felicitous in that it encourages misinterpretation of his position. Still, the shift in terminology is significant. In the 1950s, when Rouch referred to the Zabrama in Accra as "super-tribalized," he took their "tribal" identification for granted. In the 1960s, Cohen's notion of "retribalization" suggests that the occurrence of "tribal" identification in the urban setting requires an explanation.

23 Such an arrangement obviously suited the colonial administration. A mosaic of "tribes" in the city was easier to control than an African working class; there was, furthermore, the possibility of having some control exerted from the "tribal" (i.e., the rural and usually conservative) end.

24 Conversely, where military rule eclipsed electoral politics, ethnic organizations lost much of their power if they were not banned outright.

25 Hanna and Hanna (1969), in their research in Umuahia, directed attention to the role of community influentials. They emphasized the integrative role played by such key townsmen. Horizontally, they link ethnic groups within town; vertically, they connect the town with the regional and national leadership.

26 For an extensive discussion of the politics of ethnicity, with special reference to Nigeria, see Melson and Wolpe (1971). They present fourteen propositions on economic competition among ethnic groups, relations between political and ethnic institutions, changes in ethnic groups, and situational selection.

27 The ruling class in Liberia is made up largely of Americo-Liberians. But even this ethnic group, established in its privileged position by conquest, includes lower socioeconomic strata that are powerless even while they boast of their "civilized" status in opposition to the "tribal" people.

28 It is quite extraordinary to see a recent account of political events in Kano that discusses the riots in 1953 and in May 1966 in some detail pass over the organized massacres of October 1966 in one sentence (Paden 1973, p. 334). It has remained for Soyinka, Nigeria's foremost playwright, to create a monument to the victims in his novel *Season of Anomy.*

6. Three types of change

1 For what has been perhaps the most remarkable of these rural transformations, see Hill's (1963) account of how cocoa, a nonindigeneous tree that takes several years before it begins to yield, was pioneered by migrant farmers in southeastern Ghana.

2 A small intercalary group played an important role as traders, clergy, teachers, and agents for the colonial governments. They were in the main former slaves,

freed in the Americas and Europe or liberated on the high seas, who had settled as Creoles in Freetown (where Fourah Bay College was established already in 1827), as Americo-Liberians in Monrovia, as Brazilians in Lagos and Ouidah. They were joined by the descendants of the unions of European merchants and African women; their ranks swelled through adoption of local children. In Liberia, they continue to enjoy privileged social and economic position and to monopolize political power, even though they constitute only about 2 percent of the population (Liebenow 1969). For accounts of the role such groups played in the past in Freetown and Lagos, see Porter (1963) and Kopytoff (1965), respectively.

3   In the liberated areas of Guinea-Bissau, the Portuguese language has been taught from the first year (Rudebeck 1974, pp. 203f. and 216f.). In Mali, there appears to be a recent shift away from inherited French patterns, with a program of using Bambara and other local languages as the medium of instruction in primary school (Vera L. Zolberg 1974, p. 16).

4   Moore [(1963) 1974, p. 78] has suggested that aesthetic canons and forms and strictly superempirical components of religious belief are relatively autonomous. If, indeed, certain subsystems are relatively insulated from the effects of other systemic changes, then it can be further surmised that changes, including those of external origin, come more easily to them.

5   The Cornell–Aro Mental Health Research Project is sometimes cited as indicating a higher incidence of psychic disorders in urban than in rural areas, but a more detailed analysis of the data from that study does not sustain this interpretation. The study produced psychiatric ratings, based on symptoms reported in interviews, observations made during the interviews, third-party reports (usually by the village headman), hemoglobin tests, and when indicated, a medical examination for samples in Abeokuta and fourteen villages nearby. The overall results suggested a higher incidence of psychiatric disorders in Abeokuta than in the villages. A breakdown by sex and age shows indeed a substantially higher incidence of symptoms indicative of psychiatric disorders in the city, as compared with the villages, among young and even more so among old women; however, for middle-aged women and for old men, the ratings were somewhat lower in the city, and residence made little difference for young and middle-aged men (Leighton et al. 1963, p. 128).

6   Whether workers lived in Lagos or in Ibadan did not make for any significant difference either.

7   Manifold ethnic clues are available to the urban dweller confronted with a stranger: cultural modifications of physical appearance; dress, ornaments, and crafts; speech, even when a lingua franca is used; behavior ranging from traditional dances to minor physical mannerisms; occupation. Where neighborhoods are ethnically homogeneous, residence also provides an indicator.

8   The task of applying this type of analysis to West African cities and of establishing their relative position on such a continuum remains to be undertaken. For the successful application of a vast array of similar criteria to a range of rural and small urban communities in Britain and Ireland, see Frankenberg (1966).

9   Banton (1957, p. 219) has taken the position that this approach is of little assistance in analyzing trends within urban societies because of its negative definition of city living; it may be true that city life evidences characteristics opposite to those of the folk society, but it also has others that cannot be defined in counterterms of peasant society (e.g., the positive significance of voluntary associations not only as social institutions but also as embryonic

bearers and creators of culture). For a discussion of the folk–urban ideal types, see Lewis (1965) and Hauser (1965).

7. The family: continuity and change

1   We will focus on the urban couple in the context of our discussion of changes in the position of women in Chapter 8.
2   Among the variations of extended family forms encountered in West Africa are the formalized pattern of urban Yoruba family corporation (Sandra T. Barnes 1974, pp. 87f.), the urban-based complex households found in Monrovia (Fraenkel 1964, pp. 127ff.), and the mixed patterns of household and family structure encountered in Ouagadougou (Skinner 1974, pp. 90ff.).
3   Plotnicov (1970, p. 72) remarks that "home unions" operate in emergencies where relatives do not have sufficient resources to help but that unions are prepared to play only a limited role, the expectation being that substantial and prolonged support is the responsibility of the family.
4   Yet Goode had not divorced himself entirely from the earlier position. In the Preface to the paperback edition of *World Revolution and Family Patterns* in 1970, he acknowledged that "this monograph has supported a widespread hypothesis that industrialization does undermine large kin systems, and moves family systems generally toward some version of the conjugal system found in Western countries" [Goode (1963), 1970, pp. xvf.].
5   At times, net transfers are made from rural to urban areas. Such was the case in five out of the six villages surveyed by Essang and Mabawonku (1974, p. 27) in Western State, Nigeria, in 1971–2.
6   An equally or more important variable may be that the Northerners are most likely to leave their wives and children in the home area.
7   Elsewhere in Africa, Marris found that the greatest *reported* needs of Kenyan businessmen were for loans and training. He comments that "these are, in fact, the resources which the government is trying to provide, through loan schemes, a management training center, and extension workers. Yet all over the world, these obviously relevant policies have ended in disappointment" (1968, p. 30).
8   The *ìdílé* stands in contrast with the *ebi*, which is simply the pool of kindred to which individuals are tied by reciprocal obligatory relations varying in intensity by genealogical distance. However, the two terms, *ìdílé* and *ebi*, are not applied as strictly or exclusively in common usage among the Yoruba in Lagos (Sandra T. Barnes 1974, pp. 87f. and 117, fn. 1–3).
9   This is not to say that urbanites do not enjoy a certain amount of insulation from family members. Marris (1961, pp. 98ff.) reported that some newly suburban residents who had been forced to move away from relatives by urban renewal in the center of Lagos expressed relief from the constant prying and demanding of relatives. These were mostly young people who had grown to resent the control of their elders or who felt that the tensions between family members, mostly their wives and own mothers, led to the intolerable condition of disrespect toward the elder generation. Another category was made up of those who sought relief from the day-to-day demands of relatives for money. In the suburbs, they would be sought out only for loans or gifts in crises of sufficient magnitude to warrant the investment in bus fare on the part of the solicitor.
     On the whole, however, the remote rehousing estate disproportionately attracted "those who were least characteristic of the streets from which they had

been moved." Besides "the young rebel escaping from a domineering family," the estate drew to it greater than representative numbers of men from the Eastern Region who were without close family ties in Lagos. Of the total relocated, less than a third preferred the estate; whereas 57 percent wished they were back in their old homes in the center of Lagos. This last percentage would have been higher except for the fact that so many were opposed to the move (only 3 percent originally wanted to go to the new estate) and some of these simply refused the relocation and made their own way to other parts of the city, some with the aid of relatives.

10   The advance of Christianity and Islam presumably also affected the position of the old in the many societies where the ancestors held an important place. The new religions cut this link, as an inscription on a truck in Nigeria put it succinctly: "No telephone to heaven."

11   Azu (1974, p. 75) notes that in Ga lineage councils, wealthy and educated young men are now given a hearing that their age formerly would not have permitted; they are even entrusted with offices such as those of treasurer or secretary.

12   The self-selected nature of any sample of urban residents presents a problem in interpreting the data. We cannot infer from the data how important the urban experience was in changing respondents' attitudes, as against what proportion of the urban sample came to town with "modern" opinions about choosing a marriage partner.

8. Changes in the position of women

1   In an overview of the issue, Paulme [(1960) 1963, pp. 4ff.] agrees that masculine dominance in the political sphere was not entirely mythical, but she holds that the position of women in the kinship group was neither superior nor inferior to that of the men, that it was simply different and complementary. She reacts in particular against outside observers who compare African practice with the Western ideal. Indeed, it is tempting to speculate how European men delighted in trumpeting the inferior position of women in Africa in order to drown out the voices decrying the gap between ideal and practice in their own societies.

Kamene Okonjo (1976) emphasizes that a number of political systems in West Africa were "dual-sex." For example, throughout Ibo country each sex generally managed its own affairs and had its own kinship institutions, age grades, and secret and title societies. Okonjo describes the pattern among the Western Ibo where the (male) ruler had his counterpart in the *omu*, the "mother," who was charged with concern for the female section of the community. One of the main functions of the *omu* and her councillors was to oversee the local market.

Traditional Afikpo Ibo society provides an illustration of male domination made explicit. Relations between men and women were in fact characterized by strong male domination. The ideal of the innate superiority of men over women was backed by men's control over land and the supernatural and by sanctions of the village men's society, one of whose explicit purposes was to "keep the women down" (Phoebe V. Ottenberg 1959, pp. 207f.).

For a functionalist interpretation of the position of women in marriage in traditional patrilineal societies, see Dobkin (1968).

2   For a comparison with the position of women in other parts of the Third World, see Boserup (1970).

3   For a brief reference to the situation in Ghana, see Vellenga (1971, pp. 138f.).

4   However, Dobkin (1968) summarizes accounts of the dislocating effects of the very same legislation. It is not always clear, though, to what extent such changes were effects of the legislation rather than of other forces simultaneously at work. The inflation in bridewealth in particular would seem to have to be traced to the spread of the money economy.

5   For a discussion of the sources of discrimination in Ouagadougou and changes over the last two decades, see Skinner (1974, pp. 248ff.).

6   There is little information on patterns of attrition and the variables involved. Eliou (1972) shows that once in the secondary system, the survival rate of girls as against boys is significantly higher in the Ivory Coast but very much lower in Upper Volta.

7   In his overview of research on the spread of family-planning knowledge, attitudes, and practices in Tropical Africa, Caldwell (1968b, p. 618) reports that change has in fact been greatest in the large towns.

8   The journal *West Africa* has regularly carried short biographical accounts of elite women. A number of such accounts of women prominent in commerce, politics, and government administration are summarized by Little (1973, pp. 199ff.).

9   Lawson (1971, pp. 309f.), in her study of food retailing in Ghana, reports that between 1963 and 1967, retail marketing services for local foods developed better in the urban centers, particularly in Accra, than in the rural centers. She goes on to suggest that markets in the large towns and cities are likely to continue to provide a low-cost service and to remain more competitive than rural retail markets as long as there are few opportunities for the employment of urban unskilled female labor.

10 If the husband comes from a region characterized by matrilineal descent and inheritance, there is the very real fear for the wife that upon widowhood only a very small part of any household property will remain hers. Accordingly, the tendency to keep their finances separate is more pronounced when the husband belongs to a matrilineage rather than a patrilineage (Oppong 1974, pp. 90ff.).

11 In the early 1960s, a court in Ouagadougou still awarded a child to its father even though he had abandoned the mother when she became pregnant and had not supported the child for several years. In another case, a wife was granted a divorce because her husband had abused, threatened, and maltreated her; insulted his in-laws; and failed to support his children. However, custody of the children was given to him (Skinner 1974, pp. 361ff. and 376ff.).

12 Tardits found that education of ascendants made no significant difference. Omari did not control for this factor.

13 For research on changes in polygyny in the Ivory Coast, see Clignet (1970) and Clignet and Sween (1969).

14 The power of women similarly increases in rural families in which men are away in distant employment – unless male relatives take charge. Control over women by close male relatives can sometimes be found even in urban areas.

15 Women's representation in legislative bodies usually does not go beyond tokenism. The case of Guinea, where twenty out of seventy-five deputies elected to parliament in 1968 were women, is exceptional (Rivière 1971, p. 150).

16 The fact that substantial numbers of unemployed men crowd the major cities

is irrelevant to the argument here. As we have seen in Chapter 3, the urban unemployed are not a stable group; rather, there is constant movement between urban and rural areas. Opening up urban employment opportunities to women would reduce opportunities for men and hence discourage them from migrating to town. Such a policy is not likely to attract many more women, given the numbers of women who are already in urban residence and who would have considerable advantages over new arrivals in competing for jobs.

9. Stratification and social mobility

1 For detailed discussions of precolonial stratification in Subsaharan Africa, see Fallers (1964) and Southall (1970). The case studies of Ronald Cohen (1970) and Margaret M. Green (1947) illustrate two extremes of political organization and stratification.

2 Peter C. Lloyd's (1974, pp. 41ff.) account of the Yoruba case illustrates such a pattern.

3 These data give a Gini coefficient of income distribution of 0.47.

4 Differentials in money income tell only part of the story because fringe benefits are substantial. Senior civil servants in Nigeria enjoy subsidized housing and continue to receive a car allowance. Members of the elite have privileged access to medical care and to educational facilities for their children.

5 Comparative data are lacking, but by all accounts, the concentration of income in the hands of the few is most pronounced in Liberia. An American survey team estimated that approximately half of Liberia's national income accrued directly to foreign households and business firms in 1960; another quarter accrued directly or indirectly to a small group of Liberian householders (probably no more than 3 percent of the population), one or more members of which held political office or salaried positions in government (Clower et al. 1966, p. 67).

6 For a review of sources of weakness and strength of trade unions in Africa and especially Nigeria, see Robin Cohen (1974, pp. 240ff.). However, he fails to consider what may well be a crucial point: West African trade unions appear not to have provided welfare services that elsewhere have encouraged the recruitment and commitment of members. Instead, welfare functions were assumed by other groupings, frequently very effectively by ethnic associations (see Chapter 5).

7 For a summary of, and contribution to, the debate over the influence trade unions have had in wage determination in Nigeria, see Robin Cohen (1974, pp. 197ff.).

8 In his survey in Agege and Ibadan, Peter C. Lloyd (1974, pp. 148ff.) has gone beyond the sterile prestige ranking of occupations and instead focused on the reasons given for the ranking of triads of occupations with equal incomes. Apart from income, which many respondents referred to in spite of contrary instructions, four themes emerged: first and clearly predominant, a preference for self-employment; second, a man who does employ others has very high prestige, and he is accorded deference; third, many of the occupations were assessed in terms of the opportunities provided to exercise patronage or receive its benefits; fourth, learning and skill appeared to be valued for their own sake and in terms of service to the community.

9 For a more detailed discussion, see Charle (1970) who first suggested an analysis of the ratio of passenger cars to commercial vehicles.

10 Since the Civil War, Nigeria maintains an army more than twice as large as

that of any other country in Africa. Among West African countries it allocates the highest proportion of GNP, over five percent in 1973, to military expenditures, imposing the highest per capita burden on its population. The dubious distinction of having the largest army, relative to its population, goes, in West Africa, to Liberia (Sivard 1976, pp. 23 and 28).

11   See, however, Berg (1971, pp. 224f.) for questions concerning the reliability of these figures.

12   To a lesser degree, this probably also applies to the close relatives of the educated.

13   Although the secondary school enterprise in Ghana was very much larger than that in the Ivory Coast, the children of farmers, of semiskilled, and of unskilled workers were more severely underrepresented in Ghana than in the Ivory Coast (Clignet and Foster 1964b, pp. 351f. and 356). In southern Nigeria and in Mali, the children of farmers were similarly underrepresented by about half (Abernethy 1969, p. 245; Vera L. Zolberg 1974, pp. 7ff.).

14   At Ahmadu Bello University, Zaria, more than half of the students surveyed in 1970–1 reported that their fathers were farmers (O'Connell and Beckett 1975).

15   A survey of the urban upper and middle class in Ghana in 1963 found that the great majority had rejected the traditional aim of a very large family while not embracing Western very small family values. The majority advocated families of four to six children for their friends or daughters. Extra children still wanted by the respondents would, if added to their surviving children, have brought their desired family size to about one more child per family than might have been expected from their views on others' families. And in fact, those women who had already completed their reproductive span or were drawing near to its close had on average borne about six children, not appreciably fewer than was typical of Ghanaian society as a whole (Caldwell 1968a, pp. 88f. and 27).

16   The discrepancy is understated to the extent that the poor children presumably derived some benefit from the study, both because of the regular visits to the Institute of Child Health at the University College Hospital and because the mothers were given a curative dose of chloroquine for the children to take when required and some dried milk powder or other food at each visit (Janes 1974, p. 390).

17   Urban mass protest movements elsewhere have been similarly ephemeral. In Abidjan, during the summer of 1969, several unemployed Ivoiriens decided to organize the large numbers of unemployed young men throughout the city. In each of the two most populous divisions of the city, a committee of six was established that included representatives of five ethnic groups and presented itself as a cross-ethnic coalition. The leadership consisted of secondary-school graduates, many well read, some eager to discuss Dumont, Fanon, and the political charisma of Mayor John Lindsay of New York. When they called a mass meeting, some 1,600 were arrested by soldiers, detained for more than three months, and then dispersed to agricultural training camps in the interior that were run by the military. A series of "dialogues" of various occupational groups with the president, a cabinet reshuffle, and a number of policy changes ensued (Michael A. Cohen 1972; 1974a, pp. 105f., 115ff., and 145ff.).

18   Presumably because of the international prominence of Nkrumah, the case of Ghana has attracted most attention, see Kraus (1971), Kilson (1971), Berg (1971), Green (1971), Owusu (1970), and Genoud (1969).

Conclusion: The incorporation of the West African peasantry

1 The discussion here is conceptually indebted to Pearse's (1970) analysis of the incorporation of the Latin American peasant.

2 Contrast this situation with the pattern in India, where villages usually conduct their external economic affairs through specialized middlemen; frequently, their style of life is not likely to be copied by their fellow villagers (Lambert 1962, p. 126).

3 Again, the contrast is striking with India, where the urban elite in the large centers differs from the rural elite and even the elite in small towns in its education, its language of communication, its religious practices, and its attitudes and style of life (Hoselitz 1962, pp. 171ff.).

4 To the extent that a country's currency is overvalued in regard to convertible currencies, producers of export crops are shortchanged even if they are paid according to world market prices; in fact, they subsidize imports, the lion's share of which is absorbed by the urban sector.

5 For a discussion of the revolutionary potential of African peasantries, see Saul (1974).

6 For a detailed account and analysis of political actions taken by peasants in Western Nigeria see Beer (1976).

Bibliography

Abernethy, David B. 1969. *The political dilemma of popular education: An African case.* Stanford: University Press.
Abu-Lughod, Janet. 1961. Migrant adjustment to city life: The Egyptian case. *American Journal of Sociology* 67:22–32.
Achebe, Chinua. 1958. *Things fall apart.* London: Heinemann.
    1960. *No longer at ease.* London: Heinemann.
    1966. *A man of the people.* London: Heinemann; New York: John Day. Excerpt reprinted pages 175–7.
Adams, Bert N. 1968. Kinship systems and adaptation to modernization. *Studies in Comparative International Development* 4:47–60.
Adeleye, R. A. 1971. Hausaland and Bornu 1600–1800. Pages 484–530 in J. F. A. Ajayi and Michael Crowder (eds.), *History of West Africa*, Volume 1. London: Longman; New York: Columbia University Press.
Adepoju, Aderanti. 1974. Migration and socio-economic links between urban migrants and their home communities in Nigeria. *Africa* 44:383–95.
Agunwa, Clement. 1967. *More than once.* London: Longmans.
Akinola, R. A. 1963. The Ibadan region. *Nigerian Geographical Journal* 6:102–15.
Amin, Samir. 1967. *Le dévelopement du capitalisme en Côte d'Ivoire.* Paris: Editions de Minuit.
    1969. *Le monde des affaires Sénégalais. Paris*: Editions de Minuit.
    1971a. *L'Afrique de l'Ouest bloquée: L'économie politique de la colonisation 1880–1970.* Paris: Editions de Minuit. English translation, 1973, *Neo-colonialism in West Africa.* Harmondsworth: Penguin.
    1971b. Development and structural changes: African experience. Pages 312–33 in Barbara Ward, J. D. Runnals, and Leonore d'Anjou (eds.), *The widening gap: Development in the 1970's.* New York: Columbia University Press.
Anderson, Michael. 1971. *Family structure in nineteenth century Lancashire.* Cambridge Studies in Sociology 5. Cambridge: Cambridge University Press.
Ardener, Edwin W. 1961. Social and demographic problems of the Southern Cameroons plantation area. Pages 83–97 in Aidan W. Southall (ed.), *Social change in modern Africa.* London: Oxford University Press.
Ardener, Edwin; Shirley Ardener; and W. A. Warmington. 1960. *Plantation and village in the Cameroons: Some economic and social studies.* London: Oxford University Press.
Aronson, Dan R. 1970. Cultural stability and social change among the modern Ijebu Yoruba. Ph.D. dissertation, University of Chicago.
    1978. *The City is our farm: Seven migrant Ijebu Yoruba families.* Cambridge, Mass.: Schenkman. Excerpts reprinted pages 123–7.
Arrighi, Giovanni; and John S. Saul. 1969. Nationalism and revolution in Sub-Saharan Africa. Pages 137–88 in Ralph Miliband and John Saville (eds.), *The Socialist Register 1969.* London: Merlin Press. Reprinted revised pages 44–

102 in Giovanni Arrighi and John S. Saul, 1973, *Essays on the political economy of Africa*. New York: Monthly Review Press.

Awe, Bolanle. 1967. Ibadan, its early beginnings. Pages 11–25 in P. C. Lloyd, A. L. Mabogunje, and B. Awe (eds.), *The city of Ibadan*. Cambridge: Cambridge University Press.

Azu, Diana Gladys. 1974. *The Ga family and social change*. Africa Social Research Document 5. Leiden: Afrika-Studiecentrum; Cambridge: African Studies Centre.

Bachmann, Heinz B. 1974. *Senegal: Tradition, diversification, and economic development*. Washington, D.C.: World Bank.

Baker, Pauline H. 1974. *Urbanization and political change: The politics of Lagos, 1917–1967*. Berkeley: University of California Press.

al-Bakrī. 1068. *Kitāb al-masālik wa' l-mamālik*. French translation of parts dealing with the Western Sudan, pages 80–109 in Joseph M. Cuoq, 1975, *Recueil des sources arabes concernant l'Afrique Occidentale du VIIIᵉ au XVIᵉ siècle (Bilād al-Sūdān)*. Sources d'Histoire Médiévale. Paris: Centre National de la Recherche Scientifique.

Balandier, Georges. 1955. *Sociologie des Brazzavilles Noires*. Paris: Armand Colin.

[1955] 1971. *Sociologie actuelle de l'Afrique Noire: Dynamique sociale en Afrique Centrale*. Third edition. Paris: Presses Universitaires de France. English translation, 1970, *The sociology of Black Africa: Social dynamics in Central Africa*. New York: Praeger.

1960. Structures sociales traditionnelles et changements économiques. *Cahiers d'Etudes Africaines* 1:1–14. English translation, pages 385–95 in Pierre L. van den Berghe (ed.), 1965, *Africa: Social problems of change and conflict*. San Francisco: Chandler.

Banton, Michael. 1957. *West African city: A study of tribal life in Freetown*. London: Oxford University Press.

1973. Urbanization and role analysis. Pages 43–70 in Aidan Southall (ed.), *Urban anthropology: Cross-cultural studies of urbanization*. London: Oxford University Press.

Barnes, John A. 1954. Class and committees in a Norwegian island parish. *Human Relations* 7:39–58. Reprinted pages 233–52 in Samuel Leinhardt (ed.), 1977, *Social networks: A developing paradigm*. New York: Academic Press.

1969. Networks and political process. Pages 51–76 in J. Clyde Mitchell (ed.), *Social networks in urban situations: Analysis of personal relationships in Central African towns*. Manchester: Manchester University Press.

1972. *Social networks*. Module 26. Reading, Mass.: Addison-Wesley.

Barnes, Sandra T. 1974. Becoming a Lagosian. Ph.D. dissertation, University of Wisconsin. Excerpt reprinted pages 76–9.

1975. Voluntary associations in a metropolis: The case of Lagos, Nigeria. *African Studies Review* 18(2):75–87.

Bascom, William R. 1955. Urbanization among the Yoruba. *American Journal of Sociology* 60:446–54.

1963. The urban African and his world. *Cahiers d'Etudes Africaines* 4:163–85.

Baylet, R.; A. Benyoussef; and P. Cantrelle. 1972. Recherches sur la morbidité et la mortalité différentielles urbaines-rurales au Sénégal. Pages 317–37 in *La croissance urbaine en Afrique Noire et à Madagascar*, Volume 1. Paris: Centre National de la Recherche Scientifique.

Beals, Ralph E.; Mildred B. Levy; and Leon N. Moses. 1967. Rationality and migration in Ghana. *Review of Economics and Statistics* 49:480–6.

Bebler, Anton. 1973. *Military rule in Africa. Dahomey, Ghana, Sierra Leone, and Mali.* New York: Praeger.

Beer, Christopher E. F. 1976. *The politics of peasant groups in Western Nigeria.* Ibadan Social Science 7. Ibadan: Ibadan University Press.

Berg, Elliot J. 1961. Backward-sloping labour supply functions in dual economies: The Africa case. *Quarterly Journal of Economics* 75:468–92.

1971. Structural transformation versus gradualism: Recent economic development in Ghana and the Ivory Coast. Pages 187–230 in Philip Foster and Aristide R. Zolberg (eds.), *Ghana and the Ivory Coast: Perspectives on modernization.* Chicago: University of Chicago Press.

Berger, Manfred. 1975. *Industrialisation policies in Nigeria.* München: Weltforum Verlag; New York: Humanities Press.

Bernus, Suzanne. 1969. *Particularismes ethniques en milieu urbain: L'exemple de Niamey.* Mémoires de l'Institut d'Ethnologie 1. Paris: Institut d'Ethnologie.

Berry, Brian J. L. 1962. Urban growth and the economic development of Ashanti. Pages 53–64 in Forrest R. Pitts (ed.), *Urban systems and economic development.* Eugene: University of Oregon Press.

Blood, Robert O., Jr. 1972. *The family.* New York: The Free Press.

Boahen, A. Adu. 1966. *Topics in West African history.* London: Longmans.

Boorman, Scott A.; and Harrison C. White. 1976. Social structure from multiple networks II: Role structures. *American Journal of Sociology.* 81: 1384–446.

Boserup, Ester. 1970. *Woman's role in economic development.* New York: St. Martin's Press.

Bott, Elizabeth. 1957. *Family and social networks.* London: Tavistock.

Bradbury, R. E. 1967. The Benin Kingdom. Pages 1–35 in Daryll Forde and P. M. Kaberry (eds.), *West African kingdoms in the nineteenth century.* London: Oxford University Press. Reprinted pages 44–75 in R. E. Bradbury, 1973, *Benin studies.* Edited, with an introduction, by Peter Morton-Williams. London: Oxford University Press.

Brokensha, David. 1966. *Social change at Larteh, Ghana.* Oxford: Clarendon Press.

Busia, Kofi A. 1960. *Report on a social survey of Sekondi-Takoradi.* London: Crown Agents.

Byerlee, Derek. 1973. *Indirect employment and income distribution effects of agricultural development strategies: A simulation approach applied to Nigeria.* African Rural Employment Paper 9. East Lansing, Mich.: Department of Agricultural Economics, Michigan State University.

Cabral, Amilcar. 1975. La culture nationale. Pages 316–35 in Amilcar Cabral *Unité et lutte. Volume 1: L'arme de la théorie.* Paris: François Maspero. English translation: National liberation and culture. Pages 39–56 in Amilcar Cabral, 1973, *Return to the source: Selected speeches by Amilcar Cabral.* New York: Monthly Review Press.

Caldwell, John C. 1967. Migration and urbanization. Pages 111–46 in Walter Birmingham, I. Neustadt, and E. N. Omaboe (eds.), *A Study of contemporary Ghana. Volume 2: Some aspects of social structure.* London: Allen & Unwin; Evanston, Ill.: Northwestern University Press.

1968a. *Population growth and family change in Africa: The new urban elite in Ghana.* Canberra: Australian National University Press.

1968b. The control of family size in tropical Africa. *Demography* 5:598–619.

1969. *African rural–urban migration. The movement to Ghana's towns.* Canberra: Australian National University Press; New York: Columbia University Press.

Callaway, Barbara. 1970. Local politics in Ho and Aba. *Canadian Journal of African Studies* 4:121–44.

Carreira, Antonio; and Arthur-Martins de Meireles. 1960. Quelques notes sur les mouvements migratoires des populations de la province portugaise de Guinée. *Bulletin de l'Institut Francais d' Afrique Noire*, série B 22:379–92.

Cartwright, John R. 1970. *Politics in Sierra Leone 1947–67*. Toronto: University of Toronto Press.

Charle, Edwin. 1970. Some comments on the distribution of wealth in Subsaharan Africa. Paper prepared for the 13th Annual Meeting of the African Studies Association, Boston.

Childe, V. Gordon. 1957. Civilization, cities, and towns. *Antiquity* 31:36–8.

Church, R. J. Harrison. 1959. West African urbanization: A geographical view. *The Sociological Review* 16:15–28.

Clapperton, Hugh. 1829. *Journal of a second expedition into the interior of Africa, from the Bight of Benin to Soccatoo*. London: John Murray.

Clark, Colin. 1967. *Population growth and land use*. London: Macmillan; New York: St. Martin's.

Clarke, John I. 1972a. Demographic growth of cities in Black Africa and Madagascar: The mechanism of growth and general characteristics of demographic structures. Pages 65–72 in *La croissance urbaine en Afrique Noire et à Madagascar*, Volume 1. Paris: Centre National de la Recherche Scientifique.

1972b. Urban primacy in Tropical Africa. Pages 447–53 in *La croissance urbaine en Afrique Noire et à Madagascar*, Volume 1. Paris: Centre National de la Recherche Scientifique.

Clignet, Remi P. 1967. Environmental change, types of descent, and child rearing practices. Pages 257–96 in Horace Miner (ed.), *The city in modern Africa*. New York: Praeger.

1970. *Many wives, many powers: Authority and power in polygynous families*. Evanston, Ill.: Northwestern University Press.

Clignet, Remi P.; and Philip J. Foster. 1964a. French and British colonial education in Africa. *Comparative Education Review* 8:191–8.

1964b. Potential elites in Ghana and the Ivory Coast: A preliminary comparison. *American Journal of Sociology* 70:349–62.

1966. *The fortunate few: Secondary schools and students in the Ivory Coast*. Evanston, Ill.: Northwestern University Press.

Clignet, Remi; and Joyce Sween. 1969. Social change and type of marriage. *American Journal of Sociology* 75:123–45.

Clower, Robert W.; George Dalton; Mitchell Harwitz; and A. A. Walters. 1966. *Growth without development: An economic survey of Liberia*. Evanston, Ill.: Northwestern University Press.

Cohen, Abner. 1969. *Custom and politics in urban Africa: A Study of Hausa migrants in Yoruba towns*. London: Routledge & Kegan Paul; Berkeley: University of California Press. Excerpts reprinted pages 91–4.

Cohen, Michael A. 1972. The sans-travail demonstrations: The politics of frustration in the Ivory Coast. *Manpower and Unemployment Research in Africa* 5(1):22–5.

1973. The myth of the expanding centre: Politics in the Ivory Coast. *Journal of Modern African Studies* 11:227–46.

1974a. *Urban policy and political conflict in Africa: A study of the Ivory Coast*. Chicago: University of Chicago Press.

1974b. Urban policy and the decline of the machine: Cross-ethnic politics in the Ivory Coast. *Journal of Developing Areas* 8:227–33.

Cohen, Robin. 1974. *Labour and politics in Nigeria 1945–1971*. London: Heinemann; New York: Africana Publishing.

Cohen, Ronald. 1970. Social stratification in Bornu. Pages 225–67 in Arthur Tuden and Leonard Plotnicov (eds.), *Social stratification in Africa*. New York: Free Press: London: Collier-Macmillan.

Coleman, James S. 1958. *Nigeria: Background to nationalism*. Berkeley: University of California Press. Excerpt reprinted pages 101–2.

Cottingham, Clement. 1974. *Contemporary African bureaucracy: Political elites, bureaucratic recruitment, and administrative performance*. University Programs Modular Studies. Morristown, N.J.: General Learning Press.

Cronon, Edmund David. 1955. *Black Moses: The story of Marcus Garvey and the Universal Negro Improvement Association*. Madison: University of Wisconsin Press.

Cruise O'Brien, Donal B. 1975. *Saints and politicians: Essays in the organization of a Senegalese peasant society*. African Studies 15. Cambridge: Cambridge University Press.

Curtin, Philip D. 1969. *The Atlantic slave trade: A census*. Madison: University of Wisconsin Press.

Davidson, Basil. 1961. *The African slave trade*. Boston: Little, Brown.

  1974. *Can Africa survive? Arguments against growth without development*. Boston: Little, Brown.

Davis, Kingsley [1969] n.d. *World Urbanization 1950–1970. Volume 1: Basic data for cities, countries and regions*. Revised edition. Population Monograph 4. Berkeley: Institute of International Studies, University of California.

  1972. *World Urbanization 1950–1970. Volume 2: Analysis of trends, relationships, and development*. Population Monograph 9. Berkeley: Institute of International Studies, University of California.

de Graft-Johnson, K. T. 1974. Population growth and rural–urban migration, with special reference to Ghana. *International Labour Review* 109:471–85.

Diop, Abdoulaye Bara. 1965. *Société Toucouleur et migration (Enquête sur l'immigration Toucouleur à Dakar)*. Initiations Africaines 18. Dakar: Institut Français d'Afrique Noire.

Dobkin, Marlene. 1968. Colonialism and the legal status of women in francophonic Africa. *Cahiers d'Etudes Africaines* 8:390–405.

Dumont, René. [1962] 1969. *L'Afrique noire est mal partie*. Revised edition. Paris: Seuil. Quotation from revised English edition, 1969, *False start in Africa*. New York: Praeger.

  1972. *Paysanneries aux abois: Ceylan–Tunisie–Sénégal*. Paris: Seuil.

Dupire, Marguerite. 1960. Situation de la femme dans une société pastorale (Peul woDaBe, nomades du Niger). Pages 51–91 in Denise Paulme (ed.), *Femmes d'Afrique Noire*. Le Monde d'Outre-Mer Passé et Présent. Première Série Etudes 9. The Hague: Mouton. English translation. 1963, pages 47–92 in *Women in Tropical Africa*. London: Routledge & Kegan Paul; Berkeley: University of California Press.

Dupire, Marguerite; and Jean-Louis Boutillier. 1958. *Le pays Adioukrou et sa palmeraie. (Basse-Côte-d'Ivoire)*. *Etude socio-économique*. L'Homme d'Outre-Mer 4. Paris: Office de la Recherche Scientifique et Technique Outre-Mer.

Durkheim, Emile. 1897. *Le suicide: Etude de sociologie*. Paris: F. Alcan. English translation, 1951, *Suicide: A study in sociology*. Glencoe, Ill.: Free Press.

Eliou, Marie. 1972. Scolarisation et promotion féminines en Afrique (Côte-d'Ivoire, Haute-Volta, Sénégal). *Tiers Monde* 13:41–83.

Enahoro, Peter. 1974. The Nigerian census. *Africa* 35:41–7.

Epstein, Arnold L. 1958. *Politics in an urban African community.* Manchester: Manchester University Press.

____ 1961. The network and urban social organization. *Rhodes-Livingstone Journal* 29:29–62. Reprinted pages 77–116 in J. Clyde Mitchell (ed.), 1969, *Social networks in urban situations: Analyses of personal relationships in Central African towns.* Manchester: Manchester University Press.

____ 1964. Urban communities in Africa. Pages 83–102 in Max Gluckman (ed.), *Closed systems and open minds: The limits of naivety in social anthropology.* Edinburgh: Oliver & Boyd.

____ 1967. Urbanization and social change in Africa. *Current Anthropology* 8:275–95.

Essang, Sunday M.; and Adewale F. Mabawonku. 1974. *Determinants and impact of rural-urban migration: A case study of selected communities in Western Nigeria.* African Rural Employment Paper 10. East Lansing, Mich.: Department of Agricultural Economics, Michigan State University; Ibadan: Department of Agricultural Economics, University of Ibadan.

Fadipe, N. A. 1970. *The Sociology of the Yoruba.* Ibadan: Ibadan University Press.

Fage, J. D. 1969. *A history of West Africa: An introductory survey.* Cambridge: Cambridge University Press.

Fallers, Lloyd A. 1964. Social stratification and economic processes. Pages 113–30 in Melville J. Herskovits and Mitchell Harwitz (eds.), *Economic transition in Africa.* Evanston, Ill.: Northwestern University Press.

First, Ruth. 1970. *The barrel of a gun.* London: Allan Lane. Subsequent editions entitled *Power in Africa.* New York: Pantheon; Harmondsworth: Penguin.

Flanagan, William G. 1977. The extended family as an agent in urbanization: A survey of men and women working in Dar es Salaam. Tanzania Ph.D. dissertation, University of Connecticut.

Foster, Philip. 1965. *Education and social change in Ghana.* London: Routledge & Kegan Paul.

Fraenkel, Merran. 1964. *Tribe and class in Monrovia.* London: Oxford University Press.

Frankenberg, Ronald. 1966. *Communities in Britain: Social life in town and country.* Harmondsworth: Penguin Books.

Freeman, Thomas B. 1844. *Journal of various visits to the kingdoms of Ashanti, Aku, and Dahomi, in western Africa.* So-called second edition. London: John Mason.

Garlick, Peter C. 1971. *African traders and economic development in Ghana.* Oxford: Clarendon Press.

Genoud, Roger. 1969. *Nationalism and economic development in Ghana.* New York: Praeger.

Ghai, Dharam P. 1972. Perspectives on future economic prospects and problems in Africa. Pages 257–86 in Jagdish N. Bhagwati (ed.), *Economics and world order: From the 1970's to the 1990's.* New York: Macmillan; London: Collier-Macmillan.

Gibbal, Jean-Marie. 1974. *Citadins et paysans dans la ville Africaine: L'example d'Abidjan.* Grenoble: Presses Universitaires de Grenoble; Paris: François Maspero.

Gluckman, Max. 1945. Seven-year research plan of the Rhodes-Livingstone Institute of Social Studies in British Central Africa. *Rhodes-Livingstone Journal* 4:1–32.

____ 1955. *Custom and conflict in Africa.* Oxford: Blackwell & Mott.

1960. Tribalism in modern British Central Africa. *Cahiers d'Etudes Africaines* 1:55–70. Revised version of: Anthropological problems arising from the African Industrial Revolution. Pages 67–82 in Aidan W. Southall (ed.), 1961, *Social change in modern Africa.* London: Oxford University Press.

Goddard, A. D. 1974. Population movements and land shortages in the Sokoto close-settled zone, Nigeria. Pages 258–76 in Samir Amin (ed.), *Modern migrations in Western Africa.* London: Oxford University Press.

Goddard, Stephen. 1965. Town–farm relationships in Yorubaland: A case study from Oyo. *Africa* 35:21–9.

Goode, William J. [1963] 1970. *World revolution and family patterns.* New York: The Free Press.

1973. *Explorations in social theory.* London: Oxford University Press.

Goody, Jack. 1971. Class and marriage in Africa and Eurasia. *American Journal of Sociology* 76:585–603.

1972. *Domestic groups.* Module 28. Reading, Mass.: Addison-Wesley.

Grandmaison, Colette Le Cour. 1969. Activités économiques des femmes Dakaroises. *Africa* 39:138–51. English translation of excerpt reprinted pages 141–4.

1972. *Femmes dakaroises: Roles traditionnels féminins et urbanisation.* Annales de l'Université d'Abidjan, série F: Ethno-Sociologie 4.

Green, Margaret M. 1947. *Ibo village affairs.* London: Sidgwick & Jackson.

Green, Reginald H. 1971. Reflections on economic strategy, structure, implementation, and necessity: Ghana and the Ivory Coast, 1957–67. Pages 231–264 in Philip Foster and Aristide R. Zolberg (eds.), *Ghana and the Ivory Coast: Perspectives on modernization.* Chicago: University of Chicago Press.

Greenfield, Sidney M. 1961. Industrialization and the family in sociological theory. *American Journal of Sociology* 67:312–22.

Greenstreet, Miranda. 1971. Employment of women in Ghana. *International Labour Review* 103:117–29.

Griaule, Marcel. 1948. *Dieu d'eau. Entretiens avec Ogotemmêli.* Paris: Editions du Chêne. English translation, 1965, *Conversations with Ogotemmêli: An introduction to Dogon religious ideas.* London: Oxford University Press.

Griaule, Marcel; and Germaine Dieterlen. 1965. *Le renard pâle.* Travaux et Mémoires de l'Institut d'Ethnologie 72. Paris: Institut d'Ethnologie.

Grindal, Bruce T. 1973. Islamic affiliations and urban adaptations: The Sisala migrant in Accra, Ghana. *Africa* 43:333–46.

Gugler, Josef. 1969a. Identity–association–unions. Pages 89–104 in *University of East Africa Social Sciences Council Conference 1968/69 Sociology Papers I.* Kampala: Makerere Institute of Social Research.

1969b. On the theory of rural–urban migration: The case of Subsaharan Africa. Pages 134–55 in J. A. Jackson (ed.), *Migration.* Sociological Studies 2. Cambridge: Cambridge University Press.

1971. Life in a dual system: Eastern Nigerians in town, 1961. *Cahiers d'Etudes Africaines* 11:400–21.

1975. Particularism in Subsaharan Africa: 'Tribalism' in town. *Canadian Review of Sociology and Anthropology* 12:303–15.

1976. Migrating to urban centers of unemployment in tropical Africa. Pages 184–204 in Anthony H. Richmond and Daniel Kubat (eds.), *International migration: The New and the Third World.* Sage Studies in International Sociology 4. Beverly Hills, Calif.: Sage Publications.

Gulliver, Philip H. 1955. *Labour migration in a rural economy: A study of the Ngoni and Ndendeuli of Southern Tanganyika.* East African Studies 6. Kampala: East African Institute of Social Research.

Gutkind, Peter C. W. 1968. The poor in urban Africa: A prologue to modernization, conflict, and the unfinished revolution. Pages 355–96 in Warner Bloomberg Jr. and Henry J. Schmandt (eds.), *Power, poverty, and urban policy.* Urban Affairs Annual Reviews 2. Beverly Hills, Calif.: Sage Publications.

1974. *Urban anthropology: Perspectives on Third World urbanization and urbanism.* Assen: Van Gorcum; New York: Barnes & Noble.

Haeringer, Philippe. 1972. L'urbanisation de masse en question: Quatre villes d'Afrique Noire. Pages 625–51 in *La croissance urbaine en Afrique Noire et à Madagascar.* Volume 2. Paris: Centre National de la Recherche Scientifique.

Handwerker, W. Penn. 1973. Kinship, friendship, and business failure among market sellers in Monrovia, Liberia, 1970. *Africa* 43:288–301.

Hanna, William John; and Judith Lynne Hanna. 1969. Polyethnicity and political integration in Umuahia and Mbale. Pages 162–202 in Robert T. Daland (ed.), *Comparative urban research: The administration and politics of cities.* Beverly Hills, Calif.: Sage Publications.

1971. *Urban dynamics in Black Africa.* Chicago: Aldine Atherton.

Hansen, Asael. 1954. Review of "The primitive city of Timbuctoo." *American Journal of Sociology* 59:501–02.

Harris, John R.; and Michael P. Todaro. 1968. Urban unemployment in East Africa: An economic analysis of policy alternatives. *East African Economic Review* 4:17–36.

1970. Migration, unemployment and development: A two-sector analysis. *American Economic Review* 60:126–42.

Hart, Keith. 1971. Migration and tribal identity among the Frafras of Ghana. *Journal of Asian and African Studies* 6:21–6.

1973. Informal income opportunities and urban employment in Ghana. *Journal of Modern African Studies* 11:61–89. Excerpt reprinted pages 35–7.

Hauser, Philip M. 1965. Observations on the urban–folk and urban–rural dichotomies as forms of Western ethnocentrism. Pages 503–14 in Philip M. Hauser and Leo F. Schnore (eds.), *The study of urbanization.* New York: Wiley.

Herskovits, Melville J. 1954. Some contemporary developments in sub-Saharan Africa. *African Studies* 13(2):49–64.

Hill, Polly. 1963. *The migrant cocoa-farmers of Southern Ghana: A study in rural capitalism.* Cambridge: Cambridge University Press.

Hodgkin, Thomas. 1956. *Nationalism in colonial Africa.* London: Frederick Muller. Excerpts reprinted pages 30–1.

Hopkins, Anthony G. 1973. *An economic history of West Africa.* London: Longman; New York: Columbia University Press.

Hopkins, Nicholas S. 1972. *Popular government in an African town: Kita, Mali.* Chicago: University of Chicago Press.

Hoselitz, Bert F. 1962. The role of urbanization in economic development: Some international comparisons. Pages 157–81 in Roy Turner (ed.), *India's urban future.* Berkeley: University of California Press.

Hunwick, J. O. 1973. The mid-fourteenth-century capital of Mali. *Journal of African History* 14:195–207.

Hutton, Caroline. 1973. *Reluctant farmers? A study of unemployment and planned rural development in Uganda.* East African Studies 33. Nairobi: Fast African Publishing House.

Ibn Battūta. 1355. *Tuhfat al-nuzzar fī gharā'ib al-amsār wa-'ajā'ib al-asfar.* English translation of accounts of East and West African travels, Said Hamdun and Noel King, 1975, *Ibn Battuta in Black Africa.* London: Rex Collings.

Ibn al-Mukhtār. 1665. Ta'rīkh al-Fattāsh. French translation by O. Houdas and M.

210   *Bibliography*

Delafosse, 1913, *Tarikh el-Fettach ou chronique du chercheur pour servir à l'histoire des villes, des armées et des principaux personnages du Tekrour* (attributed to Mahmoûd Kâti ben El-Hâdj El-Motaouakkel Kâti and one of his grandsons). Documents Arabes Relatifs à l'Histoire du Soudan 3. Paris: Ernest Leroux.

Ifeka-Moller, Caroline. 1974. White power: Social-structural factors in conversion to Christianity, Eastern Nigeria, 1921–1966. *Canadian Journal of African Studies* 8:55–72.

Imoagene, Stephen O. 1967. Mechanisms of immigrant adjustment in a West African urban community. *Nigerian Journal of Economic and Social Studies* 9:51–66.

Inkeles, Alex; and David H. Smith. 1970. The fate of personal adjustment in the process of modernization. *International Journal of Comparative Sociology* 11:81–114.

International Labour Office. 1972. *Total involvement: A strategy for development in Liberia.* Geneva: ILO.

1973. *1973 Year Book of Labour Statistics.* Geneva: ILO.

1975. *1975 Year Book of Labour Statistics.* Geneva: ILO.

Jahoda, Gustav. 1959. Love, marriage, and social change: Letters to the advice column of a West African newspaper. *Africa* 29:177–89.

1961. Aspects of Westernization: A study of adult-class students in Ghana. *British Journal of Sociology* 12:375–86, 13:43–56.

Janes, Margaret D. 1974. Physical growth of Nigerian Yoruba children. *Tropical and Geographical Medicine* 26:389–98.

1975. Physical and psychological growth and development. *Journal of Tropical Pediatrics and Environmental Child Health* 21:26–30.

Johnson, R. W. 1970. Sékou Touré and the Guinean revolution. *African Affairs* 69:350–65. Reprinted under the title Sékou Touré: The man and his ideas, pages 329–342 in Peter C. W. Gutkind and Peter Waterman (eds.), 1977, *African social studies: A radical reader.* London: Heinemann.

Kamerschen, David R. 1969. Further analysis of overurbanization. *Economic Development and Cultural Change* 17:235–53.

Kapferer, Bruce. 1969. Norms and manipulation of relationships in a work context. Pages 181–244 in J. Clyde Mitchell (ed.), *Social networks in urban situations: Analyses of personal relationships in Central African towns.* Manchester: Manchester University Press.

Kilby, Peter. 1969. *Industrialization in an open economy: Nigeria 1945–1966.* Cambridge: Cambridge University Press.

1975. Manufacturing in colonial Africa. Pages 470–520 in Peter Duignan and L. H. Gann (eds.), *Colonialism in Africa 1870–1960. Volume 4: The economics of colonialism.* Cambridge: Cambridge University Press.

Kilson, Martin. 1966. *Political change in a West African state: A study of the modernization process in Sierra Leone.* Cambridge, Mass.: Harvard University Press.

1971. The grassroots in Ghanaian politics. Pages 103–23 in Philip Foster and Aristide R. Zolberg (eds.), *Ghana and the Ivory Coast: Perspectives on modernization.* Chicago: University of Chicago Press.

Kimble, David. 1963. *A political history of Ghana: The rise of Gold Coast nationalism 1850–1928.* Oxford: Clarendon Press.

Knight, J. B. 1972. Rural–urban income comparisons and migration in Ghana. *Bulletin of the Oxford University Institute of Economics and Statistics* 34:199–228.

Kopytoff, Jean Herskovits. 1965. *A preface to modern Nigeria: The "Sierra Leonians" in Yoruba, 1830–1890.* Madison: University of Wisconsin Press.

Krapf-Askari, Eva. 1969. *Yoruba towns and cities: An enquiry into the nature of urban social phenomena.* Oxford Monographs on Social Anthropology. Oxford: Clarendon Press.

Kraus, Jon. 1971. Political change, conflict and development in Ghana. Pages 33–72 in Philip Foster and Aristide R. Zolberg (eds.), *Ghana and the Ivory Coast: Perspectives on modernization.* Chicago: University of Chicago Press.

Lambert, Richard D. 1962. The impact of urban society upon village life. Pages 117–40 in Roy Turner (ed.), *India's urban future.* Berkeley: University of California Press.

Lander, Richard. 1830. *Records of Captain Clapperton's last expedition to Africa.* Volume 1. London: Henry Colburn and Richard Bentley.

Laslett, Peter. 1970. The comparative history of household and family. *Journal of Social History* 4:75–87. Reprinted revised pages 19–33 in Michael Gordon (ed.), 1973, *The American family in social-historical perspective.* New York: St. Martin's Press.

Laumann, Edward O. 1973. *Bonds of pluralism: The form and substance of urban social networks.* New York: Wiley.

Lawson, Rowena M. 1971. The supply response of retail trading services to urban population growth in Ghana. Pages 337–95 in Claude Meillassoux (ed.), *The development of indigenous trade and markets in West Africa.* London: Oxford University Press.

Leighton, Alexander H.; T. Adeoye Lambo; Charles C. Hughes; Dorothea C. Leighton; Jane M. Murphy; and David B. Macklin. 1963. *Psychiatric disorder among the Yoruba: A report from the Cornell-Aro Mental Health Research Project in the Western Region, Nigeria.* Ithaca, N.Y.: Cornell University Press.

Levasseur, Alain A. 1971. The modernization of law in Africa with particular reference to family law in the Ivory Coast. Pages 151–66 in Philip Foster and Aristide R. Zolberg (eds.), *Ghana and the Ivory Coast: Perspectives on modernization.* Chicago: University of Chicago Press.

Levtzion, Nehemia. 1968. Ibn Ḥawqal, the cheque and Awdaghost. *Journal of African History* 9:223–33.

—— 1971. A seventeenth-century chronicle by Ibn al-Mukthār. A critical study of Ta'rīkh al-Fattāsh. *Bulletin of the School of Oriental and African Studies* 34:571–93.

—— 1973. *Ancient Ghana and Mali. Studies in African History* 7. London: Methuen.

Lewis, Oscar. 1965. Further observations on the folk–urban continuum and urbanization with special reference to Mexico City. Pages 491–503 in Philip M. Hauser and Leo F. Schnore (eds.), *The study of urbanization.* New York: Wiley.

Liebenow, J. Gus. 1969. *Liberia: The evolution of privilege.* Ithaca, N.Y.: Cornell University Press.

Little, Kenneth. 1965. *West African urbanization: A study of voluntary associations in social change.* Cambridge: Cambridge University Press.

—— 1973. *African women in towns: An aspect of Africa's social revolution.* Cambridge: Cambridge University Press.

Little, Kenneth; and Anne Price. 1967. Some trends in modern marriage among West Africans. *Africa* 37:407–24.

Litwak, Eugene. 1959. The use of extended family groups in the achievement of social goals: Some policy implications. *Social Problems* 7:177–87.

1960a. Occupational mobility and extended family cohesion. *American Sociological Review* 25:9–21.

1960b. Geographical mobility and extended family cohesion. *American Sociological Review* 25:385–94.

Lloyd, Barbara B. 1966. Education and family life in the development of class identification among the Yoruba. Pages 163–81 in Peter C. Lloyd (ed.), *The new elites of tropical Africa*. London: Oxford University Press. Excerpt reprinted pages 165–73.

Lloyd, Peter C. 1962. *Yoruba land law*. London: Oxford University Press.

1966a. Introduction. Pages 1–85 in Peter C. Lloyd (ed.), *The new elites of tropical Africa*. London: Oxford University Press.

1966b. Class consciousness among the Yoruba. Pages 328–40 in Peter C. Lloyd (ed.) *The new elites of tropical Africa*. London: Oxford University Press.

1967. The elite. Pages 129–50 in Peter C. Lloyd, Akin L. Mabogunje and B. Awe (eds.), *The city of Ibadan*. Cambridge: Cambridge University Press.

1971. *Classes, crises and coups: Themes in the sociology of developing countries*. London: MacGibbon and Kee; New York: Praeger.

1973. The Yoruba: An urban people? Pages 107–23 in Aidan W. Southall (ed.), *Urban anthropology: Cross-cultural studies of urbanization*. London: Oxford University Press.

1974. *Power and independence: Urban Africans' perception of social inequality*. London: Routledge & Kegan Paul.

Mabogunje, Akin L. 1968. *Urbanization in Nigeria*. London: University of London Press. Excerpt reprinted pages 22–5.

McCall, Daniel Francis. 1961. Trade and the role of wife in a modern West African town. Pages 286–99 in Aidan W. Southall (ed.), *Social change in modern Africa*. London: Oxford University Press.

McNulty, Michael L. 1969. Urban structure and development: The urban system of Ghana. *The Journal of Developing Areas* 3:159–76.

Madavo, C. E. 1971. Making the cities work. *Africa Report* 16(8):18–22.

Mahmoûd Kâti – see Ibn al-Mukhtār.

Marris, Peter. 1961. *Family and social change in an African city: A study of rehousing in Lagos*. London: Routledge & Kegan Paul; Evanston, Ill.: Northwestern University Press. Excerpt reprinted pages 46–8.

1968. The social barriers to African entrepreneurship. *The Journal of Development Studies* 5:29–38.

Mauny, Raymond A. 1954. The question of Ghana. *Africa* 25:200–12.

1959. Kumbi Saleh: Ancient capital of the "Land of Gold." *UNESCO Courier* 12(10):24–5.

1961. *Tableau géographique de l'Ouest africain au Moyen Age d'après les sources écrites, la tradition et l'archéologie*. Mémoires de l'Institut Français d'Afrique Noire 61. Dakar: IFAN.

Mayer, Philip [1961] 1971. *Townsmen or tribesmen: Conservatism and the process of urbanization in a South African city*. Second edition. London: Oxford University Press.

1962. Migrancy and the study of Africans in town. *American Anthropologist* 64:576–92.

Meillassoux, Claude. 1968. *Urbanization of an African community: Voluntary associations in Bamako*. American Ethnological Society Monograph 45. Seattle: University of Washington Press.

1972. L'itineraire d'Ibn Battuta de Walata à Mali. *Journal of African History* 13:389–95.

Melson, Robert. 1971. Ideology and inconsistency: The "cross-pressured" Nigerian worker. Pages 581–605 in Robert Melson and Howard Wolpe (eds.), *Nigeria: Modernization and the politics of communalism*. East Lansing: Michigan State University Press.

Melson, Robert; and Howard Wolpe, 1971. Modernization and the politics of communalism: A theoretical perspective. Pages 1–42 in Robert Melson and Howard Wolpe (eds.), *Nigeria: Modernization and the politics of communalism*. East Lansing: Michigan State University Press.

Mersadier, Y. 1968. Les niveaux de vie. Pages 247–63 in Groupe d'Etudes Dakaroises (ed.), *Dakar en devenir*. Paris: Présence Africaine.

Miner, Horace. [1953] 1965. *The primitive city of Timbuctoo*. Revised edition. Garden City, N.Y.: Doubleday. Excerpt reprinted pages 108–15.

Mitchel, N. C. 1961. Yoruba towns. Pages 279–301 in K. M. Barbour and R. M. Prothero (eds.), *Essays on African population*. London: Routledge & Kegan Paul; New York: Praeger.

Mitchell, J. Clyde. 1956. *The Kalela dance: Aspects of social relationships among the urban Africans in Northern Rhodesia*. Rhodes-Livingston Papers 27. Manchester: Manchester University Press.

1959. The causes of labour migration. *Bulletin of the Inter-African Labour Institute* 6(1):12–47.

1962. Social change and the new towns of Bantu Africa. Pages 117–29 in Georges Balandier (ed.), *Social implications of technological change*. Paris: International Social Science Council.

1966. Theoretical orientations in African urban studies. Pages 37–68 in Michael Banton (ed.), *The social anthropology of complex societies*. London: Tavistock.

1969. The concept and use of social networks. Pages 1–50 in J. Clyde Mitchell (ed.), *Social Networks in urban situations: Analyses of personal relationships in Central African towns*. Manchester: Manchester University Press.

1973. Networks, norms and institutions. Pages 15–35 in Jeremy Boissevain and J. Clyde Mitchell (eds.), *Network Analysis: Studies in human interaction*. The Hague: Mouton.

1974. Social networks. *Annual Review of Anthropology* 3:279–99.

Moore, Wilbert E. 1951. *Industrialization and labor: Social aspects of economic development*. Ithaca, N.Y.: Cornell University Press.

[1963] 1974. *Social change*. Second edition. Englewood Cliffs, N.J.: Prentice-Hall.

Morrill, W. T. 1963. Immigrants and associations: The Ibo in twentieth-century Calabar. *Comparative Studies in Society and History* 5:424–48. Reprinted pages 154–87 in Lloyd A. Fallers (ed.). 1967, *Immigrants and associations*. The Hague: Mouton.

Mouton, Pierre. 1975. *Social security in Africa: Trends, problems and prospects*. Geneva: International Labour Office.

Mühlenberg, Friedrich. 1967. *Wanderarbeit in Südafrika: Ursachen eines Arbeitsmarktphänomens dualistischer Wirtschaftsgesellschaften*. Stuttgart: Gustav Fischer.

Nafziger, E. Wayne. 1969. The effect of the Nigerian extended family on entrepreneurial activity. *Economic Development and Cultural Change* 18:25–33.

Niemeijer, Rudo. 1973. Some applications of the notion of density. Pages 45–64 in Jeremy Boissevain and J. Clyde Mitchell (eds.), *Network Analysis: Studies in human interaction*. The Hague: Mouton.

Nimkoff, M. F. 1965. The family and the social system. Pages 61–73 in M. F.

Nimkoff (ed.), *Comparative family systems*. Boston: Houghton Mifflin.

Norris, Robert. 1789. *Memoirs of the reign of Bossa Ahádee, king of Dahomy, an inland country of Guiney. To which are added the author's journey to Abomey, the capital; and a short account of the African slave trade.* London: W. Lowndes.

O'Connell, James; and Paul A. Beckett. 1975. Social characteristics of an elite in formation: The case of Nigerian university students. *British Journal of Sociology* 26:309–29.

Ohadike, Patrick O. 1968. Urbanization: Growth, transitions, and problems of a premier West African city (Lagos, Nigeria). *Urban Affairs Quarterly* 3:69–90.

Ojo, G. J. Afolabi. 1970. Some observations on journey to agricultural work in Yorubaland, Southwest Nigeria. *Economic Geography* 46:459–71.

Okonjo, Chukuka. 1967. The Western Ibo. Pages 97–116 in P. C. Lloyd; A. L. Mabogunje, and B. Awe (eds.), *The city of Ibadan*. Cambridge: Cambridge University Press. Excerpt reprinted pages 81–5.

Okonjo, Kamene. 1976. The dual-sex political system in operation: Igbo women and community politics in Midwestern Nigeria. Pages 45–58 in Nancy J. Hafkin and Edna G. Bay (eds.), *Women in Africa: Studies in social and economic change*. Stanford: Stanford University Press.

Okonjo, Unokanma. 1970. *The impact of urbanization on the Ibo family structure.* Göttinger Philosophische Dissertation 7. Göttingen: Breger.

Omari, T. Peter. 1960. Changing attitudes of students in West African society toward marriage and family relationships. *British Journal of Sociology* 11:197–210.

Oppong, Christine. 1974. *Marriage among a matrilineal elite: A family study of Ghanaian senior civil servants.* Cambridge Studies in Social Anthropology 8. Cambridge: Cambridge University Press.

Ottenberg, Phoebe V. 1959. The changing economic position of women among the Afikpo Ibo. Pages 205–23 in William R. Bascom and Melville J. Herskovits (eds.), *Continuity and change in African Cultures*. Chicago: University of Chicago Press.

Ottenberg, Simon. 1955. Improvement associations among the Afikpo Ibo. *Africa* 25:1–27.

    1959. Ibo receptivity to change. Pages 130–43 in William R. Bascom and Melville J. Herskovits (eds.), *Continuity and change in African cultures*. Chicago: University of Chicago Press.

Owusu, Maxwell. 1970. *Uses and abuses of political powers: A case study of continuity and change in the politics of Ghana.* Chicago: University of Chicago Press.

Paden, John N. 1973. *Religion and political culture in Kano.* Berkeley: University of California Press.

Parsons, Talcott. 1937. *The structure of social action: A study in social theory with special reference to a group of recent European writers.* New York: McGraw-Hill.

    [1949] 1959. The social structure of the family. Pages 241–74 in Ruth Nanda Anshen (ed.), *The family: Its function and destiny*. Revised edition. New York: Harper & Row.

Paulme, Denise. 1952. La femme africaine au travail. *Présence Africaine* 13:116–23.

    1960. Introduction. Pages 9–22 in Denise Paulme (ed.). *Femmes d'Afrique Noire*. Le Monde d'Outre-Mer Passé et Présent. Première Série. Etudes 9. The

Hague: Mouton. English translation, 1963, pages 1–16 in *Women of Tropical Africa*. London: Routledge & Kegan Paul; Berkeley: University of California Press.

Payne, John Augustus. 1893. *Table of principal events in Yoruba history, with certain other matters of general interest, compiled principally for use in courts within the British Colony of Lagos, West Africa*. Lagos: The author.

Peace, Adrian. 1974. Industrial protest in Nigeria. Pages 141–67 in Emanuel de Kadt and Gavin Williams (eds.), *Sociology and development*. Explorations in Sociology 4. London: Tavistock.

Pearse, Andrew. 1970. Urbanization and the incorporation of the peasant. Pages 201–12 in Arthur J. Field (ed.), *City and country in the Third World: Issues in the modernization of Latin America*. Cambridge, Mass.: Schenkman.

Peel, J. D. Y. 1968. *Aladura: A religious movement among the Yoruba*. London: Oxford University Press.

Peil, Margaret. 1971. The expulsion of West African aliens. *Journal of Modern African Studies* 9:205–29.

1972. *The Ghanaian factory worker: Industrial man in Africa*. African Studies 5. Cambridge: Cambridge University Press.

1973. The influence of formal education on occupational choice. *Canadian Journal of African Studies* 7:199–214.

1975a. Interethnic contacts in Nigerian cities. *Africa* 45:107–21.

1975b. Social aspects of religion in West African towns. *African Urban Notes*, series B, 2:95–104.

n.d. Self-employed craftsmen. Manuscript.

Pfeffermann, Guy. 1968. *Industrial labor in the Republic of Senegal*. New York: Praeger.

Plotnicov, Leonard. 1962. Fixed membership groups: The locus of culture processes. *American Anthropologist* 64:97–103.

1967. *Strangers to the city: Urban man in Jos, Nigeria*. Pittsburgh: University of Pittsburgh Press.

1970. Rural-urban communications in contemporary Nigeria: The persistence of traditional social institutions. *International Studies in Sociology and Social Anthropology* 10:66–82. This issue of the journal has also been published as Peter C. W. Gutkind (ed.), 1970, *The passing of tribal man in Africa*. Leiden: E. J. Brill.

Pons, Valdo, 1969. *Stanleyville: An African urban community under Belgian administration*. London: Oxford University Press.

Pool, Janet E. 1972. A cross-comparative study of aspects of conjugal behavior among women of 3 West African countries. *Canadian Journal of African Studies* 6:233–59.

Porter, Arthur T. 1963. *Creoledom: A study of the development of Freetown society*. London: Oxford University Press.

Post, K. W. J. 1963. *The Nigerian federal election of 1959: Politics and administration in a developing political system*. London: Oxford University Press.

Powesland, P. G. 1957. *Economic policy and labour: A study in Uganda's economic history*. Edited by Walter Elkan. East African Studies 10. Kampala: East African Institute of Social Research.

Price, Robert M. 1971. A theoretical approach to military rule in new states: Reference-group theory and the Ghanaian case. *World Politics* 23:399–430.

Priestley, Margaret. 1969. *West African trade and coast society: A family study*. London: Oxford University Press.

Reindorf, Carl Christian. 1895. *History of the Gold Coast and Asante,* based on traditions and historical facts, comprising a period of more than three centuries from about 1500 to 1860. Basel: The author.

Remy, Dorothy. 1968. Social networks and patron-client relations: Ibadan market women. Manuscript.

1975a. Economic security and industrial unionism: A Nigerian case study. Pages 161–77 in Richard Sandbrook and Robin Cohen (eds.), *The development of an African working class: Studies in class formation and action.* London: Longman.

1975b. Underdevelopment and the experience of women: A Nigerian case study. Pages 358–71 in Rayna R. Reiter (ed.), *Toward an anthropology of women.* New York: Monthly Review Press. Reprinted pages 123–34 in Gavin Williams (ed.), 1976, *Nigeria: Economy and society.* London: Rex Collings.

Richard-Molard, J. 1954. Villes d'Afrique Noire. *Présence Africaine* 15:295–306.

Richards, Audrey I. 1954. The travel routes and the travellers. Pages 52–76 in Audrey I. Richards (ed.), *Economic development and tribal change: A study of immigrant labour in Buganda.* Cambridge, England: Heffer.

Richardson, Harry W. 1973. *The economics of urban size.* Farnborough, Hampshire: Saxon House; Lexington, Mass.: Lexington Books.

Rivière, Claude. 1971. Mutations sociales en Guinée. Paris: Rivière.

Rouch, Jean. 1956. Migrations au Ghana (Gold Coast): Enquête 1953–1955. *Journal de la Société des Africanistes* 26:33–196.

Rudebeck, Lars. 1974. *Guinea-Bissau: A study of political mobilization.* Uppsala: Scandinavian Institute of African Studies.

al-Sa'dī. 1655. *Ta'rīkh al-Sūdān.* French translation by O. Houdas, 1900, *Tarikh es-Soudan.* Documents Arabes Relatifs a l'Histoire du Soudan 1. Paris: Ernest Leroux.

Safier, Michael. 1970. Urban growth and urban planning in Subsaharan Africa. Pages 35–44 in Josef Gugler (ed.), *Urban growth in Subsaharan Africa.* Nkanga 6. Kampala: Makerere Institute of Social Research.

Sanjek, Roger. 1972. Ghanaian networks: An analysis of interethnic relations in urban situations. Ph.D. dissertation, Columbia University.

Sankalé, M.; R. Baylt; H. Collomb: H. Ayats; H. Ba; and J. Cros. 1968. Urbanisation et santé. Pages 264–97 in Groupe d'Etudes Dakaroises (ed.), *Dakar en devenir.* Paris: Présence Africaine.

Saul, John S. 1974. African peasants and revolution. *Review of African Political Economy* 1:41–68.

Saul, John S.: and Roger Woods, 1971. African peasantries. Pages 103–14 in Teodor Shanin (ed.), *Peasants and peasant societies: Selected readings.* Harmondsworth: Penguin. Reprinted pages 406–16 in Giovanni Arrighi and John S. Saul, 1973, *Essays on the political economy of Africa.* New York: Monthly Review Press.

Schumacher, Edward J. 1975. *Politics, bureaucracy and rural development in Senegal.* Berkeley: University of California Press.

Seck, Assane. 1970. *Dakar métropole ouest-africaine.* Mémoires de l'Institut Fondamental d'Afrique Noire 85. Dakar: IFAN.

Seibel, Hans Dieter. 1968. *Industriearbeit und Kulturwandel in Nigeria: Kulturelle Implikationen des Wandels von einer traditionellen Stammesgesellschaft zu einer modernen Industriegesellschaft.* Ordo Politicus 9. Köln/Opladen: Westdeutscher Verlag.

Seibel, Helga Renate. 1969. *Die Afrikanerin in Beruf und Familie: Eine Untersuchung bei nigerianischen Industriearbeiterinnen.* Materialien des Arnold-Bergstraesser-Instituts für kulturwissenschaftliche Forschung 24. Bielefeld: Bertelsmann.

Sembene Ousmane. 1960. *Les bouts de bois de dieu: Banty Mam Yall*. Paris: Livre Contemporain. English edition, 1960, *God's bits of wood*. London: Heinemann; New York: Doubleday.

Simmel, Georg. 1903. Die Großstädte und das Geistesleben. Pages 185–206 in Th. Petermann (ed.), *Die Großstadt: Vorträge und Aufsätze zur Städteausstellung*. Jahrbuch der Gehe-Stiftung zu Dresden 9. Dresden: v. Zahn & Jaensch. English translation, The metropolis and mental life. Pages 409–24 in Kurt H. Wolff (ed.), 1950, *The sociology of Georg Simmel*. New York: Free Press: London: Collier-Macmillan.

Sivard, Ruth Leger. 1976. *World military and social expenditures 1976*. Leesburg, Va.: WMSE Publications.

Sjoberg, Gideon. 1955. The preindustrial city. *American Journal of Sociology* 60:438–45.

1960. *The preindustrial city: Past and present*. Glencoe, Ill.: Free Press.

1964. The rural-urban dimension in preindustrial, transitional, and industrial societies. Pages 127–59 in Robert E. L. Faris (ed.), *Handbook of modern sociology*. Chicago: Rand McNally.

Skinner, Elliott P. 1965. Labor migration among the Mossi of Upper Volta. Pages 60–84 in Hilda Kuper (ed.), *Urbanization and migration in West Africa*. Berkeley: University of California Press.

1974. *African urban life: The transformation of Ouagadougou*. Princeton: Princeton University Press.

Sklar, Richard L. 1963. *Nigerian political parties: Power in an emergent African nation*. Princeton: Princeton University Press.

1967. Political science and national integration – A radical approach. *Journal of Modern African Studies* 5:1–11.

Smith, M. G. 1959. The Hausa system of social status. *Africa* 29:239–51.

Smock, Audrey C. 1971. *Ibo politics: The role of ethnic unions in Eastern Nigeria*. Cambridge, Mass.: Harvard University Press.

Songre Ambroise; Jean-Marie Sawadogo; and George Sanogoh. 1974. Réalités et effets de l'émigration massive des Voltaïques dans le contexte de l'Afrique Occidentale. Pages 384–402 in Samir Amin (ed.), *Modern migrations in Western Africa*. London: Oxford University Press. A slightly abridged and revised English version is authored by Ambroise Songre, 1973, Mass emigration from Upper Volta: The facts and implications. *International Labour Review* 108:209–25.

Southall, Aidan W. 1959. An operational theory of role. *Human Relations* 12:17–34.

1961. Introductory summary. Pages 1–66 in Aidan W. Southall (ed.), *Social change in modern Africa*. London: Oxford University Press.

1970. Stratification in Africa. Pages 231–72 in Leonard Plotnicov and Arthur Tuden (eds.), *Essays in comparative social stratification*. Pittsburgh: University of Pittsburgh Press.

1973. The density of role-relationships as a universal index of urbanization. Pages 71–106 in Aidan Southall (ed.), *Urban anthropology: Cross-cultural studies of urbanization*. London: Oxford University Press.

Sovani, N. V. 1964. The analysis of overurbanization. *Economic Development and Cultural Change* 12:113–22.

Soyinka, Wole. 1973. *Season of anomy: A novel*. New York: Third Press.

Spengler, Joseph J. 1967. Africa and the theory of optimum city size. Pages 55–89

in Horace Miner (ed.), *The city in modern Africa.* New York: Praeger.
Stanford Research Institute; School of Planning and Architecture; and Small Indus-
try Extension Training Institute. 1968. *Costs of urban infrastructure for indus-
try as related to city size in developing countries: India case study.* Menlo
Park, Calif.: Stanford Research Institute; New Delhi: School of Planning and
Architecture; Hyderabad: Small Industry Extension Training Institute.
Stiglitz, Joseph E. 1970. Rural–urban migration, surplus labour, and the relation-
ships between urban and rural wages. *Eastern African Economic Review,*
2:2–27.
Stryker, Richard E. 1971a. A local perspective on developmental strategy in the
Ivory Coast. Pages 119–39 in Michael F. Lofchie (ed.), *The state of the
nations: Constraints on development in independent Africa.* Berkeley: Univer-
sity of California Press.
1971b. Political and administrative linkage in the Ivory Coast. Pages 73–102 in
Philip Foster and Aristide R. Zolberg (eds.), *Ghana and the Ivory Coast:
Perspectives on modernization.* Chicago: University of Chicago Press.
Sussman, M. B.; and L. G. Burchinal. 1962. Kin family network: Unheralded
structure in current conceptualizations of family functioning. *Marriage and
Family Living* 24:231–40.
Tardits, Claude. 1958. *Porto-Novo: Les nouvelles générations Africaines entre leurs
traditions et l'Occident.* Le Monde d'Outre-Mer passé et présent. Première
Série. Etudes 7. The Hague: Mouton.
1963. Réflexions sur le problème de la scolarisation de filles au Dahomey.
Cahiers d'Etudes Africaines 3:266–281.
Ta'rīkh al-Fattāsh – see Ibn al-Mukhtār.
Ta'rīkh al-Sūdān – see al-Sa'dī.
Teriba, O.; and O. A. Philips. 1971. Income distribution and national integration.
Nigerian Journal of Social and Economic Research 13:77–122.
Thoden van Velzen, H. U. E. 1973. Coalitions and network analysis. Pages 219–50
in Jeremy Boissevain and J. Clyde Mitchell (eds.), *Network Analysis: Studies
in human interaction.* The Hague: Mouton.
Tidjani, A. Serpos. 1960. Note sur la migration humaine à la côte du Bénin. *Bulle-
tin de l'Institut Français d'Afrique Noire,* série B 22:509–13.
Tillion, Germaine. 1966. *Le harem et les cousins.* Paris: Editions du Seuil.
Todaro, Michael P. 1969. A model of labor migration and urban unemployment in
less developed countries. *American Economic Review* 59:138–48.
Udo, Reuben K. 1968. Population and politics in Nigeria. Pages 97–105 in John
C. Caldwell and Chukuka Okonjo (eds.), *The population of tropical Africa.*
London: Longmans; New York: Columbia University Press.
1970. Census migrations in Nigeria. *Nigerian Geographical Journal* 13:3–7.
1972. Social relations of rural–rural migrants with host communities in Southern
Nigeria. Paper prepared for the 11th International African Seminar: Modern
Migrations in Western Africa, Dakar.
UNESCO. 1976. *Statistical Yearbook 1975.* Paris: UNESCO.
United Nations. 1966. *United Nations Statistical Yearbook 1965.* New York: UN.
1968. Uncontrolled urban settlement: Problems and policies. *International
Social Development Review* 1:107–30.
1970. *Yearbook of National Accounts Statistics 1969. Volume 2: International
tables.* New York: UN.
1975. Developing countries and levels of development (E/AC.54/L.81).
1976a. *Demographic Yearbook 1975.* New York: UN.
1976b. *Statistical Yearbook 1975.* New York: UN.

1976c. *Yearbook of National Accounts Statistics 1975. Volume 1: Individual country data.* New York: UN.

1976d. *Yearbook of National Accounts Statistics 1975. Volume 3: International tables.* New York: UN.

van den Berghe, Pierre L. 1968. European languages and black mandarins. *Transition* 34:19–23.

1973. *Power and privilege at an African university.* Cambridge, Mass.: Schenkman. London: Routledge & Kegan Paul.

Vellenga, Dorothy Dee. 1971. Attempts to change the marriage laws in Ghana and the Ivory Coast. Pages 125–50 in Philip Foster and Aristide R. Zolberg (eds.), *Ghana and the Ivory Coast: Perspectives on modernization.* Chicago: University of Chicago Press.

Vernière, Marc. 1973. A propos de la marginalité: Réflexions illustrées par quelques enquêtes en milieu urbain et suburbain africain. *Cahiers d'Etudes Africaines* 13:587–605.

Vincent, Jeanne-Françoise. 1966. *Femmes africaines en milieu urbain (Bacongo–Brazzaville).* Paris: Office de la Recherche Scientifique et Technique Outre-Mer.

Wallerstein, Immanuel. 1973. Class and class conflict in contemporary Africa. *Canadian Journal of African Studies* 7:375–80. An edited version was published 1975 in the *Monthly Review* 26(9):34–42.

Weber, Max. 1921. Die Stadt. *Archiv für Sozialwissenschaft und Sozialpolitik* 47:621–772. English translation, 1958, *The city.* Glencoe, Ill.: Free Press.

Webster, J. B.; and A. Adu Boahen. 1970. *History of West Africa: The revolutionary years: 1815 to Independence.* New York: Praeger.

White, Harrison C.; Scott A. Boorman; and Ronald Breiger. 1976. Social structure from multiple networks I: Blockmodels of roles and positions. *American Journal of Sociology* 81:730–80.

White, H. P.; and M. B. Gleave. 1971. *An economic geography of West Africa.* London: G. Bell.

Wilks, Ivor. 1971. The Mossi and Akan states 1500–1800. Pages 344–86 in J. F. A. Ajayi and Michael Crowder (eds.), *History of West Africa.* Volume 1. London: Longman; New York: Columbia University Press.

1975. *Asante in the nineteenth century: The structure and evolution of a political order.* Cambridge: Cambridge University Press.

Williams, Gavin. 1970. The social stratification of a neo-colonial economy: Western Nigeria. Pages 225–50 in Christopher Allen and R. W. Johnson (eds.), *African perspectives: Papers in the history, politics and economics of Africa. Presented to Thomas Hodgkin.* Cambridge: Cambridge University Press.

1974. Political consciousness among the Ibadan poor. Pages 109–39 in Emanuel de Kadt and Gavin Williams (eds.), *Sociology and development.* Explorations in Sociology 4. London: Tavistock.

Willis, John Ralph. 1971. The Western Sudan from the Moroccan invasion (1591) to the death of al-Mukhtar al-Kunti (1811). Pages 441–83 in J. F. A. Ajayi and Michael Crowder (eds.), *History of West Africa.* Volume 1. London: Longman; New York: Columbia University Press.

Winch, Robert F. 1972. Theorizing about the family. *Journal of Comparative Family Studies* 3:5–16.

Wirth, Louis. 1938. Urbanism as a way of life. *American Journal of Sociology* 44:1–24.

Wolfe, Alvin W. 1970. On structural comparisons of networks. *Canadian Review of Sociology and Anthropology* 7:226–44.

Wolff, Hans. 1959. Intelligibility and inter-ethnic attitudes. *Anthropological Linguistics* 1:34–41.
Wolpe, Howard. 1974. *Urban politics in Nigeria: A study of Port Harcourt.* Berkeley: University of California Press.
World Bank. 1972. *Urbanization: Sector Working Paper.* Washington, D.C.: World Bank.
    1975. *Housing: Sector Working Paper.* Washington, D.C.: World Bank.
    1976a. *World Bank Atlas: Population, per capita product, and growth rates.* Washington, D.C.: World Bank.
    1976b. *World Tables 1976: From the data files of the World Bank.* Baltimore/London: Johns Hopkins.
Yeld, Rachel. 1964. Education amongst women and girls in the Kebbi emirate of Northern Nigeria. Pages 65–75 in Hans N. Weiler (ed.), *Erziehung und Politik in Nigeria (Education and Politics in Nigeria).* Freiburg: Rombach.
Young, Michael; and Peter Willmott. 1957. *Family and kinship in East London.* London: Routledge & Kegan Paul.
Zolberg, Aristide R. [1964] 1969. *One-party government in the Ivory Coast.* Revised edition. Princeton: Princeton University Press.
    1966. *Creating political order: The party-states of West Africa.* Chicago: Rand McNally.
Zolberg, Vera L. 1974. Power privilege and poverty: The case of Mali. Paper prepared for the 8th World Congress of Sociology, Toronto.

Name Index

Abernethy, David, 200 n13
Abu-Lughod, Janet, 181
Achebe, Chinua, 87, 88, 103, 175
Adams, Bert N., 120
Adebo, Simeon, 177
Adeleye, R. A., 13
Adepoju, Aderanti, 67
Agunwa, Clement, 192 n10
Akinola, R. A., 18
Amin, Samir, 161, 162, 178
Anderson, Michael, 120
Ardener, Edwin W., 108, 190 n3
Ardener, Shirley, 108, 190 n3
Aronson, Dan R., 61, 67, 70, 90, 122, 123, 187 n15
Arrighi, Giovanni, 149
Askiyā Muhammad, 10
Awe, Bolanle, 16
Awolowo, Obafemi, 102
Azikiwe, Nnamdi, 101
Azu, Diana Gladys, 128, 197 n11

Bachmann, Heinz B., 189n17
Baker, Pauline H., 190 n22
al-Bakrī, 8, 11
Balandier, Georges, 85, 104, 143
Banton, Michael, 52, 81, 86, 94, 116, 192 n1, 195 n9
Barnes, John A., 192 n9
Barnes, Sandra T., 73, 76, 78, 131–3, 196 n2, n8
Barth, Heinrich, 23
Bascom, William R., 17, 21, 107
Baylet, R., 59
Beals, Ralph E., 52
Bebler, Anton, 159
Beckett, Paul A., 200 n14
Beer, Christopher E. F., 201 n6
Benyoussef, A., 59
Berg, Elliot J., 56, 57, 200 n11, n18
Berger, Manfred, 189 n17
Bernus, Suzanne, 86, 193 n14, n18
Berry, Brian J. L., 29, 188 n4

Blood, Robert O., Jr., 119
Boahen, A. Adu, 15, 25
Boorman, Scott A., 192 n9
Boserup, Ester, 138, 147, 197 n2
Boutillier, Jean-Louis, 141
Bott, Elizabeth, 192 n9
Bradbury, R. E., 187 n14
Breiger, Ronald, 192 n9
Brokensha, David, 69
Burchinal, L. G., 120
Busia, Kofi A., 69
Byerlee, Derek, 58

Cabral, Amilcar, 179
Caldwell, John C., 52, 60, 67, 70, 128, 198 n7, 200 n15
Callaway, Barbara, 95
Cantrelle, P., 59
Carreira, Antonio, 51
Cartwright, John R., 175
Charle, Edwin, 199 n9
Childe, V. Gordon, 19, 20
Church, Harrison R. J., 33
Clapperton, Hugh, 17
Clark, Colin, 42
Clarke, John I., 40, 59
Clignet, Remi P., 103, 134, 154, 198 n13, 200 n13
Clower, Robert W., 100, 199 n5
Cohen, Abner, 91, 193 n13, 194 n22
Cohen, Michael A., 42, 95, 161, 175, 200 n17
Cohen, Robin, 152, 199 n6, n7
Cohen, Ronald, 150, 154, 199 n1
Coleman, James S., 95, 101
Cottingham, Clement, 157
Cronon, Edmund David, 100
Cruise O'Brien, Donal B., 180
Curtin, Philip D., 15, 186 n11

Davidson, Basil, 1, 186 n12
Davis, Kingsley, 32, 33, 39
de Cruz, Mattieu, 23
de Graft-Johnson, K. T., 190 n1

221

Subject Index

Aba, Nigeria, 95, 192n4, 193n12
Abeokuta, Nigeria, 16, 17, 29, 129,
  189n16, 192n4, 193n12
  population, 19
  psychiatric disorders, 195n5
  quarters in, 23
Abidjan, Ivory Coast, 27, 30, 43, 45,
  50, 95, 134, 174, 189n20
  population, 41
  primacy of, 42
  protest of unemployed (1969),
    200n17
  unauthorized housing, 45, 46
  urban–rural ties, 71–2
Abomey, Benin, 15, 22
Abuja, Nigeria, 188n6
Accra, Ghana, 17, 27, 30, 50, 59, 60,
  69, 70, 106
  contribution to education of relatives'
    children, 128
  food retailing, 198n9
  overcrowding, 45
  population, 41, 43
  self-employment, operation of
    Atinga's bar in Nima, 35–7
  Tema, 193n12
  union of Zabrama immigrants from
    Gothey, 87
Africanization, 173
African personality, 103
Agadès, Niger, 10
Agbekoya rebellion, Western Nigeria,
  182–3
Agege, Nigeria, 199n8
agriculture, effect of rural emigration
  on, 35
Ahmadu Bello University, Zaria, 200n14
Akure, Nigeria, 189n16
Alafin of Old Oyo, 16
Almoravids, jihad, 8
alternation model of change, 106
art, 17, 99

Ashanti, 14
  colonial economy, 28–9
Asia vs. Africa, cultural heritage, 99
Awdaghust, Mauritania, 7, 8

Back to Africa movement, 100
Bamako, Mali, 42, 98, 138
  population, 41
Banjul, The Gambia, population, 41
Bathurst, The Gambia, *see* Banjul
Bauchi, Nigeria, 189n16
Benin, People's Republic of
  education of women, 136
  military rule, 159
  passenger cars, 154–5
  strikes, 157
Benin City, Nigeria, 174–5, 189n16
Benin kingdom, 99, 187n14
Berlin Conference (1884–5), 26, 27, 99
biographic change, 115–17
Bissau, Guinea-Bissau, 27
  population, 41
Bornu, ancient kingdom, 12, 13, 98
Bouaké, Ivory Coast, 27
brain drain, 158
bridewealth, 198n4
  and rural–urban migration, 53
bright lights theory of rural–urban
  migration, 53
business, neighborhood, Mushin, 77–8

Calabar, Nigeria, 23, 87, 90, 189n16
Cape Coast, Ghana, 60, 103
Cape Verde Islands, projected
  unification with Guinea-Bissau,
  185n1
capital cities, 40–3
caravans, Sahara, 6
categorical relationships, 107
censuses, Nigeria, 189n13
change
  biographic, 115–17
  historical, 97–103; in Timbuktu,
    114–15

225

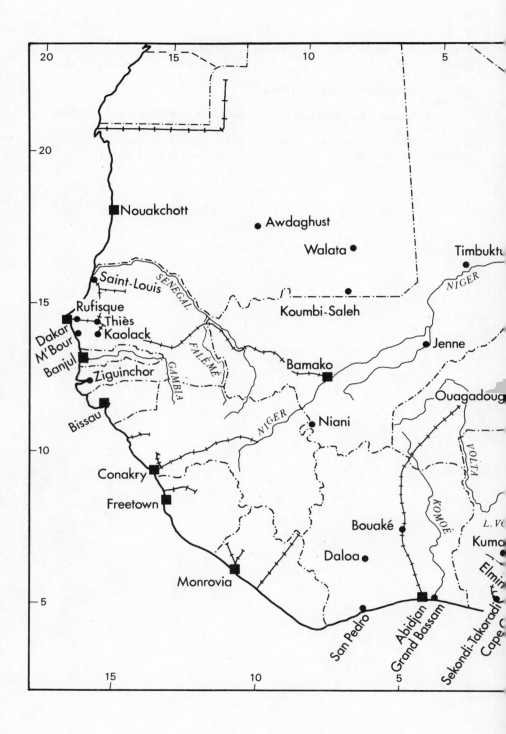

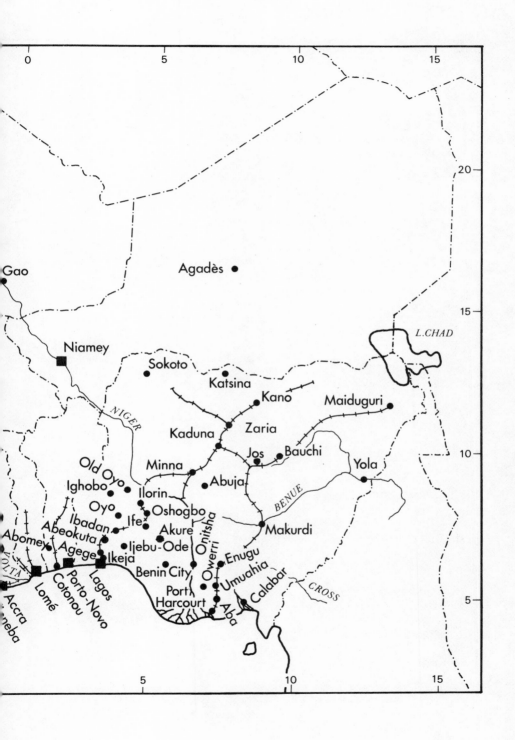